DISCARDED

AMS STUDIES IN MODERN LITERATURE
ISSN 0270-2983
Series ISBN-13: 978-0-404-61570-3

No. 25
STEPHEN K. LAND

THE HUMAN IMPERATIVE
A Study of the Novels
of Graham Greene

ISBN-13: 978-0-404-61595-6

THE HUMAN IMPERATIVE

A Study of the Novels of Graham Greene

STEPHEN K. LAND

AMS PRESS, INC.
NEW YORK

Library of Congress Cataloging-in-Publication Data

Land, Stephen K.

The Human Imperative : A Study of the Novels of Graham Greene / by Stephen K. Land.

    p. cm - (AMS Studies in Modern Literature ; no. 25)
    Includes bibliographical references and index.
    ISBN-13: 978-0-404-61595-6 (cloth : alk. paper)
    1. Greene, Graham, 1904-1991—Criticism and interpretation.
    I. Title.

PR6013.R44Z6445   2008
823'.912—dc22

2008001685
CIP

All AMS books are printed on acid-free paper that meets the guidelines for performance and durability of the Committee on Production Guidelines for Book Longevity of the Council on Library Resources.

Copyright © 2008 by AMS Press, Inc.
All rights reserved

AMS Press, Inc.
Brooklyn Navy Yard, 63 Flushing Ave. - Unit #221
Brooklyn, New York 11205, U.S.A.

www.amspressinc.com

MANUFACTURED IN THE UNITED STATES OF AMERICA

Contents

Preface   vii

1. Introduction   1
2. The Heroes   10
3. The Antagonists   131
4. Greeneland   185
5. Heroines   213
6. Detectives and Villains   239
7. Conclusion   266

Notes   273
Index   283

Preface

The matter of reference to the texts of Graham Greene's novels is not straightforward. The strictly correct procedure would probably be to refer to the pages of the first editions, or perhaps to the Collected Edition. In practical terms, however, this would be unhelpful. First editions of Greene, especially of the early novels, are rare and already often commanding four or five figure prices in auction rooms. Very few of us are likely to possess many of these books, or to have access to them outside the restrictive conditions of rare book departments in libraries. The Collected Edition, published by The Bodley Head and William Heinemann, is itself something of a rarity outside the larger libraries and, besides, does not include all of the works to which reference is to be made in this study.

On the other hand, because Greene has been, since the 1930s, a popular writer, most of his books have appeared in numerous editions and have been for some time available in paperback. (The only significant exceptions are the two early novels which Greene himself refused to have reprinted: *The Name of Action* and *Rumour at Nightfall*, neither of which will be considered here.) These later editions, new or secondhand, are easy to find, and it is almost certainly in this form that Greene's texts will be most accessible to the reader.

Although pagination varies among the many editions still current, an alternative means of reference is offered by Greene's habit of dividing and subdividing his texts into usually quite short numbered sections. The sections are variously called "parts," "books," or "chapters," or are sometimes simply given numbers, and in a few cases they also have subtitles. Ignoring the labels, however, we can achieve a simple method of reference by using a sequence of numbers to denote section, subsection, and (where appropriate) sub-subsection. Thus, "Book One, Part Two, Chapter Three" is represented as "1.2.3." While this is less specific or precise than a page reference, it stands a much better chance of being correct in its application to whatever edition the reader is using.

As a further simplification the titles of Greene's novels most frequently mentioned in this study are reduced to two-letter abbreviations, which will be used both in references and in the main text. The reader may find it helpful at this point to have a list of Greene's major writings in chronological order with the dates of first publication and the abbreviations here assigned:[1]

MW *The Man Within* 1929
    The Name of Action 1930
    Rumour at Nightfall 1931
ST *Stamboul Train* (published in the USA as *Orient Express*) 1932
IB *It's a Battlefield* 1934
EM *England Made Me* (published in the USA as *The Shipwrecked*) 1935
    The Basement Room and Other Stories[2] 1935
JM *Journey Without Maps* 1936
GS *A Gun for Sale* (published in the USA as *This Gun for Hire*) 1936
BR *Brighton Rock* (published in the USA as *Labyrinthine Ways*) 1938
LR *The Lawless Roads* (published in the USA as *Another Mexico*) 1939
CA *The Confidential Agent* 1939
PG *The Power and the Glory* 1940
MF *The Ministry of Fear* 1943
    The Tenth Man (apparently written in 1944) 1985
HM *The Heart of the Matter* 1948
TM *The Third Man* 1950
EA *The End of the Affair* 1951
    Loser Takes All 1955
QA *The Quiet American* 1955
OM *Our Man in Havana* 1958
BC *A Burnt-Out Case* 1961

UG "Under the Garden" (published in *A Sense of Reality*) 1963
TC *The Comedians* 1966
TA *Travels with my Aunt* 1969
SL *A Sort of Life* 1971
HC *The Honorary Consul* 1973
HF *The Human Factor* 1978
DF *Doctor Fischer of Geneva* 1980
WE *Ways of Escape* 1980
MQ *Monsignor Quixote* 1982
    Getting to Know the General 1984
CE *The Captain and the Enemy* 1988

Even in the 1930s Greene's novels were widely discussed and reviewed. Since the War Greene has been recognized as an important literary figure, and academic and general studies of his work have been appearing at an ever-increasing rate.[3] A milestone, which will serve to stimulate yet further critical study, is the three-volume biography of Greene by Norman Sherry.[4] The present study is not an academic thesis but is intended to interest not only the student of the modern novel but also the reader of Greene who wishes to bring his appreciation of the novels into a single perspective. Technicalities have been kept to a minimum. The few notes, which are placed at the end of the text, offer (along with elaboration on several matters of detail) some suggestions for further reading and research.

Quotations are from the Penguin editions. The author is grateful to Random House (UK) for permission to include extracts from the novels of Graham Greene.

1. Introduction

The present study rests upon the premise that Greene's major fiction can usefully be considered as a corpus, a body of writing united by a complex of interrelated motifs which is significantly present in most of his novels. From the examination and attempted justification of a number of these motifs will emerge what may be called the underlying conceptual form or structure of Greene's fiction. Although individual novels and stories will be discussed, parts of them in some detail, the final purpose here is not so much the interpretation of individual works as the argument of the case for seeing them (or most of them) in terms of this common form. Insofar as the argument is persuasive, the underlying form may then become a powerful factor in the further interpretation of individual novels.

Most general studies of Greene's work begin by offering a number of generalizations, and about the validity of a number of these there has been widespread agreement among Greene's critics. Such generalizations include, for example, Greene's view of life as fundamentally unhappy and of humanity as corrupt (a view which may be related to the theological notion of "original sin"), and his consequent tendency to set his stories against backgrounds of pervasive misery and conflict.[5] Greene's heroes, it is often noted, are usually men in spiritual or actual flight from guilt. Many of the novels focus upon matters of personal obligation, in the context of which default or betrayal are possibilities often realized. Certain characters, such as priests and childlike heroines, tend to recur. Like many of Conrad's novels, Greene's plots present crucial issues of the individual's social and political action in the framework of an adventure-story.[6]

That some such generalizations about the work of a novelist should be possible is no more than one would expect, for the ultimately trivial reason that all his work proceeds from a single creative intelligence. The present study looks for those generalizations about Greene's work which go beyond the merely adventitious and which may, in the end, be brought together to display a unified underlying pattern of ideas at the heart of his fiction. Specifically, it examines features of character and patterns of action which run through most of the major novels and in the light of which some of the already recognized constants of Greene's stories—such as betrayal, flight, and the "terror of life"[7]—may be brought into a new coherence.

Greene himself gives some encouragement to those who would view his work as a coherent whole, and he does this in several ways. In 1971, for instance, he offered a single epigraph for all his novels, suggesting a possible interpretation of his fiction in the light of the "dangerous edge of things," of moral, social, and political borders astride which the action takes place. A number of his later novels, moreover, particularly *TA* and *MQ*, abound in "cross-references," in allusions which deliberately remind the reader of earlier novels or else, with hindsight, may be seen as anticipating those still to come. In *MQ*, for instance, Monsignor Quixote hearing confession in a lavatory echoes not only the mock-confession of the Nazi general in *TA* but also Javitt's throne in *UG*, the conclusion of "The Destructors" (a short story published in 1954), and perhaps also the death of Hilfe in *MF*. Again, Quixote's reference to himself as potentially a "whisky priest" (*MQ* 1.5.1) reminds us of *PG*. In *TA* the Brighton episode and the train journey to Istanbul are reminiscent respectively of *BR* and *ST*, while the ending, among South American arms smugglers, looks forward to *CE*. A number of comparable authorial self-references have been traced in *TM*.[8] The bomb which perhaps kills Bendrix in *EA* echoes other similar explosions in *CA* and *MF*. The abundance of these self-allusions, along with the many recurring situations and character types in Greene, add up to a strong suggestion of underlying unity beneath the diversity of the stories.

Some of these similarities and allusions are either trivial or mere literary jokes, confidential asides to the initiated reader. Yet the search for such repeated motifs can sometimes lead us to deeper waters. The profiteer Sir Marcus in *GS* is echoed in Lord Benditch in *CA* and Lime in *TM*, and it is but a short step from these to the smugglers Carlyon in *MW* and Yusef in *HM*, or to the fraudulent Krogh in *EM*. The concealment of cruelty beneath a veneer of friendship, such as is seen in Carlyon, Krogh, and Yusef, can be traced also in Pyle in *QA* and even in Rycker in *BC*. Thus there begins to appear a line of morally dubious but powerful figures, of men in each case exerting a strong influence upon the hero.

Again, it is easy to see in the Captain's first meeting with Baxter in *CE* an echo of Carlyon's initial encounter with Andrews in *MW*: in both cases an older, more experienced man removes the boyish hero from the tedium of school life and offers him instead a life of risk and adventure. But the crucial relationship between the charismatic and active mentor and the more hesitant, self-critical hero appears centrally not only in these two cases but also between Anthony and Krogh in *EM*, Martins and Lime in *TM*, and Fowler and Pyle in *QA*; and it requires only a little thought to see further variants of it in other novels. There is nothing superficial or whimsical about the features indicated here, which concern the moral relationships at the heart of a good number of Greene's novels.

It is with the elaboration of observations of this kind that the present study will begin. Many general studies of Greene begin with his life, moving from a brief biographical outline to the isolation of certain elements, such as childhood fears or adolescent attempts at suicide, which are then used in the interpretation of the novels.[9] Here, however, we are concerned only with features internal to Greene's fictional world, and not with the external frames of reference offered by the author's life, his personal beliefs, or his nonfictional works. We are searching for the structure and dynamics of the world of Greene's fiction, not for the powers or forces, in Greene's own circumstances, psychology, or philosophy, which may have conditioned that world or brought it into being.

A special case of this exclusion is Greene's Catholicism, which requires particular mention here since a number of impressive studies have been written about Greene specifically as a Catholic writer, interpreting his novels in the light of Catholic doctrine.[10] Greene's Catholicism is a matter for his biographers, and the present study takes at face value his often-reiterated and much-quoted statement that he is "not a Catholic writer but a writer who happens to be a Catholic" (*WE* 2.4). In practice this amounts to the denial that, because he was a Catholic writing (in some cases) about Catholic issues and characters, his novels (or some of them) must be assessed by special criteria; that a particular body of knowledge, other than (or besides) that of the secular critic, must be employed in their interpretation.[11] It may be that this is the way in which Catholics choose to read Greene, but insofar as they do so what they are doing has more to do with theology than with literature.

Greene's novels may be seen to involve a "religious sense" and even a "treatment of supernatural evil," qualities Greene praises in the work of Henry James;[12] but the novels are not therefore about good and evil, any more than they are intrinsically "Catholic." Just as a "Catholic novel" would in reality be theology, not fiction, so a novel *about* good and evil would be a sermon or an essay in moral philosophy. Greene himself again states the point clearly: "One gets so tired of people saying that my novels are about the opposition of Good and Evil. They are not about Good and Evil, but about human beings."[13] Any novel must concern itself fundamentally with character and action, and whatever else is to be included must evolve from this foundation. The characters may well hold and act by religious beliefs, and will almost certainly invoke moral judgement upon their actions. Their stories may also suggest values and powers which, relative to the world in which the characters move, figure as supernatural. Yet the ontological divide between fiction and fact remains in place, and the critic is under no obligation to frame his judgement of the novel in terms of the beliefs of its characters. Fiction may reflect reality but it remains essentially hypothetical. We do not judge the characters and doctrines in a novel in the same way as we judge the conduct and ideas of our neighbors or of political or religious leaders.[14]

The present study is concerned with the development of generalizations about internal features of Greene's fictional world. It does not, however, consider all of Greene's fictional writings, but only the central core of published novels. Largely in order to keep within manageable limits a text already long enough, it leaves out of account all of the other writings (which may be considered as in some sense "minor"), including the plays, poems, film scripts, and children's stories. Short stories are also not considered, with the exception of *UG* and "The Basement Room," two of the longer stories which bear particularly close relation to the novels. For the same reason no account is taken of suppressed or unpublished novels.[15]

Each of the twenty or more novels and stories to be discussed has at, or somewhere close to, its heart a variant of the underlying pattern of character and action to be disclosed here. This does not imply, however, that Greene's career as a novelist was static, that he spent over fifty years repetitively reworking the same ideas. It is sometimes said that whereas Beethoven wrote nine symphonies Bruckner wrote the same symphony nine times; and the germ of truth behind this rather glib aphorism is that, while Beethoven's symphonies are radically different from one another in conception and design, Bruckner pursues and develops a single formal ideal which receives ever more powerful and individualistic statement in his successive symphonic works.[16] Greene's career can be seen in something of the same way as Bruckner's, as a gradual development and unfolding of a single central concept of the novel form; and it is part of the purpose of this study to plot the course of this development.

Greene's first six published novels (including here the two novels later suppressed) are evidently experimental. After making a start with three "romantic" stories of heroic action in historical settings, Greene turned, in *ST* and *IB*, to contemporary settings and a more fast-moving narrative style. While still experimental (in, for example, its occasional use of stream-of-consciousness narrative), the next novel, *EM*, abandons the fragmented structure and diversity of characters of *ST* and *IB*, and emerges as Greene's first successful telling of a single, unified story with a contemporary setting. It is no great surprise, with hindsight, that

Greene moved rapidly on to a succession of masterpieces in *BR*, *PG*, and *HM*. These three major works form a group (some critics even consider them a "trilogy"[17]) and also mark a watershed in Greene's development.

His career after *HM*, from about 1950, is marked by diversification. While *QA* announced a new approach to the themes of human obligation and personal loyalty, an approach which was to be further explored in *BC*, *TC*, *HC*, *HF*, and *CE*, Greene began at the same time to experiment with other forms. *EA* is a love story and stands alone as such among his novels. In *OM* he turned to comedy, and several of his later works are largely comic, often with strong doses of irony and satire included. *OM* was followed in this mood by *TA* and the collection of stories under the title *May We Borrow Your Husband?* (1967), and there is much ironic comedy in both *TC* and *MQ*. *Loser Takes All*, which turns upon a highly improbable set of characters and circumstances and involves a heavy moral judgement, is more of a fable than a novel; and in this it belongs with *DF*. (It is perhaps anticipated as a fable by *The Tenth Man*, which was apparently written in 1944.) At the same time Greene turned also to the theater, and the succession of plays he wrote in the 1950s and 1960s absorbed much of his time.[18]

This synopsis suggests a three-phase classification of Greene's novels as "early (or experimental)," "middle," and "late," a division which more or less coincides with that offered by Greene himself in terms of the novels' subjects. "For one period I did write on Catholic subjects: from *Brighton Rock* to *A Burnt-Out Case*. . . . *The Comedians* is essentially a political novel. My period of Catholic novels was preceded and followed by political novels . . . . Even the early thrillers were political."[19] The identification of a middle "Catholic" period has been widely accepted by writers on Greene's novels, although there is less agreement on exactly where this period ends. Greene includes *BC*, and presumably *EA*, among the "Catholic" novels; yet neither *QA* nor *OM*, both written before *BC*, are at all "Catholic," but belong rather with the later "political" novels such as *HC* and *HF*.

A comparable blurring of the division between the first and second phases is occasioned by the "entertainments" *GS*, *CA*, and *MF*. These novels are evidently "political" rather than "Catholic," yet they are not "experimental" in the same sense as are the first four or five published novels. On the contrary, although they do have some new features, they are largely simplified versions of the stories and techniques Greene had already evolved; and it was precisely this which made them "entertainments," novels written rapidly, to win wide appeal and make money, rather than serious essays in the novel form comparable with *BR*, *HM*, or even *EM*. Both *CA* and *MF*, however, were written after *BR*.

The widely accepted use of the term "Catholic novels" to denote and distinguish the novels of Greene's middle phase is not ultimately satisfactory. It proposes a classification based upon theme or subject, but what we need for a study of Greene's development as a novelist is one based rather upon underlying principles of plot structure and composition. In these terms, as will be argued here in Chapter 2, while *GS* and *CA* belong with the early novels, *MF* belongs with *BR*, *PG*, and *HM*. Again, despite its Catholic subject, the pattern of its action places *BC* closer to *QA* and *TC* than to the Catholic "trilogy." *EA*, which is really a different kind of novel altogether, is closer to the later group; and *MQ*, another idiosyncratic piece, may be left in its chronological place among the later novels. This yields a broad threefold division of Greene's works which, apart from the cases of *CA* and *TM* [20] (which both come after *BR* in the order of time), is chronologically tidy and reflects the main stages in Greene's development.

The arguments for this classification will be set out more fully in the next chapter, but a preliminary table showing what is proposed may be helpful:

EARLY	MIDDLE	LATE
MW (1929)		
ST (1932)		
IB (1934)		
EM (1935)		
GS (1936)		
	BR (1938)	
CA (1939)		
	PG (1940)	
	MF (1940)	
	HM (1948)	
TM (1950)		
		EA (1951)
		QA (1955)
		OM (1958)
		BC (1961)
		TC (1966)
		TA (1969)
		HC (1973)
		HF (1978)
		MQ (1982)
		CE (1988)

This listing provides a useful frame of reference, but the present study is topical rather than chronological in approach. Whereas most general studies of Greene follow the traditional method of examining the novels, singly or in groups, in chronological sequence, the chapters which follow here will each explore a particular feature of Greene's fictional world. Chapter 2 looks at the heroes and the way in which their story is treated in successive novels. The radically different ways in which, at different times, Greene set out the hero's story will provide the chief criteria for the division of his fictional work into three periods or phases. The third chapter looks at the figure who, in almost all of the novels, functions as the hero's primary "antagonist." The business of the novels and their moral implications arise largely from the interaction of these two figures. Chapter 4 looks at the fictional world within which Greene's characters act out their stories. It is concerned not so much with the very varied locations which occur as settings in the different novels as with the set of moral and ontological premises which can be seen as common to them all. The fifth and sixth chapters respectively examine two further roles which appear significantly in most of the novels: that of the female characters who exert moral influence upon the heroes, and that of the investigator or "detective" by whom the hero is pursued. Chapter 7, by way of summary, looks at the overall pattern of action involving the character types already discussed, and at the fundamental "laws" of Greene's fiction.

2. The Heroes

I. INTRODUCTORY

The "hero" of a novel is the character at the focal point of the story's moral situation. The identity of Greene's heroes is quite clear in most cases, but a list of the characters who will be so called in this study may nonetheless help to avoid misunderstanding. In chronological order, the heroes are: Andrews (*MW*), Czinner (*ST*), Conrad (*IB*), Anthony (*EM*), Raven (*GS*), Pinkie (*BR*), D (*CA*), the Priest[21] (*PG*), Rowe (*MF*), Scobie (*HM*), Martins (*TM*), Bendrix (*EA*), Fowler (*QA*), Wormold (*OM*), Querry (*BC*), Brown (*TC*), Pulling (*TA*), Plarr (*HC*), Castle (*HF*), Quixote (*MQ*), and Baxter (*CE*). The only cases of possible doubt are among the early novels, where Greene sometimes places the hero's story among the competing stories of other characters (as in *ST* and *IB*), or views the hero through the eyes of another (as in *GS* and *TM*).

Czinner is the hero in *ST* because his capture and death are at the structural climax and moral center of the story. Although he fails, Czinner is attempting morally significant action; whereas Myatt, who also receives a good deal of narrative attention, remains morally unconcerned. Czinner dies for a cause, whereas Myatt is deflected from his attempt to rescue Coral, an attempt which ends ironically when he rescues Grünlich instead and rapidly turns his thoughts from Coral to Janet. In much the same way Conrad is the hero of *IB*. Conrad's action in loving Milly and attempting to shoot the Assistant Commissioner, although in many ways wrong, contrasts positively with the feeble loves and passive lives of Jules and Surrogate. The Assistant Commissioner himself, with his assignment to report on the Drover case, provides the framework for the narrative, but fails to affect the course of events.

To the Assistant Commissioner's role in *IB* may be compared the business between Mather and Anne in *GS*. Their love, interrupted at the beginning, threatened by the action, and finally re-established at the end, is the narrative frame. The focal character, the man upon whose success the preservation of peace depends, and whose life is sacrificed in the struggle to restore the moral balance, is Raven. Again, although the narrative voice in *TM* is not Martins's but Calloway's, it is Martins who, anticipating Fowler in *QA*, takes the morally crucial decision to betray his friend. In the other cases the hero's identity is not open to doubt.

The heroes of Greene's novels are generally quiescent, introspective men with a preference for persistence in an established routine of life. In the course of the story they are galvanized, often reluctantly, into activity through contact with another man (the "antagonist," whose role is the subject of Chapter 3 below), sometimes with the further object of impressing or placating a particular woman. The thread which unites the heroes, from Andrews to Baxter, is their initial preference for a sheltered, sometimes even covert, way of existence, a wish to stand aside from, or even to hide beneath, the mainstream of action. This impulse may take the form of geographical withdrawal (as with Fowler, Querry, Brown, and Plarr), of a quiet life within the routine of work (as with Czinner the schoolmaster, Conrad the clerk, D the scholar, Scobie the plodding policeman, Wormold the salesman, Pulling the bank manager, and Castle the civil servant), of the security of the priesthood (as with the heroes of *PG* and *MQ*), or even of an undercover life of crime or deception (as with Raven, Pinkie, and Anthony). Consequently, as has often been observed, Greene's heroes tend, when faced with harsh realities, to become men pursued, to be maneuvered into unaccustomed lines of action which frequently result in some sort of crime or betrayal.

By examining the succession of heroes in the context of the increasingly elaborate patterns of action developed in the novels we can arrive at a threefold grouping, the proposed division outlined in the previous chapter. Heroes in the early novels are simply displaced or disadvantaged characters faced with dilemmas they cannot resolve. Their difficulties, it is usually suggested, may have roots in childhood deprivations.[22] In the middle novels, however, the heroes' weaknesses are explored, not only in terms of a possibly disadvantaged past (as remains a factor in Pinkie's case), but rather through their tendency to weigh the present situation against an idealized version of the past in such a way as significantly to inhibit positive action. In the later novels this habit of mind becomes an overtly formulated plan. What in Pinkie, the Priest, Rowe, and Scobie remains a dream memory of a childlike "peace," becomes in Fowler, Querry, Brown, Plarr, and Castle a consciously devised strategy of withdrawal from the conflicts of life to the position of an observer on the sidelines.

The structure of the successive stories reflects these three phases of the heroic character. The early novels relate rapid, uninterrupted sequences of events compressed into the span of a few days and with only brief flashbacks or narrative summations to alert us to conditions or events prior to the main action. The middle novels operate within much longer spans of time and are characterized by distinctive, symbolic, quest-like episodes in which the heroes confront the images of the past which still haunt them. In the later novels this symbolic journey back gives place to the irruption of characters from the past, or representative of the heroes' past—characters such as Rycker, Jones, Leon, Muller, and Baxter's father. These figures, intruding into the present, tend to upset the heroes' policy of withdrawn noninvolvement.

II. THE EARLY NOVELS

The heroes of the early novels—Andrews, Czinner, Conrad, Anthony, and Raven—tend to be disadvantaged, downtrodden, and socially displaced. They are men with no fixed position in society, inclined to drift, open to influence, and without firm commitment to established codes of law or morality. They are either without legitimate employment or else desperately unhappy in their work. Their lack of social roots is, in several cases, underlined by an unhappy childhood and want of effective parental care.

When they do eventually take decisive action they tend to be precipitate, unpredictable, and a potential danger to both the guilty and the innocent. Their stories follow a common basic pattern. Under mounting pressure of circumstances the hero commits himself to a course of action. The action he takes is morally ambiguous, and may be seen as brave, foolhardy, and dangerous, as being at once altruistic and treacherous. At the same time he comes into contact with a woman, usually an actual or potential lover, and (in all cases except that of Czinner) the woman's presence helps to prompt the hero's crucial action. All of these early heroes meet death in the end, a death which can be seen as at once a retribution for folly or betrayal and a worthy self-sacrifice.

The pattern is clearly exemplified by Andrews in *MW*. Still an immature young man when his story opens, Andrews had lost both his parents while only a schoolboy. He had, in any case, hated his father as a "bully" and a "brute" (1.1–2). Led by Carlyon, he has abandoned his schooling and joined a band of smugglers, but he is unhappy in the rough life at sea and feels constantly inferior within the shadow of his father's memory. Under these circumstances Andrews takes the step which sets the main action of the novel in motion: he sends a letter betraying the smugglers' plans to the authorities; and in the ensuing ambush an exciseman is killed, and several of the smugglers are taken prisoner.

Andrews's action has the moral ambiguity which becomes characteristic of the heroes' undertakings in Greene's major fiction. From one point of view the sending of the letter is a betrayal of Carlyon's friendship and of Andrews's place as a member of the gang. From another point of view it is justifiable as an act in support of law and order, the deed of a young man sickened by the violence of a criminal life from which he wants to escape. Greene's concentration on the mixture of the hero's motives is reflected in his choice of title, which draws attention to the duality of a selfish, driven "outer" man and the higher, more altruistic impulses of the "man within." Although Greene soon abandoned the heavily explicit terms in which the moral struggle is presented in *MW*, the same conflict of motives can be found in virtually all the subsequent heroes.

When his story opens Andrews is being impelled by personal feelings of fear and vengeance. He is in flight, both as a suspected smuggler from the law and as a suspected traitor from Carlyon. In his flight he encounters Elizabeth, and through his meeting with her he becomes more courageous and decides to take the grave risk of surrendering himself to the law and giving evidence at the captured smugglers' trial. Andrews's encounter with his heroine helps to raise his moral aspirations, but it also propels him towards his death. After the trial he has still to face Carlyon. He has risked his own safety to serve the public interest, and he risks it still further in confronting his betrayed friend. His death is at once a self-sacrifice and the retributive outcome of his earlier weakness and vindictiveness.

In *MW* Greene first laid down the patterns of action he was to follow and elaborate in many of his subsequent works, but this first published novel also contains salient features which its author soon abandoned. The "man within" idea, reflected in passages of interior dialogue between higher and lower selves, was rapidly outgrown as Greene found ways more subtle than overt debate to communicate moral conflict. Also untypical of Greene is what might be called the full close in a major key at the end of *MW*. As Andrews approaches death the reader is led to the view that, by giving himself up, the hero has allowed Carlyon to escape and so atoned for his original betrayal; while at the same time he has satisfied Elizabeth's expectations by liberating the "man within" and is about to achieve some sort of spiritual union with her in death. It was probably on account of these features that Greene later repudiated *MW* as "very young and sentimental" (*SL* 10.6).

ST differs in pattern from *MW*, and from most of Greene's novels, chiefly in that it has no "antagonist" (no character corresponding to Carlyon), and in that it lacks significant moral interaction between the hero and heroine. Coming after the resounding failures of *Rumour at Nightfall* and *The Name of Action*, *ST* was a new departure in both style and subject. It represents for Greene a decisive step away from the Conradian mannerisms and historical settings of his first three published novels, towards a terse, fast-moving narrative style in a contemporary setting. Writing under pressure to achieve sales and make money, Greene produced his first "entertainment" and, at the same time, began to find his distinctive voice. Within these limitations the novel was a success, and it remains entertainingly readable; but it lacks something of the moral intensity of *MW*, chiefly because of the fragmented structure and the failure of the hero to interact significantly with other major characters. Despite its financial success, Greene was himself not happy with *ST*,[23] and it is best seen as another experimental work.

Along with the adoption of a plainer narrative style, the experiment consists chiefly in the use of a kind of montage technique of storytelling. A group of assorted characters are brought together by circumstances, in this case a train journey, and the narrative moves among them in short, sometimes fragmentary passages. It was a technique Greene was to use again in his next novel, *IB*, but not—at least, not to the same degree—again thereafter. The deliberate breaking of the story into small sections, with the narrative focus shifting rapidly from one to another among a large group of diverse characters, tends to foster an overall picture of social disintegration. Each character pursues his own interests with little knowledge of or regard for the affairs of others. In this way the narrative experiment of *ST* is skillfully conducted so as to generate the kind of deeply ironic view of humanity which was to become one of the hallmarks of Greene's fiction.

The fragmented narrative of *ST* helps Greene to represent a society in which aims are frustrated by failures of communication, potentially positive relationships are fortuitously interrupted, and evildoers escape detection while the deserving but weak go unnoticed to the wall. The technique serves its purpose well, but at a cost. *ST*, for all its brilliance, remains basically three distinct storylines (along with a handful of character vignettes), cunningly, but in the end not very tightly, stitched together. The central characters—Czinner, Coral, and Grünlich—are brought together by circumstances, but they stop short of morally significant interaction. The result is indeed ironic but, looking ahead to the great novels of Greene's middle and later periods, we can see that he wanted much more in his fictional world than mere irony.

The three stories which largely make up *ST* are easily distinguished. One involves four characters and follows the process whereby Myatt and Mabel change partners. Myatt loses Coral to Mabel while at the same time Mabel loses Janet to Myatt, in a symmetrical sexual comedy which might, by itself, have made a neat, cynical short story. Another tale in *ST* is that of Czinner, returning to lead a popular uprising in Belgrade which, as he learns en route, has already failed. He journeys on nonetheless, hoping at least for the chance to plead the cause in a public trial, but is intercepted and shot as he crosses the border into Yugoslavia. The third story is that of Grünlich who joins the train at Vienna, having just killed a man in the course of a robbery.

The three storylines intersect on the train. Mabel recognizes Czinner and follows him on the journey. Czinner, a doctor, attends Coral when she is taken ill, and later he interrupts Grünlich in the act of stealing from his luggage. Greene makes a real attempt to bind the three stories together in what he called the "key scene" of the novel (*WE* 1.4). In a device borrowed from the theater, Greene says, he structured some of his early novels so as to reach a dramatic climax in a "key scene" in which the central characters are isolated together for some time. This device recurs in *GS*, and can be seen also in a number of the later novels, notably *QA* and *HC*.[24] In *ST* this is the episode in Subotica where Coral, Czinner, and Grünlich are locked up together overnight. They break out and make a dash for freedom. Grünlich escapes, but Czinner is wounded and Coral stays to help him. They spend the night hiding in a barn.

The trouble is that, having rather laboriously brought Coral and Czinner together at this point, Greene does nothing further to give the scene significance. Nothing of consequence passes between the two. Czinner is badly hurt, only semiconscious, and says nothing intelligible. Coral does what she can to make him comfortable, but he is hardly aware of her presence. In the morning they are discovered by the soldiers from whom they had escaped. Czinner, who was to be shot anyway, is finished off with a bullet through the head, and Coral, who was in any case to be released that day, is allowed to go. The only consequence of the overnight episode is that Grünlich is able to take Coral's place in Myatt's car, but this escape precedes the "key scene" in the barn, which then merely occupies the time remaining before morning.

The scene has some significance: it underlines Coral's humanity in her attitude towards Czinner, and his dying thoughts, related by the narrator, emphasize the sad futility of his life. The point remains, nonetheless, that nothing is made of the potential for interaction between the two key characters. On the contrary, Czinner's condition, the language barrier between them, and the darkness, all simply accentuate the isolation not only of the two of them from the world at large but also each from the other. By contrast the "key scene" in *GS*, where Anne and Raven hide overnight in a shed while the police gather outside, is very different in its effect. Anne and Raven hold lengthy conversations, developing a degree of mutual understanding, and they exchange information which affects their subsequent courses of action. Much the same is true of the "key scene" in *QA*, where Fowler and Pyle converse deeply in the guard tower. The relatively static and empty quality of the barn scene in *ST* is symptomatic of Greene's problem with the overall concept of the novel at this early stage of his work. In seeking to portray a fragmented society he has been unable to avoid writing a fragmented novel.[25]

ST is therefore three stories and a number of character vignettes, held together within the framework of the train journey. Czinner's story rises above the others because of its involvement in a wider arena (Czinner's political plans and his communist ideals) and because he is the novel's most fully drawn figure. We know, for instance, a good deal about his earlier life, the development of his ideas, and his aspirations, whereas Myatt and Grünlich are portrayed within the narrower limits of the immediate present. It is also Czinner who shares the prominent features common to most of the early heroes.

Czinner is a displaced person, a refugee, of downtrodden, rather impoverished appearance. He is a lonely figure, ridden by anxiety. He has not been at all happy in his work as a schoolmaster. He is a hunted man, pursued first by Mabel and then by the Yugoslavian police. Like Andrews and Conrad, he has bravely but foolhardily decided to face his enemies, and his story ends with his consequent death. There is an element of self-sacrifice in Czinner's fate, which invites comparison with Andrews and Raven. Like the other early heroes he is also reckless and a danger to others: just as Andrews endangers Elizabeth and Raven brings harm upon Anne, so Czinner inadvertently involves Coral in his fate.

What separates Czinner from the other heroes are the structural features just mentioned, as a result of which he remains an isolated figure who has only trivial interaction with other characters. Whereas other heroes are radically affected by their encounters with their respective heroines, Czinner remains unmoved by Coral. He makes quite a difference to her, being the cause of her arrest and therefore of her separation from Myatt; but she has no effect upon him, altering neither his thoughts nor his course of action. There is, moreover, no antagonist in Czinner's story, and therefore no personal betrayal. The other heroes each betray someone—Andrews betrays Carlyon, Conrad his brother, Anthony Krogh, and even Raven in a sense betrays his employers by turning his gun against them—but Czinner betrays no one, nor is it clear that he has ever done so. Czinner is unusual among Greene's heroes in that (despite his name, recalling the English word "sinner") there are no very specific feelings of guilt bound up with his heroic action.

Although *IB* employs a disjointed narrative technique similar to that of *ST* in its rapid movement among a number of characters, the novel avoids the overall fragmentation of *ST* and, with its English setting and somber theme, recovers something of the intensity of *MW*. The story is framed by the Assistant Commissioner's task, the compilation of a report, and the subject of that report, the fate of Jim Drover, is the common starting point for the actions of all the other major characters. All the several storylines—Conrad's activities, Milly's attempt to win media attention, the business among Jules, Kay, and Surrogate, and Lady Caroline's intervention—are anchored and held together by the focal image of Jim in his cell. Despite the diversity of characters, there is an effective unity in *IB* which makes some sections of *ST*, particularly its portrayal of minor characters, seem frivolous by comparison.

With Conrad Drover we return to the full pattern of action exemplified in Andrews and followed in the subsequent novels. Conrad is deeply affected by his encounter with the heroine, which encounter is also a serious betrayal, since Milly is Jim's wife. Conrad is, moreover, a typical hero of the type outlined. "Pale, shabby, tightly strung" (2.2), he is a lonely and insecure figure. Although he has a place as a chief clerk he feels threatened, even paranoid, in his work. As a child he suffered general persecution from which he was saved only by the strength of his brother. As a man he has a strong sense of injustice (1.7) and an almost pathological response to human suffering (4.6). (Conrad's exaggerated feeling of pity sounds a theme which reappears with variations in Anthony, Scobie, Fowler, Castle, and the Captain.) Although not an actual fugitive when the story opens, Conrad becomes a homeless outlaw when he acquires a gun and begins to stalk the Assistant Commissioner.

Much as Carlyon has killed a man (the exciseman Rexall) and is betrayed by Andrews, so Jim Drover has killed a man (the policeman Coney) and is betrayed by Conrad. Conrad's betrayal is of a different kind—he does not give Jim away to the authorities but sleeps with his wife—but the consequent feeling of guilt is comparable. Conrad and Andrews have each turned against a protector and mentor. In the end, and largely in a state of remorse, both men die. Conrad's career therefore exhibits all the ingredients of the heroic pattern: an initial state of moral confusion arising from his feelings for Jim and Milly after Jim's imprisonment; an impulse to further action, altruistic but ill considered, after his encounter with the heroine; a sense of guilt, following his adulterous dealings with Milly; and a fatal conclusion which is at once a retribution for earlier moral weakness and an act of atonement.

The pattern is apparent again in the hero of *EM*. Anthony Farrant is thirty-three but still has a face "no more mature than when he was a schoolboy" (1.1). This immature appearance reflects his character, for he is a drifter who has failed to find a place or role in life. He has held no long-term job, has been more or less continuously on the move, and has no ties except to his sister, whom he sees only rarely. He survives on his "child's cunning" and petty "dishonesty" (1.1), which is enough to keep him alive and out of major trouble, but no more. Like Andrews and Conrad, he is a weak and defensive character with no sense of purpose or direction.

Much as Andrews finds shelter in the protection of Carlyon, so Anthony prepares to settle with Krogh. Krogh has nothing of the personal magnetism of Carlyon, but in each case the older, more powerful man offers the unsteady hero employment and a potential foothold in life. In each case the benefactor turns out to have a sinister aspect, to be involved in crime and violence and to be expecting the hero's active support. Meanwhile Anthony meets Loo, who expresses suspicions of Krogh and tries to draw Anthony away from him and back to England.

Anthony betrays Krogh, not only because of Loo but also because he discovers Krogh's fraudulent dealings and because he sympathizes with the exploited workers, represented by young Andersson. Anthony's unwillingness to work with Krogh becomes apparent when he refuses to take part in the assault on Andersson at Saltsjöbaden, but this refusal is symptomatic of a deeper, contemplated betrayal. Anthony has already made an arrangement to sell information about Krogh to Minty, and he does in fact inform Minty of Krogh's secret engagement to Kate. Knowledge of the fraud gives Anthony something much more valuable to sell, and, with Minty in place as a potential buyer, Anthony is in a position to blackmail his employer. When Anthony announces his intention to join Loo in England—to leave Sweden, where his actions may be monitored and controlled by Kate—Krogh has to act. Anthony's death at the hands of Hall is at once a precaution against the threat of blackmail and a retribution for Anthony's support for the workers. The hero's death is again both the penalty for betrayal and the consequence of his having attempted to protect the helpless victims.

GS is another potboiler, another rapidly written "entertainment" very much along the lines of *ST*. Greene himself called it a "shocker,"[26] meaning presumably that it has a simple, dramatic storyline heightened with liberal doses of sex and violence. There is violence, for example, in the opening section, in the detailed account of the killing of the minister's secretary, and sexual titillation arises from the later scenes involving chorus girls. The story itself lies on the level of John Buchan and Ian Fleming in its fundamental assumption that the evil plot of one greedy villain might, in a matter of hours, plunge the world into catastrophe unless the hero succeeds against all odds in his desperate counteraction.

In many ways *GS* is another patchwork novel, and a number of its pieces are reworked from earlier stories. Much comes directly from *ST*: the background of Balkan politics, the train journey, the traveling chorus girl and the chorus line, a murder, and the night in a shed beside a railway. Sir Marcus, as a powerful and corrupt industrial magnate, echoes Krogh, while Mather, in his straightforward dedication to the task of criminal investigation, echoes the Assistant Commissioner. Structurally, *GS* suffers from the occasional looseness that pervades *ST*. While the gasmask drill and even the street rioting (an echo of *IB*), contribute to the sense of tension and social unrest which forms the background to the story, the specific business concerning the bully Fergusson and his persecution of Watts is something of a digression. The main story is suspended for some ten pages, and the only material outcome relevant to the plot is that Raven has acquired an effective disguise. Again, Acky and Tiny, brilliantly portrayed as they are, do not fit into the story. It is not clear, for instance, why these two grotesques should be so passionate in the concealment of Cholmondeley's attempted murder of Anne, particularly when, as is revealed at the end, they seem strangely unaware that he is also Davis, a prominent citizen whose face is well known to local policemen and doormen.

On the other hand, despite its flaws, *GS* in some ways anticipates the next step forward in Greene's development as a novelist. Raven, as a small-time racecourse crook, embittered by childhood hardship and lately guilty of a brutal murder, is a sketch for Pinkie, a comparison underlined by Greene's use of the name Kite in the background of both stories. Again, although *GS* is in many ways a reworking of ingredients from *ST*, it goes significantly beyond *ST* in its development of a relationship between hero and heroine. The scene between Raven and Anne in the railway shed explores in some depth Raven's character and motivation, charting territory which Greene was to develop in the character of Pinkie in *BR*.

The overnight scene between Raven and Anne is a reworking of the Coral-Czinner situation in *ST*, both scenes set in small buildings adjacent to railway yards. In *GS*, as in *ST*, the fugitive hero whose action threatens to ignite the Balkans meets by chance on a train an English chorus girl on her way to her next job. In each case the hero entangles the girl in his affairs, and as a result she falls under suspicion of being his accomplice. She accompanies him in flight in both cases, and in both stories a nighttime pursuit across railway yards results in their taking shelter in a small deserted building, while the pursuers gather outside waiting for daylight.

This is the "key scene" of *GS*.[27] Whereas in *ST* Coral only watches helplessly as Czinner is dying, Raven and Anne converse at length. He "confesses" to her, telling her about his childhood and admitting his responsibility for the murder of the minister. She enables him to see the moral implications of his action and to realize that he has been used by his employers to act against the interests of people like himself. Anne also gives Raven the information he needs to track down Sir Marcus. She agrees to act as a decoy, allowing him, in the morning, to make his escape through the surrounding cordon of police. This scene between Raven and Anne is therefore crucial to the success of Raven's search for Sir Marcus and to the prevention of the anticipated war.

Raven himself is an extreme example of the outcast, displaced hero previously represented in Andrews and Conrad. His father was hanged for murder, and his mother committed suicide when he was only six. His upbringing in an orphanage and a disfiguring harelip have isolated him from human affection, leaving him "a sour bitter screwed-up figure" (1.1). Like Andrews and Anthony, Raven is still immature, an unformed personality, led by circumstances and bitterness and easily prey to the influence of others. He has drifted into crime and become a hired killer. His murderous potential is another link with the other early heroes. Anthony is a hired bodyguard, and although he never has a gun of his own he demonstrates his skill as a marksman at a shooting gallery. Pinkie shows the same talent in the same way, although he prefers more subtle weapons in his killing. Conrad carries a gun and tries to use it against the Assistant Commissioner. Andrews shares responsibility for Rexall's death, and the knife he carries kills Elizabeth. Raven's murder of the minister and his secretary serves as a prelude to the main action of *GS*, much as Pinkie's murder of Hale introduces the story in *BR*.

Raven's career in *GS* conforms in outline to the pattern followed by the other early heroes. He begins as a homeless fugitive. The betrayal in *GS* is mutual: Raven disobeys instructions in keeping the gun after the murder, and he uses this against his employers when he discovers they have paid him in stolen money. His encounter with the heroine gives him a new depth of insight and enables him to continue his retributive hunt for his enemies. Like the other heroes Raven is at once a danger, an outlaw to be hunted down, and a sacrificial innocent whose death arises from an attempt to shield others.

In death Raven goes further into self-sacrifice than his predecessors. Like Andrews, he risks himself to save the heroine from dangers he has himself brought upon her, and like all the earlier heroes he dies in a broadly humanitarian cause. Czinner dies trying to help the underprivileged of his country, Anthony's death is the result of his refusal to collaborate with the fraudulent, oppressive capitalism of Krogh, and Conrad is struck down while trying—however wrongheadedly—to retaliate against the injustice inflicted upon Jim and Milly. Raven risks his own life and safety in rescuing Anne, whom he believes to be his friend, in an episode which goes a long way towards winning him the reader's sympathy. His subsequent pursuit of Davis and Sir Marcus is initially undertaken from motives of personal revenge, but after he has learnt the truth from Anne his quest for private vengeance becomes also an urgent crusade to prevent these men from involving Europe in war for their own profit.

Raven's pursuit of vengeance becomes, in effect, humanity's one hope for peace. Greene gives this aspect of Raven a religious coloring much stronger than anything of the kind connected with the earlier heroes. This coloring arises from the story's Christmas setting, and particularly from Raven's musing over the image of the infant Christ (1.3), an element which recurs at crucial points (4.1 and 7.2). Raven is not himself religious, as he tells Anne (5.1), but he sees the figure of Christ as a symbol epitomizing human suffering and victimization, and therefore commanding sympathy. Raven displays his own humanity in his care for the kitten (1.3), his concern for Anne's welfare, and his "horrified tenderness" for the infant Christ (4.1). His capacity for love, his care for the victim and the helpless, extends itself into his quest when he learns that the minister, like Christ, had been a champion of the poor. When Raven dies in the act of killing Sir Marcus, incidentally exposing his own complicity in order to reveal the truth which can alone prevent war, he may be said to sacrifice himself to save others. The point is underlined by an allusion in the narrative to Matthew viii:20, comparing Raven to Christ (7.2). The use of religious symbolism is another of the ways in which *GS* looks forward to *BR*.

Greene turned to a very different kind of novel in *BR*, an innovation which he then developed in *PG*, *MF*, and *HM*. He returned, however, to the simpler pattern of his early novels in *CA* and *TM*. It remains, therefore, to look briefly ahead to these two before examining the more complex novels which belong properly, by virtue of structure and design, to his mature middle period. Both are stories of the early type, their actions each covering a span of only a few days during which the hero follows the pattern observed in *MW*, *IB*, *EM*, and *GS*.

D in *CA* is another fugitive. He has a careworn, victimized air, and does indeed seem to attract misfortune and persecution. He is engaged on a mission which, however politically sympathetic, is technically illegal: he is to arrange with Lord Benditch for the export of coal to the republican forces in the Spanish Civil War. The expected help from Benditch (who is another profiteer, akin to Sir Marcus) does not materialize. In a chain of events closely similar to *GS*, the conspirators turn against their own "agent," who then retaliates against them with murderous consequences. Benditch rejects D and does a deal with his enemies, and D then sets out to expose the plot. Like Raven, he causes such havoc that the true state of affairs is revealed and the plot is thereby foiled. He is materially aided at several points by a heroine, Rose Cullen, who also arranges his escape. The conventional "happy ending" of *CA*, in which D regains his freedom and is joined by the heroine, is atypical—and is indeed offset by a reminder that, as an ageing man returning empty handed to his severe political masters in war-torn Spain, he is unlikely to find long-term happiness.

The pattern of complicity, betrayal, love, and murder, is again played out in *TM*. Martins goes to Vienna, invited by Lime, whom he expects to meet there. Suspected by the police and implicated in a murder, he becomes for a while a fugitive. He establishes a relationship with Anna. When he learns the truth about Lime's criminal activities he agrees to help the police to catch him. For all its justice, Martins feels this act to be a betrayal of his former friend. Lime is killed, and Martins survives, but only after risking his life in the pursuit of Lime through the tunnels.

For some years in the 1950s *TM* enjoyed a celebrity disproportionate to its place among Greene's works. This was on account of the film with Orson Welles, its haunting tune, and the masterful direction of Carol Reed. The book of *TM* is really the last of Greene's simple "thrillers" on the lines of his early novels. Nonetheless, it also looks forward. Its story, turning upon the hero's reluctant realization that he must put a stop to the activities of a friend by betraying him, anticipates in several details the situation of Fowler in *QA*.

III. THE MIDDLE PERIOD

One characteristic of Greene's middle period is a two-track approach to fiction, the production of a series of simpler, more popular novels, with the avowed intent of earning money, while investing longer stretches of time on the composition of more complex, more serious novels, perhaps less likely to win rapid popularity. The adoption of this method also indicates Greene's growing confidence and mastery of his craft. After the completion of *EM*, which may be regarded as the last of his experimental works, he alternated a series of rapidly written potboilers (*GS, CA, MF,* and *TM*), works which he publicly labeled "entertainments" and privately called "shockers," with the series of great novels upon which his reputation still largely rests (*BR, PG, HM*). After 1950, however, with a body of acclaimed work behind him and a degree of financial security, Greene abandoned the "shocker" and allowed himself to diversify his talents into other forms of writing, including plays and comic novels.

The deliberate alternation of serious and popular, major and minor novels affected the nature of Greene's work in the middle period. Sales and film rights of the "entertainments" gave him the freedom to devote longer periods of sustained attention to his major novels. He no longer had to rush these into print to make money, or to worry too much about tailoring them to meet his publishers' tastes. He could be reasonably confident by this time that any work of his would be published, and his popular novels ensured his financial security meanwhile. The result is evident: after a group of imaginative, experimental, competent, but not, in the end, brilliant or enduring works, we enter a new world altogether with *BR*. If Greene had stopped writing after *GS* his work would by now almost certainly be long out of print and largely forgotten. On the other hand, *BR* alone secures him a place among the major English novelists of the mid twentieth century, and the same could be said of each of *PG* and *HM*.

The minor novels of this period are not unrelated to these major achievements. They are somewhat shorter, less tightly constructed, with emphasis on pace and incident rather than character and concept. They tend, moreover, to rework character types and situations from the earlier novels. On the other hand, Greene can be seen with hindsight to have used these "entertainments" to sketch out ideas which he then carried over into the major novels. *GS*, as has already been observed, while reworking characters and situations from *ST* and *IB*, also presents in Raven a sketch for Pinkie. Although not a boy (he is twenty-eight), Raven is immature, has the same background in racetrack crime, and is associated with a murdered man named Kite. He even anticipates Pinkie's taste for a distorted simplification of Christian theology.

In *CA*, written contemporaneously with *PG*, we have the story of a middle-aged man driven by a sense of duty and pursued by enemies through a country indifferent to his fate, a story which clearly anticipates that of the Priest. Both men have their once-quiet lives uprooted by political turmoil, and both are placed in the position of having to take great risks in the service of others, despite a sense of personal inadequacy. An even closer anticipation is the figure of Else, the child in *CA* who helps the hero and is then murdered by his enemies. She reappears as Coral Fellows in *PG*.

In *MF* Greene succeeds in making the "entertainment" into something more than a potboiler. It has the same sort of creaky plot mechanisms as *GS* and *CA*, being another improbable scamper through a John Buchan world of killings, abductions, double identities, and fanatical conspiracies; yet it wins from the reader a willing suspension of disbelief as the fantastic events of the plot become elements in a drama more psychological than circumstantial. Rowe is a fugitive not so much from his enemies as from his own feelings of guilt and pity, feelings which have effectively brought his life to standstill. What matters in *MF* is not simply that, like Raven and D, Rowe should save the world from the wicked plots of the story's villains, but rather that, in the course of doing this, he should work through and resolve his inner problems.

Rowe's remarkable story, the study of a man afflicted with a deep sense of pity and personal responsibility, while it owes something to the Priest and some of the early heroes, is a clear foreshadowing of Scobie and, more generally, of Bendrix, Fowler, and Querry. Rowe's compelling sense of pity, and particularly his need to reconcile his sense of responsibility for his wife's death with his new love for Anna, anticipates Scobie's situation between Louise and Helen. Again, Rowe, caught up in the London

Blitz and in love with a woman who has died, foreshadows Bendrix. Fowler and Querry, each with residual feelings of guilt over women abandoned, are driven by sensibilities akin to Rowe's to cut themselves off from the mainstream of life in ways which echo Rowe's withdrawal into himself at the opening of *MF*. Moreover, the figure of Hilfe, a plausible and apparently gentle idealist who is in fact engaged in monstrous cruelties, attempting to reshape the world according to a vision, is an early version of Pyle.

If one approach to the change which came over Greene's writing in the mid 1930s is by way of the two creative channels, those of the serious novels and the "entertainments," and the interaction between them, another approach is by way of the progressive maturation of the heroes. Whereas all of the early heroes up to and including Pinkie, with the exception of Czinner, are youthful, immature, and boyish, the heroes of the novels which followed *BR* (D, the Priest, Rowe, Scobie) are all men mature in both years and personality. At the same time the early displaced fugitive type gives way to men with established places in society. Pinkie, as a criminal dodging the law, is the last of the displaced fugitives. D and the Priest are, indeed, men pursued, but their being so arises from particular circumstances, from the effects of war and political persecution, not from their own acts or failings. Both D, as a professional scholar, and the hero of *PG*, as a parish priest, have in the recent past been men of position and status. The same is true of their successors: Rowe was a journalist before his wife's death, Scobie is a police officer, Bendrix a well-known author, and Fowler is a journalist successful enough to be offered promotion. Among Greene's heroes only those of the early novels are by nature "hunted men." The later hero is more likely to be a well-established professional man who becomes "hunted" only in exceptional circumstances or, like Querry, by his own choice.

The physical ages of the heroes, however, and even the degrees of personal maturity attributed to them, are only symptomatic. What really matters is that the heroes of the novels Greene wrote in the 1940s and after are much more deeply explored as characters than are those of the novels written before 1936 (leaving

GS, *BR*, and *CA* as in this respect transitional cases). This depth manifests itself chiefly in two ways: the detail and complexity of motivation revealed, and the degree of direction and control assumed by the character over events.

The motivation of the early heroes is in each case relatively simple. Andrews wants to liberate the "man within" and to impress Elizabeth; Czinner wants to do whatever he can for the poor of his country; Conrad loves Jim and Milly and suffers from feelings of persecution; Anthony is feckless but feels a strong bond with the common man, with people like Loo and Andersson; and Raven is vindictively driven to strike back at those who have hurt or betrayed him. There is more to say in each case, but perhaps not very much. Anthony's background is given some depth through his relationship with Kate, and his motives are further explored in terms of the duality developed in the novel between the Englishness to which Anthony owes his origins and the internationalism of Krogh, which he ultimately rejects. Again, Raven's motivation acquires an added dimension from his rudimentary religious speculations.

We are at once in a different world with Pinkie, the complexity of whose motivation is attested by the volume of interpretive criticism written about it. Relevant factors include his impoverished childhood, his early experience of Catholicism, his abandonment as a boy, his memories of Kite, his experience of crime, his desire to avenge Kite and run the gang, his feelings about sex, his feelings towards Rose, and his satanistic creed. Even D, a much simpler man than Pinkie, remains nonetheless more complex in his motivation than the early heroes. His initial sense of duty to his party and, more widely, to the human cause, is quickly complicated by resentment of his opponents, a growing liking for Rose, a desire to avenge the death of Else, and a rising need to assert himself. The relative motivational complexity of the Priest, Rowe, Scobie, and the later heroes needs no demonstration.

As the heroes become more mature and more elaborately motivated, so they become less passive, more assertive in the face of events, more dynamic in their respective confrontations with fate. The early heroes, typically "hunted men," tend to be driven by events and to make only sporadic efforts to assume direction. They tend, like Andrews and Anthony, to be open to the influence of others, often subject to manipulation, and slow to resist or take independent action. Having sent his letter, Andrews is halted in flight by Elizabeth, who sends him to Lewes, where Lucy persuades him to give evidence. His only independent decisions within the course of the main action are to return to Elizabeth in an attempt to save her and, when this has failed and she is dead, to give himself up. In an even simpler story, Czinner's sole material decision lies between returning to his miserable obscurity in England or sacrificing himself for the popular cause. Conrad is hardly in control of his actions, which are scarcely deliberate. He sleeps with Milly on impulse, acquires a gun as a joke, and by the time he begins to stalk the Assistant Commissioner he is evidently unstable and is, in any case, acting under the mistaken impression that the man he is after bears responsibility for Jim's plight. Anthony is a passive drifter, taken in tow by Kate. His only real decision, to break with Krogh after the Andersson affair and to follow Loo back to England, leads directly to his death.

Raven is a little more dynamic. He remains a "hunted man," but he sets the pace of the pursuit and accomplishes several things before he is finally cornered: he rescues Anne from the chimney, tracks down Davis, kills his enemies, and in so doing exposes their plot and averts a war. Again, however, it is in Pinkie that we encounter the first of a really new breed of hero. Throughout his story Pinkie is struggling to hold his collapsing world together. He fails in the end, but the course of his protracted effort is packed with action and initiative. The story begins when he kills Hale. He does this not, as Raven killed the minister, because someone else told him to, but in an assertive act of vengeance intended to establish himself as Kite's successor. To maintain this position he associates himself with Rose, attempts to deal with Colleoni, kills Spicer, arranges Drewitt's disappearance, and plans the fake suicide. Even D, a figure closer to the early heroes in many ways, assumes control of the course of events halfway through his story, when he turns from being "the hunted man" to become "the hunter."

The Priest is, indeed, another "hunted man," but like Pinkie, and like D in Part Two of *CA*, it is he who dictates the course and speed of the chase. The novel opens with his decision to remain voluntarily within reach of his enemies. Subsequently, for his own reasons, he returns to his old home and then takes the road to Carmen. He dodges the *mestizo* and enters the capital in quest of wine. When at last he has made good his escape across the border, he again decides, without compulsion, to return and face capture. Even in flight, moreover, the Priest continues to exercise his ministry. He abandons the attempt after his release from prison, but soon resumes it across the border, and having resumed it promptly returns to the danger zone. Every one of his encounters in the course of his flight—with Coral, his own daughter, the Indian woman, the Lieutenant—is pregnant with significance and involves him in spiritual activity or psychological growth. There is every imaginable difference between the dynamic, symbolically progressive flight of the Priest and the merely responsive or impulsive flights of Andrews, Conrad, and Anthony. The same urgent wrestling with destiny characterizes the other heroes of the middle phase, Rowe and Scobie, in ways too obvious to need discussion.

The greater dynamism of the heroes of the middle period and their more studied motivation are reflected in a structural change first apparent in *BR*. This consists essentially in the spread of the main action over a much longer time span than is used in the early novels, allowing the hero to experience significant growth and development within the period of the story. All the early novels (including *CA*) have plots which, with only occasional brief flashbacks or passages of narrative background, occupy a few days. Indeed, with only two exceptions, one an obvious "prologue" and the other an "epilogue," to the main action, each of these stories covers less than a single week. The exceptional episodes are the murders of the minister and his secretary at the start of *GS*, which take place one week before the action proper opens in London; and Anthony's funeral at the end of *EM*, which, although the interval is not specified, may be presumed to take place several days after the previous scene. These two exceptions aside, *ST* occupies three days, *IB* and *MW* four days each, *CA* five days, and the main action of *EM* five or six days.

It is well worth looking in detail at the tight schedules followed by the early plots, because it is a significant feature of Greene's early work and easily passed over at a cursory reading. In the schemes that follow, days are counted from evening to evening because (probably no more than an odd coincidence) the actions of all of these novels open in the evening. (This is true of *GS* whether we take it to open with the murders or with the London scene a week later.)

MW
DAY 1:   Andrews arrives at Elizabeth's cottage at nightfall. Next day he attends Jennings's funeral and hides from Carlyon.
DAY 2:   Andrews walks to Lewes and meets the lawyers. He then spends the night alone at an inn.
DAY 3:   The trial. Andrews spends the night with Lucy.
DAY 4:   Andrews returns to the cottage. At nightfall the smugglers arrive, Elizabeth dies, and Andrews is arrested next morning.

ST
DAY 1:   The train departs from Ostend in the evening. Myatt gives Coral his compartment. Next day Mabel interviews Czinner. In the evening the train arrives in Vienna. Grünlich comes aboard.
DAY 2:   Coral and Myatt spend the night together. When the train reaches Subotica Coral, Czinner, and Grünlich are detained.
DAY 3:   Overnight Grünlich escapes with Myatt, but Coral and Czinner hide in a barn. In the morning they are found. Later the same day Myatt arrives in Istanbul, where he is dining as the story closes.

IB
DAY 1:   The Assistant Commissioner meets the minister's secretary in the late afternoon. A little later the communist meeting takes place, and afterwards Kay goes

home with Surrogate. That night the Assistant Commissioner arrests a murderer. Next day Surrogate visits Caroline Bury and Milly obtains Mrs. Coney's signature to the petition.

DAY 2: Conrad spends the night with Milly. Next day he acquires a gun. Jules and Kay drive into the country.

DAY 3: Conrad follows the Assistant Commissioner, who has dinner with Caroline Bury. Conrad tries to shoot him as he leaves her house. Later that evening Conrad dies in hospital.

EM

DAY 1: Kate and Anthony meet in the evening at a London station. They apparently travel overnight to Gothenburg. There, next day, they meet the Davidges.

DAY 2: Kate and Anthony arrive in Stockholm. Anthony meets Krogh and spends the night in a hotel.

DAY 3: A Tuesday. Anthony is hired by Krogh. That evening they go to the opera and on to Tivoli.

DAY 4: Anthony meets Loo in the morning. Kate and Krogh become engaged. Dinner at the hotel in Saltsjöbaden. Andersson is beaten by Hall.

DAY 5(?): The day of the card party, after which Anthony is drowned, is almost certainly the Thursday or Friday of the same week. (His funeral would then take place sometime during the week following.)

GS

DAY 1: The main action begins, a week after the murder of the minister, with Mather and Anne in London one evening. Raven meanwhile meets "Cholmondeley." Anne takes the midnight train to Nottwich. Next morning she is captured by Raven and escapes. She reports for work and is taken out by Davis, who leaves her for dead in the chimney.

DAY 2: Mather arrives in Nottwich at 11:00 p.m. and begins his search overnight. Raven rescues Anne. Mather spots him. Raven and Anne hide in the railway shed.

DAY 3: In the morning Raven escapes from the shed. The air raid drill. Raven kills Davis and Sir Marcus and is himself shot down. Anne and Mather return to London in the evening.

CA
DAY 1: D arrives at Dover in the evening and travels to London overnight. Next morning he makes contact with K. He spends the evening with Rose, after which he is attacked by the manageress in his hotel.
DAY 2: A Saturday. D meets Benditch. Else is killed. D escapes from the police and captures K.
DAY 3: D takes an early morning train to the coalfields. In the evening, after the explosion, he is arrested and brought back to London.
DAY 4: D remains in police custody. (This day is not recounted in the narrative, but its passage is alluded to.)
DAY 5: D appears before a magistrate and is granted bail. By nightfall he is on a boat with Rose.

The tight schedules within which all of these early plots operate allow no time for significant character development. The heroes are already well embarked on potentially fatal courses when the novels open, and the situations which will soon seal their fates are already in place. From the early pages the reader is aware that the hero is on a course towards catastrophe. Character development in these stories is elementary and consists chiefly in such features as the hero's reactions to the attempts of his enemies to capture or control him, response to the heroine, and gathering courage for the final decision which then rapidly precipitates his end. While the psychological or conceptual interest of these heroes is minimal, the novels are carried along chiefly by a question of suspense: what can the hero do to avoid the forces gathering to oppose him, and how long can he postpone his inevitable fate?

All this changes in *BR*. The element of suspense remains, but is subordinate to the interest of Pinkie's growth and motivation. The focus of the novel is upon this boyish figure and upon the question of how he will respond to the increasing challenges of adult life. The reader learns of Pinkie's state of mind, of the early life which brought this about, of the influence upon him of Kite, and of his role as Kite's successor. Within the story Pinkie faces the pressures of adult life: the challenge to his status from Colleoni, the demands of human sympathy represented by Rose. To attempt all of this within a span of three or four days would be absurd. The greatly expanded time scale of *BR* is the structural precondition for the new kind of novel Greene began to write in his middle period.

The importance of the point again deserves detailed examination. Here, in contrast to the compact schedules of the early novels, is the much more expansive time scheme of *BR*:

PART I:	The Whitsun holiday. The murder of Hale. Pinkie first meets Rose. Several days later, after the inquest, Ida attends Hale's cremation. (This section may be regarded as "prologue" to the main action.)
PARTS II & III:	Ida arrives in Brighton. There follows a complex of events which seem to occupy two consecutive days: Ida goes to the police; Pinkie visits Brewer; next day Colleoni sends for Pinkie; Pinkie is taken to the police station; he then takes Rose to the country.
PART IV:	The races, a considerable time later. Pinkie is attacked by Colleoni's men, and Spicer is killed.
PARTS V & VI:	Part V opens some days later, after the inquest on Spicer. (The events from this point to the end could be read as continuous, in which case they would occupy five days, but the experience of reading gives the impression of a longer passage of time.) The evening at the pub. Pinkie and Spicer's girl. Pinkie visits Rose's parents. Cubitt deserts. The wedding. The day after the wedding (a Sunday). The suicide pact. Pinkie's death. The closing section (7.10–11), which may be regarded as "epilogue," occurs an unspecified time after Pinkie's death.

The longer time span of *BR* is necessary, not only to accommodate such mechanical requirements as inquests and marriages, but more importantly to allow scope for the growth of the hero. In the course of the story Pinkie undergoes a number of crucial experiences: he murders Hale, faces Colleoni, courts Rose, has his first sexual encounters, is beaten and wounded, revisits the scene of his childhood, murders Spicer, gets married, and faces the possibility of becoming a father. The novel requires that Pinkie be allowed time to absorb his experiences. He has to grow from the vindictive, vicious boy who kills Hale to the tormented soul struggling to preserve his way of life and fit the growing chaos of experience into his narrow conceptual framework of good and evil.

Much the same is true in the case of *MF*, despite its being only an "entertainment." The action of Part I, "The Unhappy Man," occupies four consecutive days: the day of the fête, the day ended when a bomb falls on Rowe's house, the day of the séance, and (after his night in the Underground) the day on which Rowe loses his memory in an explosion. Parts III and IV, "Bits and Pieces" and "The Whole Man," take only two consecutive days, at the end of which the novel is concluded. Between these two short blocks of time, however, comes the long Part II, "The Happy Man," set in the sanatorium, which evidently occupies several weeks. This central lapse of time is crucial, not for the unfolding of events (since very little of importance happens in the outside world during Rowe's time with Doctor Forrester) but to allow a credible interval for Rowe's healing and growth. The "unhappy man" of the fête has to become the "whole man" who accepts Anna's love at the end. Nothing in Rowe's material circumstances is changed by his stay in the sanatorium: he has still killed his wife, the war continues, and inevitably, one way or another, he will soon be reminded of his whole past history. What has changed is the new perspective Rowe has gained from his temporary return to an arcadian, childlike state, and from his realization that this kind of innocence, which he had formerly desired, is ultimately illusory. If this radical inner change is to be credible it has to be gradual, hence the progression of well-spread episodes in Part II from which Rowe gradually acquires a new outlook on life.

The enlarged time scales of the subsequent novels need not be set out in detail. It is obvious that *PG* occupies several weeks, *HM* several months, and *EA* several years; and in each of these novels it is equally clear that the main reason for the extended time span is to accommodate significant growth and development in the character of the hero.

An integral aspect of the hero's growth and development in the middle novels is his reappraisal of the past. There is a marked difference between the early and middle novels in the matter of the hero's past and its relation to the present. In each of the early novels up to *BR* we have a brief sketch of the hero's early life, sufficient to indicate a deprived or unhappy childhood or youth. Andrews had an unhappy boyhood, blighted by his mother's early death and the brutality of his father. Czinner devoted himself to his work from an early age, cutting himself off from parental affection. Conrad suffered as a child from the persecution of other children and relied upon his brother for protection. Anthony was miserable at school (from which he once ran away) and felt that he disappointed his father. Raven, son of a hanged father and a suicide mother, grew up unhappily in an orphanage. Childhood misery and a want of parental affection are the common inheritance of the early heroes from Andrews to Raven.

The deprived childhood is still present in Pinkie's story. His memories of his parental home are entirely negative; he evidently grew up in poverty, and we infer (from the fact of his rescue, while still a boy, by Kite) that he became either abandoned or a runaway. Already in *BR*, however, there is also a very different picture of the hero's past, a much more emotionally positive image. There are certain aspects of his early life which Pinkie regards with nostalgia. Music recalls for him "a whole lost world" associated with his childhood participation in the rituals of the church (2.1). He remembers with longing the prayer for "peace" at the conclusion of the Mass (7.7), and he recalls with "nostalgia" his early experience of Confession (4.1). Thus, while Pinkie is striving to maintain his distance from the kind of life he associates with his parents and his early home, he has also at the back of his mind a vague notion, based upon these more positive memories, of a lost condition of calm happiness, a state often called, in *BR* and in the other novels of this period, simply "peace."

As in the other heroes of the middle novels, Pinkie's vague, occasional nostalgia becomes a confirmed longing for a lost world of innocence. The Priest carries with him happy memories of his days in the seminary and in his first parish, when he was still young and self-satisfied. Scobie looks back to a time before his daughter's death, before Louise joined him in Africa, when he pursued his work without constraining feelings of guilt or pity, and when he enjoyed particularly his lonely treks through the jungle. Even in the "entertainments" of this period the heroes show the same sort of nostalgia. D recalls his happy married life before the war, and Rowe looks back to his childhood, to a time before he was burdened with the guilt of his wife's death.

The early heroes are men whose nature is largely conditioned by unhappy childhood. Character in these early novels is determined by environment. Andrews's initial cowardice and the moral vacillation he displays almost to the end are evidently the result of his upbringing by an indulgent mother and a bullying father and of his later existence in the shadow of his father's memory. Czinner's cultivation in youth of an unemotional idealism leaves him the isolated, ineffectual figure we see. Childhood persecution developed in Conrad the bitterness, paranoia, and fanatical devotion to Jim which activate him in his story. Anthony's unhappy school days and uneasy relations with his father make him a rootless, unreliable character, unable to commit himself for long to any task, person, or line of conduct. Raven's traumatic loss of parents and subsequent unhappiness in an orphanage make him the vicious and vindictive man willing to become a hired assassin and determined to kill those who betray him.

Pinkie's case in *BR* is already different. Although his drift into crime and his inherent cruelty can reasonably be seen as the outcome of childhood hardship and negative feelings towards his parents, there is also in Pinkie's past a significant body of positively remembered experiences which still color his thinking. Pinkie's early membership in the church gave him an alternative course: he might have remained a practicing Christian and even have become a priest, as he had at one time intended (6.2). The reality of this alternative, and the importance of its continued bearing upon his life, are evident not only from the selected trappings of Catholicism in which he still believes—damnation, hell, Satan—but also in his yearning, usually awakened by music, for the sense of peace he had occasionally known as a boy (2.1).

Although Pinkie's deprived childhood may explain his present anarchic, vindictive nature, it has not *determined* that nature to the extent that the childhood of, for example, Anthony has determined the man. Pinkie's past included an alternative, a different kind of life, the memory of which remains with him, even if only as a vague occasional regret. In a similar way each of the heroes of the next four novels also carries a sense of nostalgic regret for past happiness now lost. Each of them longs in secret for an alternative life and feels some guilt or remorse over his failure to have maintained this remembered innocence.

The Priest, Scobie, D, and Rowe can each to some extent ascribe this feeling to circumstances, although this does not eliminate the element of personal guilt. In Pinkie's case we are simply given no account of the factors which turned him away from the church and left him prey to Kite, but in each of *PG*, *HM*, *CA*, and *MF* there is a definite circumstantial divide between the remembered life of innocence and the unhappy present. In D's case it is war (apparently the Spanish Civil War) which deprived him of his much-loved work and caused the death of his wife. For the Priest the crucial event was the onset of religious persecution in Mexico (begun in reality under President Calles in the 1920s). The turning point in Rowe's case was the death of his wife, an event which, although only fortuitously, coincided roughly with the outbreak of the Second World War. The chief watershed in Scobie's life was the death of his daughter, a death once again associated coincidentally with a transition in the wider world to a state of war. Of these four heroes, each is separated from his respective past by political turmoil, in each case events from historical reality. In three cases there is also a death for which the hero feels some responsibility. There is a common feeling here, found also in *BR*, of a regrettable and probably irreversible transition from a state of happy innocence to one of guilt-laden experience.

Whereas in the early novels, up to and including *GS*, the hero's past takes the form of an unhappy or loveless childhood or youth, the effects of which have created in him the flaws which make him a subject of tragedy, in the novels of the middle period (including here *CA*) the hero's past is seen in a very different light. In these novels the hero's childhood or youth includes elements of contentment which figure, in the adult memory, as a state of "peace" or "innocence." Childhood has not determined the man, since at the heart of each of these heroes is a feeling that things might have been different, that a chance of personal happiness has somehow been missed. The inner growth of the hero, which is the main business of the expanded time scale of these middle period novels, is conducted chiefly in terms of his reappraisal of this vision of the past.

Each of the heroes from Pinkie to Scobie may be said to be seeking, or at least regretting, a lost past innocence. In a simpler novelist than Greene we might then expect to make our final judgement of the hero in terms of his success or failure in recapturing the innocence he has lost; but Greene is rarely simple, and the straightforward conclusion that lost innocence is a condition to be desired cannot, in his mature novels, be taken for granted. The hero himself, in each of these cases, sets out with a deep yearning for the world he has forfeited, but in the course of the action he learns (or is expected to learn) that his ideal is insufficient, that the goal of peace and contentment he had set himself is not now realistically attainable nor even desirable.

This reappraisal of their vision of the past lies at the heart of the heroes' growth and development in the middle novels. In each case the hero is faced with the necessity of turning from a backward-looking yearning for lost innocence to an acceptance of the limitations of experiential reality. In each case (excepting that of *CA*, which in this respect remains in the more simplistic ambit of the early novels) an integral part of this reappraisal is an episode in which the hero makes a symbolic journey back to confront his personal past. In *BR* Pinkie goes back to the scene of his childhood in his visit to Rose's parents; Rowe returns to a state of childlike innocence in the arcadian setting of the sanatorium; Scobie's trip to Bamba recreates the conditions of his early treks which he remembers with fondness, and the young Pemberton, whom he finds at the end of the journey, is a symbolic representation of his former self; and the Priest, in the first stages of his flight, retraces his past life, returning first to his former home and then setting off for his birthplace, where his parents are buried.

These episodes each stand a little aside from the main flow of the narrative. They are not strictly required by the action and have consequently the character of digressive episodes. Pinkie does indeed need the consent of Rose's parents before he can marry her, but the scene in which he obtains it is not essential to the story, much less the account of his journey to their house through the streets in which he grew up. (The business might, for instance, have been accomplished by Drewitt, without Pinkie's personal involvement, an expedient which might have been more in line with Pinkie's character than the personal visit.) The Priest, in flight from the soldiers, has no particular reason for his return to his former home. He is no safer there than anywhere else. Indeed, because he is known there, and because he has acquaintances and a daughter there whom his presence might compromise, we might have expected him to avoid this place. The Priest is already in flight, but the direction he takes after he leaves Coral Fellows and until he abandons his intention of entering Carmen forms an episode concerned primarily with his need to confront his past. Book Two of *MF*, which covers Rowe's period in the sanatorium, is plainly episodic. The hero is temporarily withdrawn from the action by amnesia and confined to an isolated location. The main storyline resumes only when, as his memory begins to return, he escapes from the sanatorium and goes back to the scene of the action in London. Scobie's trek to Bamba is also an interlude, a journey made to investigate the death of a character who does not otherwise figure in the story, a journey on which Scobie is sent but which, as Louise points out (2.2.2), should more properly have been assigned to a junior officer.

D's journey to Benditch in *CA* does not belong with these primarily symbolic journey-episodes from the middle novels. *CA* belongs structurally with the early novels by virtue of its tightly scheduled plot, which allows no place for digressive episodes and no time for significant character development. D's trip to Benditch is an integral part of the plot, undertaken for straightforwardly practical ends: to hinder the delivery of the coal to his enemies. Although there are symbolic elements in this part of the story, such as the arid landscape, and although there is an association with childhood in D's meeting with Rose's old nurse, the journey has no immediate connection with D's personal past, nor does any self-scrutiny arise from it. The digressive backward-journey-episode, therefore, is a feature exclusive to the middle novels. It does not occur in *CA* or the novels before *BR*, and neither is it used in novels after HM. It remains to see how, in each of the four middle novels, the journey episode works to reveal the hero's dynamic revaluation of his past.

Pinkie remembers two very different childhood worlds. One memory involves a yearning for spiritual peace, associated with his boyhood membership of the church, and particularly with Confession.

> [H]is heart weakened with a faint nostalgia for the tiny dark confessional box, the priest's voice, and the people waiting under the statue . . . to be made safe from eternal pain. (4.1)

> The words, "Dona nobis pacem," came again to mind; for the second time he felt a faint nostalgia, as if for something he had lost or forgotten or rejected. (4.1)

> [The] boy began to weep. He shut his eyes to hold in his tears, but the music went on—it was like a vision of release to an imprisoned man. He felt contrition and saw—hopelessly out of reach—a limitless freedom: no fear, no hatred, no envy. It was as if he were dead and were remembering the effect of a good confession. (6.2)

> "Why, I was in a choir once," the Boy confided, and suddenly he began to sing softly in his spoilt boy's voice: "Agnus Dei qui tollis peccata mundi; dona nobis pacem." In his voice a whole lost world moved.... (2.1)

This vision, encompassing the church, Confession, and peace, is one of innocence. Diametrically opposed to this is the demonic memory of Pinkie's home life, which has its geographical center in "Paradise Piece." The name is simply ironic: any suggestion of innocence in Paradise Piece is flatly rejected: "*there* was not innocence: you had to go back a long way farther before you got innocence" (5.3). Pinkie, indeed, embodies a rejection of the Wordsworthian-Platonic notion of primal innocence: "He trailed the clouds of his own glory after him: Hell lay about him in his infancy" (2.2).[28] Paradise Piece, despite its name, is hell, a place of violence, desolation, and suffering:

> The Salvation Army Citadel marked with its battlements the very border of his home.... A flapping gutter, glassless windows, an iron bedstead in a front garden the size of a table top. Half Paradise Piece had been torn up as if by bomb bursts: the children played about the steep slope of rubble; a piece of fire-place showed houses had once been there.... The children were scouting among the rubble with pistols from Woolworth's; a group of girls surlily watched. A child with its leg in an iron brace limped blindly into him....
> (5.3)

This waste land is Pinkie's birthplace, a place not of innocence but of grim experience.

Paradise Piece represents the realm of experience not only because of its physical attributes of poverty and destruction but also because, in Pinkie's mind, it is associated with human familial relationships and particularly with sexuality. Pinkie remembers "the room at home, the frightening weekly exercise of his parents which he had watched from his single bed" (3.3). The "horror" (5.3) with which Pinkie regards the place stems not only from his natural desire to escape from so drab and impoverished environment but more deeply from a revulsion against any kind of human intimacy or interpersonal emotion, a revulsion which arises ultimately from his childhood observation of sexuality.

Pinkie's character rests upon these two opposed visions, of innocence and experience, each rooted in his past. On the one hand he yearns for the peace he knew as a choirboy, while on the other he rejects the horror of his boyhood life at home in Paradise Piece. Like other heroes of Greene's middle fiction, Pinkie longs for a lost innocence, but his conception of innocence, conditioned by these two childhood visions, takes on a peculiar nature. Pinkie's idea of innocence is not so much a positive concept as a negative idea, consisting in a determined rejection of what he sees as the heart of human corruption. At the center of Pinkie's vision of hell is the copulation of his parents. To avoid this, Pinkie rejects not only sexuality but also adulthood, with its connotation of human bonding in any kind of close sympathy or intimacy. This is why Pinkie's age, his adolescent immaturity, upon which the narrative so often insists by referring to him simply as "the Boy," is essential to him. Pinkie's character is one of deliberately arrested development, of one who refuses to cross the threshold into the adult world.

Pinkie is engaged in an emulation of Peter Pan, a refusal to grow up. This is the basis of his asceticism, which he learned from Kite: he does not participate in any of the activities specific to the adult world. He does not drink, he does not work for a living, he does not enter into intimate relationships. On the contrary, he remains emotionally childlike. He is spiteful, vengeful, self-willed, with no stronger feelings for others than are involved in simple gang loyalty. This is also the reason why Pinkie avoids music: he cannot tolerate music because it arouses emotions, strong emotions which he cannot handle and which, in his mind, belong to the world of human intimacy, the world of his parents and Paradise Piece.

Pinkie's "boyish" immaturity is described as a lack of imagination, meaning specifically that he has not developed the capacity for sympathy, for sharing or appreciating the feelings of others.

> The imagination hadn't awakened. That was his strength.
> He couldn't see through other people's eyes, or feel with

their nerves. Only the music made him uneasy, the cat-gut vibrating in the heart; it was like nerves losing their freshness, it was like age coming on. (2.1)

Pinkie's avoidance of emotion, particularly of feelings of human sympathy, associates him with other heroes of this period, especially with Rowe and Scobie. It might seem that this boyish criminal could have little in common with a mature police officer; but Scobie's vision of peace consists essentially in a freedom from human emotion and is therefore not far removed from Pinkie's.

Like so many religious sects, Pinkie confuses spiritual innocence with physical abstinence. He sees the church not as a road to any kind of higher spirituality but rather as a haven from the snares of human emotion. In an important piece of conversation with Dallow while they stand waiting for Rose outside the registry office, Pinkie reveals that as a "kid" he "swore" that he would become a priest. When Dallow laughs Pinkie argues, "What's wrong with being a priest? . . . They know what's what. They keep away . . . from this"—"this" being the world of experience and particularly, as the context makes clear, human sexuality and reproduction. Pinkie, who is himself about to be married, indicates a copy of Marie Stopes's *Married Love* in a nearby shop window, and goes on to tell the story of Annie Collins, a fifteen-year-old girl who committed suicide rather than bear a second child (6.2). For Pinkie the essential aspect of priesthood is celibacy and, more widely, isolation from involvement in everyday life. This also explains Pinkie's theology: his god is not a god of love and mercy but a god concerned with the punishment of carnality. Hell exists, typified in Paradise Piece, and Satan is the presiding deity of animal passion. One reaches towards God by denying, and even inflicting cruelty upon, carnal humanity.

Pinkie is trying to regain something of peace and innocence by remaining adolescent, by deliberately rejecting adulthood in the form of sexuality or indeed of any form of emotional involvement. The only emotions he allows himself are simple, childlike feelings of grateful affection towards a protector (Kite) or of vindictive hatred of those who threaten him (Hale, Spicer, and eventually Rose). Ironically, however, the story requires of him precisely what he will not do. In order to protect himself after the murder of Hale, Pinkie is obliged to form a relationship with Rose. Rose, in Pinkie's mind, stands for everything he is struggling to avoid.

> She got up and he saw the skin of her thigh for a moment above the artificial silk, and a prick of desire disturbed him like a sickness. That was what happened to a man in the end: the stuffy room, the wakeful children, the Saturday night movements from the other bed. Was there no escape—anywhere—for anyone? (3.3)

Much as in Scobie's case, therefore, the heroine, the potential lover who, in a traditional story, might be expected to bring the hero to full maturity, even to a metaphorical redemption, figures in the hero's mind as a distraction from his private spiritual goal. Although Rose represents "goodness" and, in a sense is "something which completed him," and although he is aware of this (4.3), Pinkie cannot help seeing Rose in the end as a mortal threat.

There is deep irony, even an element of mystery, in the relationship between Pinkie and Rose. He meets her as a direct result of his attempt to conceal the murder of Hale. With uncanny insight, despite his largely successful efforts to destroy or hide evidence, she rapidly divines the truth that Pinkie is a murderer. She is unmoved by his initial attempts at intimidation, and eager for his friendship—which he dare not withdraw. Even marriage, he feels, will not guarantee her silence, and he fears her even when, as the reader knows, her loyalty to him is absolute. The obvious expedient of using violence against her is never seriously considered. Spicer is killed out of hand on mere suspicion after years of service, but Rose walks unscathed amongst the gangsters who have just murdered Hale and "carved" Brewer. When Pinkie at last conceives the idea of the false suicide pact it turns even Dallow, his last ally, against him, and brings Ida and the police down upon him.

Whatever more abstract allegorical or symbolic interpretation may be given of Rose, it is clear that she represents for Pinkie an irresistible, irremovable compulsion. As he sees it, his only alternative to ever-closer association with Rose, and to final acceptance of marriage, parenthood, and family life, is extinction, the discovery of his crime and consequently his execution or (if he is indeed a minor) life imprisonment. What Rose is compelling him to do is the very thing which his nature revolts against, to enter the world of adult relationships and responsibility, a world which is for him identified with the hell of Paradise Piece. Nor is Pinkie wholly wrong, for Rose comes from the same place, from the neighboring street, Nelson Place. It is another extraordinary irony that, in order to marry her, Pinkie must first go back there and confront her parents in the place of his own birth.

Pinkie needs to marry Rose for reasons both practical and symbolic. His safety from the consequences of his past crime of murder rests, as he sees it, upon her silence, since she is the only witness not an accessory who can connect him with Hale. She is also, in psychological terms, giving him the opportunity to embark on a normal adult life. She is a natural and proper partner for him: she is twice said to "complete" him (4.3 and 6.2). She is, moreover, prepared to accept damnation for his sake: "I'd rather burn with you," she says, "than be like Her [Ida]" (4.1). All of this suggests that Rose offers Pinkie some form of salvation and that his marriage to her, irrespective of his own feelings about it, is a desirable, even necessary step for him to take.

This being so, his walk through the slums of Brighton, along the streets of his childhood to Rose's home in Nelson Place, assumes the characteristics of a quest. If Rose is the heroine whom Pinkie must win for himself, his journey across the landscape of Paradise Piece, described as a waste land of violence and suffering, is a symbolic rescue. Rose, like Pinkie, dreads her home, and marriage, even marriage with him, would secure her from the possibility of having to return there. Rose's parents, therefore, stand as the guardians of this unhappy place, preventing her escape into the wider world. They are the Pluto and Persephone whom this unlikely Orpheus must confront if he is to return with his Eurydice.

In the event Rose's parents turn out to be a pair of minor grotesques—related, in the context of Greene's fiction, to Acky and Tiny and to Javitt and Maria—with whom Pinkie deals without much difficulty. The real hardship for him in this episode lies, not with Rose's parents, but in the traumatic journey. "He was scared, walking alone back towards the territory he had left—oh, years ago. . . . Every step was a retreat. He thought he had escaped for ever by the whole length of the parade. . . . He began to fear recognition and feel an obscure shame . . . " (5.3). What he has to do to "win" Rose is in line with what she herself will require of him: he has to face his past, to acknowledge in himself the basic humanity, the capacity for love and sympathy, through which he may achieve maturity. The difficulty and distress he experiences in the journey are closely related to the resistance he makes against Rose herself.

In the end Pinkie is unable to accept Rose, although for a while his attitude towards her remains uncertain. At times he feels that she "completes" him, and when he trusts her he even "felt an odd sense of peace, as if—for a while—he hadn't got to plan" (7.2). Even as he plans her death he feels a momentary "tenderness" for her (7.7). He cannot rid himself of suspicion, however, and is unable to believe that she could not be made to betray him. Marriage makes no difference to this abiding mistrust, nor does sexual union with her alter his attitude to love. Afterwards he "was shaken again with his nocturnal Saturday disgust. He couldn't blame his father now . . . it was what you came to. . . . It was life getting at you" (7.5). The realization that he himself might become a father inspires him only with "terror and disgust" at the thought of "another life already pinning him down" (7.4).

Despite Rose's efforts Pinkie fails to achieve the transition to maturity. In his last journey with her, to Peacehaven where he plans that she should die, he makes a symbolic retreat back into boyhood. At the hotel he meets Piker, an old school mate, and remembers old feuds: "I used to give him hell in the breaks" (7.7). As he makes the final arrangements for the "suicide" he is like "a boy playing a game," and when he is finally burned with his own acid he "shrank into a schoolboy, flying in panic and pain" (7.8).

The Heroes

BR is the story of a young man dominated by two notions he has formed upon the basis of his childhood experience. On the one hand he retains a vision of "peace" or lost innocence, associated with his period as a choirboy; on the other hand he has conceived a horror of adult human relationships, derived from the squalor of his boyhood home and from observation of parental sex. His solution is an attempt to preserve in himself something of his vision by cultivating priest-like asceticism and celibacy and, at the same time, avoiding action characteristic of emotional maturity. Events in the story urge him to abandon this program and to engage, through a relationship with Rose, in a normal adult life of marriage and parenthood, but he is unable to do so. At the center of this pattern of action lies Pinkie's journey back to his boyhood home, a painful confrontation with what he has rejected, a confrontation which he has to undergo if he is to marry Rose.

Pinkie stands at a turning point in the line of Greene's heroes. His immaturity and inability to confront the responsibilities of adult life are developed from the early heroes, particularly from Andrews, Anthony, and Raven. His deliberate refusal to accept the demands of adult relationships foreshadows the noninvolvement cultivated by later heroes such as Fowler, Querry, and Plarr. His confrontation with his past life anticipates the same motif in the immediately succeeding cases of the Priest, Rowe, and Scobie.

The story of *PG* can be seen as one of a man who has to revaluate his past life. The past life of the Priest is represented in the newspaper photograph "taken years ago" at a first communion party in his parish.

> It was obscure, but you could read into the smudgy photograph a well-shaved, well-powdered jowl much too developed for his age. The good things of life had come to him too early—the respect of his contemporaries, a safe livelihood. The trite religious word upon the tongue, the joke to ease the way, the ready acceptance of other people's homage ... a happy man. (1.2)

The picture, seen in the early pages of the novel, represents the

Priest in his youth. It conveys an easy, worldly conception of the priesthood, in which spirituality becomes only a shallow formality. It was just this conception of priesthood, we later discover, that had attracted him as a boy: "he had believed that when he was a priest he would be rich and proud—that was called having a vocation" (2.1). He had been happy as a young priest and had, he later felt, even achieved a kind of innocence, albeit of a selfish and loveless kind: "in those days he had been comparatively innocent.... Then, in his innocence, he had felt no love for anyone" (2.3). There is a close similarity to Pinkie here in the Priest's abiding memory of youthful innocence within the church, an innocence of which abstention from emotional contact with others was an integral part.

By the time of the action of the story, however, innocence has been lost and has receded into memory. Rather like Pinkie, the Priest is haunted by the vision of lost peace and contrasts it with the harsh reality of present experience.

> Suddenly he remembered—for no apparent reason—a day of rain at the American seminary, the glass windows of the library steamed over with the central heating, the tall shelves of sedate books, and a young man—a stranger from Tucson—drawing his initials on the pane with his finger—that was peace. He looked at it from the outside: he couldn't believe that he would ever again get in. He had made his own world, and this was it—the empty broken huts, the storm going by, and fear again.... (2.4)

Although he can have little practical hope, the Priest, as we find him at the beginning of the story, still has in mind as his ideal this remembered life of peace and comfort in a priesthood respected and secure but free from personal involvement with human corruption. *PG* is the story of the process whereby this ideal is reappraised, a process which, as in *BR*, requires the hero to review and reassess his past.

The story consists essentially of the Priest's attempts to elude capture, and these fall into two distinct stages, separated by the pivotal episode, more or less midway, of the night he spends in a prison cell. He sets out, having failed to catch the boat to safety, with the goal of personal comfort and security very much in mind. What he still desires, and what he might actually achieve if and when he crosses into a different state, across a border into a territory where the church is not persecuted, is a return to his former way of life as a comfortable parish priest. In token of this he still carries with him from those days, very much in evidence, a briefcase in which are a few trivial papers relating to parish administration.

The actual journey mapped out for the Priest, the course he takes in his flight from the soldiers, may appear random but is really significant. The course he selects for himself in Part One is a retracing of his steps into the territory of his past life, much in the manner of Pinkie's return to Paradise Piece but treated in much greater narrative detail. After leaving Coral Fellows, the Priest heads first for "the very place he most wanted to be," the place he thinks of as his "home" (2.1). This is where he had taken refuge years before, when persecution first drove him from his parish. He had lived there in obscure poverty, given way to drink and despair, and fathered a child. Shortly after the birth of this child, about six years before the time with which the novel deals, he had left the place and had not returned since. Like Pinkie's Paradise Piece, therefore, this "home" is a place of shame and misery associated with carnality and parenthood.

What the Priest finds there, and indeed the main thing which draws him to the place, is his daughter. Here again, as in *BR*, any expectation the reader may hold that childhood will represent innocence is quickly shattered. The Priest's daughter is vicious and unresponsive, an even more poignant portrait than the poor, deformed children mimicking acts of crime and violence among the rubble of Pinkie's home. The Priest loves his daughter, feels responsible for her and, anticipating an action of Scobie's, offers God his own damnation in return for the salvation of the girl; but he has to face the fact that in reality there is little he can do for her. It is hard to escape the conclusion that this child, whose corruption must be innate and not acquired, represents original sin, the sin of the father in particular. Begotten in sin and despair, she confronts the Priest with his own complicity in evil.

The Priest's encounter with his daughter is also the first step in his revaluation of the past. Maria (the girl's mother) throws his briefcase onto the village rubbish heap. He protests and goes to retrieve the papers from it.

> He sighed: it had been quite a good case: one more relic of the quiet past.... Soon it would be difficult to remember that life had ever been any different....
>
> The papers were there; reluctantly he let the case fall—a whole important and respected youth dropped away among the cans—he had been given it by his parishioners in Concepcion on the fifth anniversary of his ordination. (2.1)

At the same moment the Priest sees his daughter watching him, and their final unsatisfactory interview takes place beside the rubbish heap. The meaning of the abandoned briefcase is clear: the shock of seeing his daughter has begun the process whereby he will eventually reject the dreams of his old life.

The Priest's "journey back" is not yet complete. From his "home" village he sets out for Carmen, the place "where he had been born and where his parents were buried" (2.1). What exactly he planned to do there is never apparent, since he is deflected by the *mestizo* and so never arrives. What is interesting here is the impulse to return to his roots, back even as far as the place of his birth, although it has no practical outcome in the story. Again, the journey is primarily symbolic: the process of returning to his humble origins among the common people prepares him for the sense of communion with humanity he experiences shortly afterwards in the prison cell.

The "journey back" is a necessary part of the Priest's spiritual progress, but significant events in Greene's fictional world are rarely unambivalent. Just as Pinkie finds images of death in Paradise Piece (particularly the child who threatens him with an imaginary gun), and just as Scobie's trek to Bamba ends with a prefiguration of his own death in the suicide of Pemberton, so on the Priest's road to Carmen he meets the *mestizo*, the Judas who will eventually betray him to his enemies. In *PG*, as in each of *BR*, *MF*, and *HM*, the "journey back," however necessary, is far from safe and is, indeed, in most cases, fatal in the outcome.

The Heroes 53

At this point in the story, however, the Priest finally renounces his past. On the road to Carmen he still carries with him the paper reclaimed from his briefcase. "Now that his case was gone, it was the only evidence left that life had ever been different: he carried it with him as a charm, because if life had been like that once, it might be so again" (2.1). However, as he is about to be arrested he drops the paper unnoticed: "it was like the final surrender of a whole past" (2.2). This "surrender" takes place outside the house of Padre José, a priest who has given in to the persecution and accepted married life and a pension in return for renunciation of his priesthood. It may at first seem that the Priest's "surrender" of his past is comparable to José's, but it soon becomes clear that we are looking here at a contrast rather than any real similarity. José has renounced his priesthood: he refuses to pray for the dead child in the cemetery (1.4), and he refuses to hear the dying confession of his fellow priest (3.4). The Priest, although he has given way to despair and failed, like José, to remain celibate, does not abandon his ministry. This becomes immediately clear in the prison cell.

The Priest's night in the cell is his turning point. Here he openly avows his calling, in the words "I am a priest," and his reward is a new kind of "peace."

> It was like the end: there was no need to hope any longer. The few years' hunt was over at last. There was silence all around him. This place was very like the world: overcrowded with lust and crime and unhappy love, it stank to heaven; but he realized that after all it was possible to find peace there, when you knew for certain that the time was short.
>
> (2.3)

In the microcosmic world of the cell he has come to terms with ordinary life. He has abandoned his dream and reconstituted his ideas of priesthood on a new basis. Here the formalities do not matter, and his office can bring him no gain or comfort; on the contrary, his admission that he is a priest places him at the mercy of everyone present and makes his betrayal almost certain. Yet here he finds "a sense of companionship which he had never experienced in the old days when pious people came kissing his black cotton glove" (2.3). He has been led to this point, gradually discarding the tokens of his old concept of priesthood, in the course of his journey back over the scenes of his past life.

He is not betrayed in prison and, to his surprise, is released. At this turning point, as the second phase of his flight is about to begin, he is confronted with the photograph described to the reader in the second chapter. His reaction to this image of his past self reveals how much he has altered: "What an unbearable creature he must have been in those days—and yet in those days he had been comparatively innocent.... Then, in his innocence, he had felt no love for anyone; now in his corruption he had learnt..." (2.3). "Innocence," as in *BR*, is not enough: now, in the light of painful experience, the Priest has attained a greater humanity and, as becomes apparent in the second phase of the story, a deeper faith.

It remains for the Priest to complete the second phase of his flight and make good his escape. Now, with his experience of the cell behind him, he is given an insight into "the dark and magical heart of the faith" (2.4) in the Indian cemetery, a faith whose roots go further down than the dogmas or traditions of any church. Then, when he has crossed the border and found safety with the Lehrs, the restoration of his old way of life, the ideal to which he was still clinging at the start of the story, becomes a real possibility. "He felt respect all the way up the street: men took off their hats as he passed: it was as if he had got back to the days before the persecution" (3.1). He no longer feels easy in this way of life, and when the *mestizo* appears again he promptly renounces it for a priesthood based upon service to humanity. He finds that "he had never really believed in this peace" (3.1).

Greene's "entertainments" tend to be in some respects patch works, made up from ideas and motifs in novels already written; but at the same time he used them to try out new ideas, some of which figured more elaborately in subsequent serious novels. *MF* borrows from the early novels the central figure of the hunted man. Rowe, like Raven and D, is pursued across a landscape permeated with conspiracy and echoing with the rumble of war, as he tries desperately to vindicate the truth he is meanwhile uncovering. He also reminds us of the Priest in his burden of personal guilt. At the same time Rowe is clearly a preliminary sketch for Scobie and, more remotely, for Fowler and Querry, as a man whose extreme sensitivity comes close to making life impossible.

Although an "entertainment," *MF* follows *BR* and *PG* in using a long time span and portraying a hero whose character and thought develop significantly during the story, and particularly as a result of reconsideration of the past. *MF* still has the adventure-story characteristics of *GS* and *CA*: a fast-moving plot of highly improbable events and coincidences (e.g., the bomb blast causing amnesia, a fiendish conspiracy which only the hero can expose, and a rather perfunctory love story). What raises this novel above the general level of the earlier "entertainments" is its subordination of these adventure-story elements to the study of the hero's developing state of mind. The main events of the plot—the fête, the séance, the bomb, the sanatorium episode—are presented as largely symbolic stages in a drama which is more psychological than real.

Rowe begins, like the Priest, with a sense of lost innocence. In Rowe's case this is associated particularly with childhood. The whole story, the entire sequence of adventures, is initiated by his effort to regain this lost world. He goes, on the spur of the moment, to a fête which "called him like innocence: it was entangled in childhood" (1.1.1). Rowe's yearning for innocence arises chiefly from his distress and guilt over the death of his wife, a mercy killing prompted by his own horror of suffering. He is constantly asking himself whether he killed Alice to free her from pain or to free himself from the agony of seeing her suffer (1.2.2). Along with this confusion and guilt, which has so paralyzed Rowe that he lives in complete isolation and idleness, goes the background of war. There is, of course, no causal connection, but here, as in *EA*, the coincidence of the events of the story with the onset of war is meaningful. The hero's loss of innocence is reflected in the chaotic state of the wider world, and the hero's mission in the story is at once to help end the chaos and to set himself on the road to spiritual recovery. As Rowe contributes to the effort to bring the war to a satisfactory conclusion so, like Raven, he expiates his personal guilt.

At the fête he acquires a copy of *The Little Duke* by Charlotte M. Yonge. Originally published in 1854 and now quite forgotten, this book, as is clearly established in Greene's narrative, represents for Rowe the moral simplicity of his childhood world. In a brilliant stroke Greene uses this book as a source for chapter epigraphs throughout *MF*, sounding a kind of ground note of innocence beneath all the doings of the plot.

Rowe's childhood innocence is reminiscent of Pinkie's, but not quite the same. Whereas Pinkie seeks a prolongation of childhood irresponsibility in order to avoid adult relationships and duties, Rowe looks back with longing to the moral simplicity of childhood. Rowe remembers childhood as a world of good and evil, heroes and villains, a world of clear moral distinctions such as is found in boys' adventure-stories and particularly in *The Little Duke*. Evil certainly existed in that world, but it was recognizable and separable. In adult life, Rowe has found, this is not so, and the world is full of moral ambiguities and dilemmas, such as that he himself faces over his wife's death. Is it right to kill to end suffering? Can one do evil to achieve good?

> That is why no later books satisfy us like those which were read to us in childhood—for those promised a world of great simplicity of which we know the rules, but the later books are complicated and contradictory with experience; they are formed out of our own disappointing memories. . . . The Little Duke is dead and betrayed and forgotten; we cannot recognize the villain and we suspect the hero and the world is a small cramped place. (1.7.1)

Moral simplicity is characteristic of innocence, while with experience comes complexity and moral uncertainty.

Rowe's attempt to maintain the moral vision of childhood into adult life, to find a simple answer to all moral questions in terms of either good or evil, is the root of his distress. In the course of the novel it is shown that moral simplicity is not in reality a tenable ideal and that, for effective action in the real world, compromise is necessary. This relates to Rowe's personal problem. He learns in the end to accept his wife's death as, in the circumstances, a necessary moral compromise.

The story thus requires Rowe to reevaluate a view of the world based upon a notion of past innocence and to adapt himself to present experience. In this respect *MF* follows the pattern of *BR* and *PG*. Like Pinkie and the Priest, Rowe must go back, make a symbolic journey to the past he remembers, and must recognize as a result that this memory is not a sound basis for life. Rowe's journey back begins as he enters the fête, stepping "back into adolescence, into childhood." "It was as if Providence had led him to exactly this point to indicate the difference between then and now" (1.1.1). Realization of "the difference between then and now," the progression from a dream of lost innocence to acceptance of imperfect reality, is the task of the heroes of the middle novels.

The fête, of course, is not as innocent as it appears. It reminds Rowe of childhood and yields a copy of *The Little Duke*, but it is also his point of contact with the conspiracy. As he receives the fateful cake, Rowe feels "as if the experience of childhood renewed had taken a strange turn, away from innocence" (1.1.1). The practical inseparability of good from evil, of innocence from corruption, is already apparent.

From this beginning Rowe's adventure takes him through a number of gardens—echoes of the original garden in which the fête is held, and, of course, of the lost garden of Paradise—and through several reenactments of the "murder" of his wife—the primal sin in Rowe's life, which entailed his loss of innocence. After the fête and a series of enquiries Rowe traces Mrs. Bellairs. To enter her house he must cross a "little patch of dry and weedy garden" where "a piece of statuary lay . . . chipped and grey with neglect" (1.4). Rowe is evidently entering a fallen world. After his escape from the house, where he has apparently committed another murder, he spends the night in the Underground and dreams of the garden of his childhood home. In the dream he is "having tea on the lawn at home behind the red brick wall and his mother was lying back in a garden chair eating a cucumber sandwich." Into this English Eden, while Rowe is trying to explain to his mother that his world is no longer one of idyllic innocence, enters "the vicar's wife carrying a basket of apples" (1.5), another allusion to the Fall. Rowe's task in this dream reflects his mission in the novel: to force himself out of nostalgic longing for lost innocence and to bring himself to a realistic reckoning with adult life.

Next day Rowe is followed by an odd man who identifies himself as Fullove, a dealer in antiquarian books, but who is actually one of the enemy. Fullove specializes in old books on landscape gardening, and in an apparently casual piece of conversation Rowe observes that a garden is a place where one might expect to feel safe. Fullove points out, to the contrary, that eighteenth-century gardens were full of "tricks," "machinery," and even "tombs." "Why, in a good garden you weren't safe anywhere," he says (1.7.2); and this is appropriate, because his case, supposedly packed with books on gardens, actually contains the bomb which is to cause Rowe's loss of memory and which is intended to kill him.

The last of the gardens of *MF* is that of the sanatorium. This is "Arcady," according to the chapter heading (2.1), but from the start it is clear things are not quite right. The garden is "of a rambling kind which should have belonged to childhood and only belonged to childish men" (2.1.4). Rowe's first walk here brings him upon Major Stone, who is concerned about evil doings on the island in the pond. Rowe is at first inclined to dismiss Stone as unbalanced, but the Major turns out to be right. The remains of the murdered Jones are buried on the island: there is death even in Arcady.

The gardens of *MF* all allude in a general way to the remembered garden which is the focus of Rowe's vision of childhood innocence. The several deaths he encounters allude more specifically to the death of Alice, to the source of Rowe's guilt. First of these is the "murder" of Cost at the séance, which occurs just as Rowe hears his wife's voice. The voice is not his wife's, and Cost is not dead, but this attempt of the conspirators to play on Rowe's guilt is nonetheless effective. He becomes a fugitive and dreams that night of the dying rat and his lost childhood.

Next day he searches out Henry Wilcox and arrives coincidentally at the moment of Henry's wife's funeral. Henry's mourning for his wife, the victim of a wartime accident, echoes Rowe's continuing distress over the death of Alice. The name Henry Wilcox is borrowed from the central male character in E. M. Forster's *Howard's End*, the death of whose wife is a major event in the novel. *Howard's End* also prominently features a garden, symbolic of innocence, of which the deceased wife was the owner. Rowe's second meeting with Henry, much later, towards the end of the novel, indicates the progress he has made. Henry has recovered his equilibrium and observes that "It's no use mourning someone all your life" (4.1.1). Although they are talking for the most part at cross purposes, Rowe's casual assent indicates that, as events will soon show, he is himself coming to terms with Alice's death.

The final death is Hilfe's. By this time Rowe is ready to face the truth. Hilfe reveals to him (or reminds him) that he killed his wife, but Rowe can now accept this without relapsing into his former state of paralytic guilt. Instead he reaffirms his action by reenacting it: out of pity he gives the cornered Hilfe the means to kill himself before being captured. Rowe's action, another mercy killing, demonstrates his acceptance of the need to incur the guilt of action in an inherently imperfect world. His reward is Anna, a symbolic restoration of his lost wife.

While the frequent references to gardens and to murder make Rowe's whole adventure a kind of review of the past, the focal episode, the true "journey back," is the period he spends in the sanatorium. Here, relieved of all memory of his adult life, he reverts to the state of childlike innocence of which he had dreamed. Yet the innocence of the sanatorium, like that of Rowe's dream, is unreal; and as he becomes more aware of his new surroundings he begins to discover sinister signs. The sanatorium is a larger version of the several garden images in the novel: what should be a place of safety and peace turns out to be a place of mortal danger. The sinister aspect of the sanatorium is the "sick-bay," run by the demonic Poole. "It was like the underside of a stone: you turned up the bright polished nursing home and found beneath it this" (2.2.2).

The outcome of Rowe's investigations in the sanatorium is his rejection of this false innocence. He makes his escape and heads back to war-torn London, beginning a psychological return journey in the course of which he gradually re-assumes the experience, the memories, and the guilt from which he had formerly longed to be relieved and which had been artificially taken away in the sanatorium. As he does so he comes to accept that his old demand for a simple world of moral absolutes is impractical. In reality, he now feels, one must love "people" rather than ideals, and in the human realm it is inevitable that "happiness should always be qualified by a knowledge of misery" (3.2.3). The philosophical issues are not, of course, argued closely or in any depth; but it is clear that, by the end, Rowe has given up his effort to see the world, and to judge himself, in simple terms of good and bad. As a result he can now accept the role he played in Alice's death and move forward into a new life.

The rather odd ending of *MF* illustrates the point. One would think that, after his final encounter with Hilfe, Rowe had only to go back to Anna and tell her everything. Yet he conceals from her that he now knows that he killed Alice. The concealment appears pointless in practical terms, since he could surely be expected to discover this truth sooner or later, and he has, in any case, managed to accept it without undue distress. We have to suppose that Anna wants at all cost to preserve Rowe's "innocence," and that he, knowing this, hides from her the fact that he has already lost it, hoping by concealment to save her from pain. As a result, while she lives in perpetual anxiety lest he discover a truth which he already knows, he is forever apprehensive lest he should reveal to her that he already knows it. The point behind this rather improbable contrivance is to show that Rowe has accepted the necessary element of unhappiness in human relationships. "If one loved one feared" (4.1.4). Love for another entails a degree of apprehension of the other's suffering. Knowing this in advance, as he embarks upon a new life with Anna, Rowe has overcome the trauma of his first wife's death and no longer mourns for a lost innocence.

Rowe has therefore traveled a great distance in psychological terms since the beginning of his story, and it is this inner growth which most distinguishes him from D and Raven, the heroes of the two previous "entertainments," as well as from the heroes of the other early novels. Like the Priest, he accomplishes this growth chiefly by means of a revaluation of his past. The particular issue upon which this revaluation turns in *MF* is often associated in the narrative with "pity," meaning not simply the everyday "feeling sorry for" the unfortunate, but rather a highly developed sensibility and capacity for sympathy, an acute perception of the pain of others. This idea of pity is further developed in *HM*.

As Raven the gangster is a sketch for Pinkie, and D the hunted middle-aged scholar is a sketch for the Priest, so Rowe, the man tormented by pity, is a sketch for Scobie. Scobie is in many ways the most puzzling and ambiguous of the three heroes of Greene's so called Catholic trilogy. Pinkie is an obviously negative character, vicious and destructive, for whom a degree of sympathy is painfully constructed by giving so much of his point of view in the narrative and by portraying his principal opponent, Ida, in slightly grotesque or mocking terms. The Priest, on the other hand, engages the reader's sympathies by his self-critical humility and his sense of duty, and his personal weaknesses are more than subsumed in the dignity and heroism of his end. Scobie's case is not so straightforward and is open to widely differing interpretations. Some readers sympathize with Scobie, even to the point of seeing him as a Promethean figure attempting to shield humanity from the cruelties of an indifferent god; others see him as hopelessly weak, a man of no real fibre who drifts into complicity in crime and murder for wholly inadequate reasons, and who commits suicide rather than decide between a wife and a mistress.[29]

Scobie's point of view is followed for the greater part of the narrative. The qualities he has in common with the Priest—a great compassion, a sense of duty, a self-critical humility—endear him to most readers. Greene himself, however, was initially surprised by the largely favorable impression Scobie created. "The character of Scobie," he wrote, "was intended to show that pity can be the expression of an almost monstrous pride. But I found the effect on readers was quite different" (*WE* 4.2). Greene admits to a "technical fault" in this respect, making Scobie too likable and other characters, especially Louise, too colored by Scobie's own view of them.

Greene tried to create a more balanced view of Scobie by including in later editions of *HM* a section (1.2.2.1) left out of the first. Here Louise and Wilson go off on their own for a walk; the point being not that Scobie's marriage is threatened by their relationship (which it is not), but that the reader should have a chance to see them, and particularly Louise, other than through Scobie's eyes. As soon as we see Louise apart from Scobie, as we do both here and briefly after his death, she immediately becomes a much stronger, more decisive, and independent character than the miserable, whining figure we see through Scobie's perception. Indeed, Scobie's view of Louise is quite wrong, as we discover in the end, when it becomes clear that she has known for some time about Helen and that she has coped with this knowledge as rationally as she is evidently coping with Scobie's death.

In the same way we discover finally that Helen too is much tougher than Scobie gave her credit for, and that for her too life will go on without him. There is thus a real sense in which Scobie's feelings of responsibility and "pity" rests upon a serious misjudgment of others. Presumably this exaggerated sense of his own responsibility for the lives of others is what Greene intended to be seen as "monstrous pride."

Scobie's misjudgment of others (he doesn't see very far into Wilson or Yusef either) is only one aspect of his limited nature. Another is revealed in the "process of reduction" by which he constructs his preferred environments (1.1.1.2), his office and the bathroom of his home. On the surface this asceticism is a strength, a willingness to make do without luxuries, a desirable characteristic in a colonial administrator; but it is also reminiscent of Pinkie's coldheartedness, and breeds in Scobie a preference for solitude which is part of the reason why neither his marriage nor his affair with Helen is ultimately satisfactory.

At heart Scobie is not unlike Pinkie, in that they both long for a state of "peace," a life without emotion, which is in each case associated with an idealized memory of the past. Where Pinkie remembers his boyhood attendance at church, Scobie recalls the treks of his younger days, when he lived alone with Ali and without family. It is Scobie's natural tendency to avoid emotion which helps him to survive in the local climate (1.1.1.4) and to be tolerant and fair in his duties as a police officer. Like Pinkie, he prefers an ascetic lifestyle, making his surroundings austere and empty of personal associations. This "process of reduction" is really an attempt to exclude or minimize the elements of human association in his life: "He had cut down his needs to a minimum, photographs were put away in drawers, the dead were put out of mind" (2.1.1.3). In particular among the dead, he tries to forget his daughter. His needless guilt over her death echoes Rowe's painful memories of his wife.

Scobie avoids "bare relation of intimate feeling" (1.1.1.7). His retreat from his wife's poetry sessions echoes Pinkie's distress over sentimental music. Scobie does not share Pinkie's horror of the sexual act, although it is clear that he has little interest in it. Neither his relationship with Louise nor that with Helen is founded upon sexual attraction: on the contrary, it is rather the unattractiveness and consequent pathos of these women that draws Scobie to them (1.1.1.3; 2.1.3.1; 3.2.3.2). Both Scobie and Pinkie, however, are revolted by the idea of domesticity, the concept of the conjugal home. In Pinkie's case this revulsion goes back to childhood recollections of his parents' "Saturday night" activities, and surfaces in his outraged reaction to Rose's innocent rearrangement of his room. Scobie has a similar attachment to his bathroom, the only part of his house unaltered by Louise and therefore "like a relic of his youth" (1.1.1.7). Hence Scobie's dread of retirement.

> The thought of retirement set his nerves twitching and straining: he always prayed that death would come first. . . .
> He thought of a home, a permanent home: the gay artistic curtains, the bookshelves full of Louise's books, a pretty tiled bathroom, no office anywhere—a home for two until death, no change any more before eternity settled in.   (1.1.1.8)

This is the middle-class equivalent of Pinkie's horrified vision of married life. Both Scobie and Pinkie take a road leading to death rather than accept the offered alternative of domesticity.

Scobie has an idea of "peace," which he comes closest to realizing in the isolation of his office. He "dreamed of peace by day and night . . . by day he tried to win a few moments of its company, crouched under the rusting handcuffs in the locked office" (1.1.2.4). Peace for Scobie is approached through asceticism and the impersonal duties of work in a climate which effectively forbids strong emotion. He is satisfied with the life he leads, except with respect to his marriage. "If he had become young again this was the life he would have chosen to live; only this time he would not have expected any other person to share it with him" (1.1.2.4). Scobie's dream of peace is located specifically in his younger days as an officer in Africa before he was joined, after the death of his daughter, by Louise.

The narrative of *HM* is punctuated by Scobie's two journeys away from his base on the coast, both on official business, the first to Bamba to investigate the death of Pemberton (1.3.1.1), the second to Pende to observe the arrival of the survivors from the torpedoed ship (2.1.1.1–5). The two trips mark stages in Scobie's moral decline: after the first he borrows the money to send Louise away, and from the second stems his association with Helen. Both trips, and particularly the first, are important not only for the business they accomplish but for the light they shed on Scobie's character.

The trip to Bamba is a "journey back" similar in function to Pinkie's walk to Paradise Piece. In both cases the journey itself is made into a narrative episode heavily covered with nostalgia. Scobie is not returning to childhood, but he is recreating a lost past, seeking "peace." On the journey he has an idyllic dream of "walking through a wide cool meadow with Ali at his heels," and when he awakes, the journey reminds him of "the old days" in Africa, before his wife's arrival.

> It seemed to him that this was all he needed of love or friendship. He could be happy with no more in the world than this—the grinding van, the hot tea against his lips, the heavy damp weight of the forest, even the aching head, the loneliness. (1.3.1.1)

The aching head, which develops into a fever, is the clue that Scobie's dream is not entirely a healthy one.

The "journey back" serves to show that the apparent innocence of the past is not as wholesome as it may seem. Pinkie is shown in Paradise Piece that *"there* was not innocence" (*BR* 5.3), and the Priest, returning home after six years as a fugitive, finds corruption in the person of his own daughter. What Scobie finds is the body of Pemberton, a suicide. In Pemberton there is a clear premonition of Scobie's own fate. The young officer, living in isolation, has become financially indebted to Yusef, has probably been subjected to blackmail or other pressures to compromise his integrity, and has killed himself rather than continue an unhappy, guilty existence. This, in essence, is to be Scobie's story too.

The image of Pemberton refers not only forwards to Scobie's fate but also backwards to his past. Pemberton is much the kind of young man Scobie recalls himself to have been, living alone in Africa with a strong but vulnerable sense of personal integrity. In the confusion of his fever he even muddles their names, Ticky and Dicky (1.3.1.1). This is the life Scobie wants to return to, but its inherent weakness, its openness to corruption, is exhibited in Pemberton's fate. Significantly it is at Bamba that Scobie succumbs to Yusef's temptation: as soon as he returns to the coast he commits himself to Louise's departure and so to placing himself in Yusef's debt. Scobie's return to the old days, the trek to Bamba, has as its outcome his first step along the route already taken by Pemberton.[30]

Scobie's second journey, to Pende, is not in itself a "journey back," but it does involve a sudden irruption of children. Scobie is confronted not only by Helen, a "child" who "only left school a year ago" (2.1.2.1), but also by the two younger children, the boy to whom he reads and the girl who dies. Here, in these children, Scobie finds a starker instance of suffering innocence than in the dubious case of Pemberton, and is led to ponder here upon "the heart of the matter," the problem of evil itself (2.1.1.3). The point of the episode, beyond accomplishment of the business of bringing Helen into Scobie's world, is to show his capacity for sympathy and his frustration over helplessness in the face of suffering, preparing the ground for his later inability to hurt either Helen or Louise.³¹

Unable to cope with the fact of suffering in an imperfect world, Scobie, much like Rowe, attempts to retreat into an artificial world of moral simplicity where every problem has its answer. Scobie finds such a world in routine police work, whereas Rowe finds it only in the sanatorium. Both men measure the miseries of present-day life in wartime against a probably falsely remembered dream of past innocence, and both are quite incapable of handling the discrepancy.

Scobie is s good policeman only until he comes across real personal suffering (in the case of the Portuguese captain), and he is hopelessly incompetent in the government of everyday emotional life. Confronted with the sufferings of others, and incapable of finally freeing himself, as Rowe manages to, from his obsessive vision of emotional tranquillity, Scobie places himself in an impossible situation: he is unlikely to be able to proceed without causing suffering, and there remains, in the improbable event of his managing to conceal his actions from all parties who might be hurt, the problem of Communion, the notion that his actions are sinful and as such cause suffering to God, even when no one else knows of them. In the abstract, Scobie's problem is the same as Pinkie's. Although Scobie's impulses tend towards the morally good, while Pinkie's are towards evil, both are driven ultimately by an inability to face the complex and often unsatisfactory facts of human emotional nature.

The extremity of Scobie's reactions, particularly his inability to accept the necessity for an element of suffering in human affairs, and his very literal interpretation of religious symbolism, remain problematical for many readers. Many will agree with George Orwell that the character as depicted is psychologically improbable: a man who truly believed in damnation would not risk it so casually as Scobie does; his actual conduct belies his claim to believe. Again, a man in Scobie's situation, particularly a man practical and capable enough to have become a respected police officer, would make a decision about his personal life rather than allow a deteriorating situation to lead to an end disastrous for all parties.[32]

While Orwell's psychological contention is hard to dispute, the wider point made in this 1948 review is more debatable. Orwell accuses Greene of presenting in Scobie, and perhaps also in Pinkie and the Priest, a kind of "sanctified sinner," a man who is a sinner and who as such is said to be superior to others who are not. This is a type, Orwell suggests, that Greene may have found in Baudelaire, although the idea certainly goes back to Byron, for whom Greene also had great admiration. The notion, in the context of narrative realism, is inherently paradoxical: if sin is really *better* than goodness, then sin becomes goodness, and two concepts, distinct and opposed by definition, become confused. The paradox demands resolution: if the sinner is indeed superior and assuming he has really committed acts which are sinful, then he must either be freed from blame for his actions or else his superiority must be derived from some quality other than his sin.

Orwell accuses Greene, in effect, of maintaining the paradox unresolved, but, to the extent that Greene does present the paradox of the sanctified sinner in these novels, he is doing so in order to invite the reader to look for its resolution. Each of the novels of the middle period is concerned to make the reader reevaluate moral ideas, ideas of sin, and of good and evil. What may at first appear evil, or a character who might at first sight seem sinful, may in the end be viewed if not with tolerance then at least with doubt. Far from being confronted dogmatically with a paradox, the reader is being challenged to reconsider accepted moral boundaries. This process of reconsideration is related to that which is made explicit in *MQ*, where codified moral concepts, exemplified in the writings of Heribert Jone, are constantly exposed to the corrosive wit of the Monsignor.

The sins remain sins: actions such as the killing of Spicer and the attempted killing of Rose do not become in any way acceptable or other than wrongful. One separates the action from the man; and while the action remains evil the man is presented as a complex of motives, emotions, ideals, and vices. In this way we resolve the paradox, by allowing the possibility of forgiveness.

The man may be a sinner in the literal sense that he has committed sinful actions, yet without these actions being condoned it may nonetheless be that in the end the man is forgiven. This is what Greene suggests as a possibility, at the end of both *BR* and *PG*, when he alludes to the mercy of God.

This does not return us to Orwell's "sanctified sinner," because it is the man, not the sin, who is sanctified. If Pinkie, the Priest, and Scobie are in some way redeemed, it is in spite of their faults, not because of them. As naive characters, each in his own way seeking "peace" and personal integrity in a morally corrupt world, each of these heroes, through his simplicity, comes to commit greater offenses than most men. What may redeem them are not the offenses but the original sincerity and "the purification of the motive"[33] as revealed in the whole character of each.

If a nineteenth-century model be sought for these heroes, a more promising candidate than Baudelaire or the Byronic hero would be Wagner's Parsifal. Parsifal is initially naive, ignorant of human love and suffering. His ancestry, in the romances of Chrêtien de Troyes and Wolfram von Eschenbach, also includes the "holy fool," the man of radical simplicity, such as was perhaps St. Francis of Assisi. At first his foolishness leads him into sin, but in the end, through suffering and revaluation of his past experience, he achieves sanctity. The sin and the sanctity are distinctly separate: Parsifal has to recognize and repudiate his past failings in order to succeed. Greene's middle heroes are also naive, inexperienced in human affairs, dreaming of a "peace" consisting essentially of an unattainable moral simplicity. Ill-equipped to face a complex reality, they fall easily into guilt or wickedness, despite the best intentions. For these men, as for Parsifal, "the way forward is the way back":[34] to progress beyond sin they must look again at where they started from. Parsifal's meeting with Kundry in the garden where he learns of his parentage and childhood corresponds in this respect to the "journey back" which figures in each of these novels. Just as Parsifal must reject the temptations of Kundry, the temptation to remain in the garden of apparent innocence, so Greene's middle heroes need to leave the shelter of their dreams of peace and confront the reality of suffering in a corrupt world.

The novels of Greene's middle period are not simply better than his early novels, but different from them in kind. There is a sharp difference between *EM*, *GS*, and *CA* on the one hand and *BR* and *PG* on the other, a difference involving the very concept of the novel. Central to the new departure of the middle novels is the enlarged role of the hero in an expanded time span. The longer time span not only allows scope for significant development of character but also permits the hero to undertake a "journey back" to confront his past. These novels therefore include not only a narrative movement forward but also a considerable amount of retrospection. The requirement that the hero review his past in a symbolic return is an essential distinguishing feature of this group among Greene's novels.

Although the pattern is worked out very differently in each of the four novels, there are common features. Each hero begins with an idea of innocence, which he tends to call "peace" and which he associates with childhood or youth, but which, from another point of view, may be dangerous naivety. In each case, attempting to live by this idea, the hero falls into trouble: Pinkie accepts the influence of Kite and drifts into crime; the Priest becomes vain and worldly and despairs when the position he enjoyed is taken away; Rowe's inability to face suffering leads him into the moral dilemma of Alice's death; and Scobie, similarly unable to contemplate pain, allows himself to be drawn into corruption and deceit. In each case we see that innocence is not enough, and the course of the narrative, involving a symbolic "journey back," invites the hero to reconsider.

The process is not a mechanical one, there is no guaranteed outcome, and the heroes' fates vary considerably. Rowe manages to put the past behind him, to tear himself away from the garden of innocence, and to become an effective participant in the struggle of life. His, however, is the simplest case. The Priest alters his outlook radically, as is clear from his conduct in the cell and from his final surrender; but his reward is not a new earthly life, such as Rowe is granted, but rather a martyr's death. Pinkie, on the other hand, clearly fails in the end to adapt to life's demands. His rejection of Rose ensures his own destruction, and although his death has a tragic dimension, the inflexibility of his nature has made it morally inevitable. Scobie's case is harder to summarize. Like Pinkie, he refuses to adjust: he ignores the warning represented by the fate of Pemberton and persists in his ideal of peace, refusing to accept the necessity of pain. On the other hand, since his motives are so evidently selfless, his death can be construed as an act of love and therefore as having more in common with the martyrdom of the Priest than with the accident whereby Pinkie's evil engine turns against its operator.

The moral depth of the middle novels, and their concentration on the hero's need for self-appraisal suggest an association with Greene's first travel book, *Journey Without Maps*, published in 1936 and written, more or less at the same time as *GS*, in the latter half of 1935. *BR*, the first of the newly conceived novels, followed immediately after. *JM* tells the story of Greene's trek across Liberia in the early months of 1935, a journey which was evidently, although Greene was already in his thirties, a formative experience.[35] The experience can be seen as reflected in the novels he wrote in the dozen years following his return.

In *JM* Greene presents the Liberian expedition as "a long journey backwards," comparable to the process of psychoanalysis, in which the object is "to face the general idea, the pain or the memory" (2.1). The journey can be difficult, and the outcome is not necessarily pleasant. Greene did not have a sentimental attitude towards the primitive: he did not accept the Wordsworthian view of natural man (3.3), nor did he expect in Africa to meet the "noble savage" (1.3). Just as the backward journeys in *BR*, *PG*, *MF*, and *HM* bring the hero face to face with stark facts of evil, decay, and death, so in the jungle Greene faced terror and disease, and as a matter of fact was saved from death only by the care of his companions. The journey back may take you in the direction of childhood, but childhood for Greene, as is evident in *BR* and "The Destructors," can be the seat of violence and fear. In Africa he "had the sensation of having come home, for here one was finding associations with a personal and racial childhood, one was being scared by the same old witches" (2.1).

JM presents Greene's Liberian journey not only as a "journey back" but also as the scene and stimulus for a kind of "conversion," a new attitude to life. Here, as in *SL*, Greene portrays himself as having been, from adolescence, inclined to world-weariness, bored by the necessary routine of life, and sometimes driven to extreme behavior, even to suicidal risks and games. Deep in the Liberian jungle, however, ill and facing the fact that he might well be dying, he "made a discovery": he discovered in himself "a passionate interest in living." This, he says, surprised him, since he had previously always assumed, "as a matter of course, that death was preferable" (3.4). Again something similar can be seen in the middle novels. The heroes are initially inclined to world-weariness, to be, like Rowe, incapable of participating in life, or, like Scobie, desirous of a "peace" which would consist in the elimination of worldly concerns. The journey back confronts them with a stark image—the Priest's daughter, the dead body of Pemberton, the desolation of Paradise Piece—which may, if the hero is, like Rowe, responsive, spur him to a renewed vitality.

The roots of Greene's brilliant creative flourish in the middle novels do not lie in the facts of the Liberian journey. What does take us at least a step closer to those roots is the narrative of *JM*, which reveals that the predisposition to structure experience in a manner comparable to that revealed in the novels was already in Greene's mind as he reflected on the journey and wrote about it. It is in *JM*, more clearly than in the early novels, that we can see the raw concepts which form the basis of Greene's mature fiction: the rejection of the Wordsworthian notion that innocence lies behind us in our origins, the consequent moral need to confront the actual corruption of human nature at its very root, and the conviction that the only effective response is acceptance of compromise and involvement in action.

Greene's Liberian experience may have helped him to focus these ideas, but he did not find them there. No doubt he found something of them in religion, as the Catholic themes of these novels would suggest, particularly in the theological concept of original sin; but we are considering the novels as literature, not as theology, and literary sources are readily apparent. Here, as usual when Greene's sources are the issue, the name of Conrad stands out above all others. It seems fair to conclude that sometime in the mid 1930s Greene arrived at a deeper understanding of *Heart of Darkness* and succeeded in making this the basis for a new departure in his own work.[36] He discovered in Conrad's story what is probably the most powerful creation of the "journey back" motif in modern English literature, and its use in his own subsequent work—not only in the middle novels, but also, most obviously, in *UG*, *BC*, and *TA*—is perhaps best seen as another step in Greene's progressive establishment of himself as Conrad's heir.

IV. THE LATER NOVELS

The third phase of Greene's career as a novelist properly begins with *QA*, which sets the pattern for most of the major works which follow, especially for *BC*, *TC*, and *HC*. Before *QA*, however, by a clear four years, comes *EA*, which belongs, on account of its genre and structure, with none of the other groups. *EA* stands aside from the mainstream of Greene's fiction because it is a love story—a very unusual one, but nonetheless a story in which the emotional relationship between the hero and heroine is the focal issue. In the other novels, although a love story element is usually present, it is never more than a part, and often not the chief part, of the hero's concern in the plot. The complex relationship between the hero and the figure we shall call his antagonist, crucial in the other novels, is simply not present in *EA*. In *EA* Bendrix has no concern outside his relationship with Sarah and, after her death, his attempts to come to terms with her loss.

EA is also perhaps the most problematic of Greene's major novels, raising difficulties beside which the improbabilities of Scobie's character become almost negligible. Greene himself was uncertain about *EA* and decided to allow its appearance only after Edward Sackville-West had urged him to "publish the bad as well as the good" (*WE* 5.3). "Bad" can be only a relative term here, for while *EA* certainly has shortcomings there remains much that is good in it, particularly in its techniques and in the character of Bendrix. The shortcomings, however, arise chiefly from Greene's decision to make belief in the existence of God the subject of a story.

Fiction being hypothetical, the question of whether or not God exists, and whether or not the reader personally believes in God's existence, should not matter. In *EA*, however, we are presented not with the (hypothetical) question of the existence of God, but with two central characters who, in the course of the story and as a direct result of the events which are the subject of the story, become convinced of that existence. When characters in a novel are required to form opinions based upon evidence given in the novel, the evidence which convinces them must also convince the reader, or else the characters forfeit credibility. When Greene in *EA* sets out to tell the story of the conversion of two rational agnostics to theism he creates a special problem: he cannot allow his characters to be convinced by arguments which do not also convince the impartial reader, or else his characters will lose sympathy and the novel as a whole fail to carry conviction. This, for most readers, is what happens in *EA*.

In a moment of stress, thinking her lover has been killed by a bomb, Sarah, a worldly-wise woman of no religious tendencies, prays and undertakes to end her affair with him if he is (as she sees it) restored to life. (Exactly why she formulates the prayer in this way is not clear. Would she not have been more likely to undertake to leave Henry and marry Bendrix?) When Bendrix surprises her by surviving the explosion, Sarah quite improbably takes this, not as evidence that he was never really dead, but as a miracle placing her under an obligation to keep her part of the bargain. Seeking a way out, Sarah tries to convince herself on rational grounds that God does not exist—although once again a more obvious and direct route to the same end would be to convince herself that Bendrix never died and that therefore no miracle occurred. Sarah never even looks at this question: having assumed, after a most cursory check, that Bendrix was dead, she never so much as enquires about evidence that his survival might have had a natural explanation. Greene leaves open to the reader the conclusion that Bendrix was not killed by the bomb but was saved by the door which fell on top of him. Sarah's failure even to consider this possibility makes her subsequent conduct seem perverse.

A similar set of problems then occur over the character of Bendrix as he seems gradually to succumb to a further accumulation of odd events. The difficulty is even more acute in him, since the option available in Sarah's case of assuming she has had some kind of spiritual experience or psychological breakdown, is not available in the case of Bendrix, whose cynical, precise, detached narrative voice continues evenly to the end. Bendrix is faced with a series of odd events concerning Sarah after her death, and pressure is upon him to construe these as miracles. Here again Greene has raised insuperable problems for himself: if he allows Bendrix to be convinced more readily than the reader is convinced the novel's central character and narrator will forfeit credibility, while if Greene increases the weight of evidence to render Bendrix's conviction more plausible, he will be open to the charge of blatant authorial manipulation. Greene, in doubt as to how to proceed, altered his original plan and shortened this section considerably, and made further alterations in later editions (*WE* 5.3). As it stands the novel simply tails off, with Bendrix uncertain after a number of these "miracles" and apprehensive that more may yet occur.

EA is interesting as the first major novel in which Greene used a first-person narrator as hero. There is a first-person narrator in *TM*, published some three years before *EA*, but it is not the hero. Calloway is simply an observer, little more than a bystander, who deputizes for the author. Employment of the hero as narrator is at once part of the peculiar technical problems of *EA* and the way forward to the new concept of the central character which distinguishes Greene's later novels. The problem is that making Bendrix the narrator of his own story in *EA* means that the very nature of the story comes to depend upon the question of Bendrix's conversion, which is a possible event within it. In fact, despite the apparent uncertainty over this, the thoughtful reader knows that Bendrix cannot be converted to a genuine belief in God before the end of *EA*, because a converted Bendrix, a believing, theistic Bendrix, would have told the whole story in a very different way from the beginning.

Making Bendrix the narrator of his own story is also a new departure, particularly since he tells the story in a manner which is not only competent, with considerable narrative skill, but also perceptively analytical in the presentation of his motives. It is no mere coincidence that he is a professional writer: it is just because he is a good storyteller that he is able to tell his own complex story well. Bendrix is the first of the middle-aged, intelligent, ironic, self-critical, would-be dispassionate heroes characteristic of the later novels. His most obvious successors include Fowler, Brown, and Henry Pulling. They differ from the early and middle heroes chiefly in this matter of articulateness and capacity for self-scrutiny. It is inconceivable that Andrews, Conrad, Anthony, or Raven should tell their own stories. They are men of too limited, immature outlook to encompass anything like the breadth of the narratives in which they figure. (Czinner and D, as older, more experienced and self-possessed characters, might be felt capable of the task; but their stories are simpler, much simpler even than those of Andrews and Conrad.) Much the same is true of the middle heroes. They include men of greater maturity but still of essentially limited outlook, whose natural simplicity would prevent them from telling their own stories. They tend to be taciturn figures, shy of emotion. Indeed, their initial inability to face the facts of human feeling—of love, guilt, or suffering—is the crucial issue in their characters. We cannot imagine *BR* narrated by Pinkie, *PG* by the Priest, or *HM* by Scobie, without these novels becoming radically different, different not merely in "point of view" but in overall purpose and concept. Rowe, a former journalist, might be up to the task, except that halfway through his story he is required to forget his past adult life, which leaves him with even less capacity for autobiography than Pinkie.

In one way or another all of the heroes before Bendrix, except perhaps those of the much simpler novels conceived as "thrillers" or "entertainments," are men inherently incapable of expatiation on the complexities of the human heart. The Priest, of course, preaches powerful sermons and engages in penetrating dialogue on occasions, but this does not make him an exception here. Although he can speak well and wisely to others he remains himself an emotional novice and a very poor judge of his own case. His own relationships, with Maria and his daughter, are catastrophic, and even at the end, by which time his awareness has enlarged considerably, he remains a very simple man with little notion of personal individuality. Among the later heroes, on the other hand, there are professional writers (Bendrix, Fowler, and Baxter), five who tell their own stories as first-person narrators (Bendrix, Fowler, Brown, Pulling, and Baxter), and the others are all mature, educated men who might quite conceivably have told their own stories and who do each manage to engage in extensive "confessional" dialogues: for example, Querry's conversations with Colin and Parkinson and the autobiographical story he tells to Marie, Plarr's discussions in the hut with Leon and Fortnum, and Castle's conversations with Boris.

The difference between the relatively inarticulate heroes of the middle phase and the relatively highly articulate heroes of most of the later novels is not merely superficial. The inarticulateness of men like Scobie and Pinkie reflects their inability to handle the moral complexity of human emotion. These heroes are men of inherently limited outlook, and despite the fact that in some cases, notably those of Rowe and the Priest, the outlook is broadened in the course of the story, they remain to the end men for whom detailed self-analysis would be out of character. Their stories turn essentially upon the disparity between their limited outlook, conditioned by a notion of "peace" and a yearning for moral simplicity, and the wider awareness and the moral flexibility necessary for survival in a radically imperfect world. The later heroes, on the other hand, tend to begin from a position of deep experience and developed awareness. They are men of the world who have, in most cases, already experienced emotional crises and come through the kinds of personal entanglements which Pinkie and Scobie fail to negotiate.

The pattern and purpose of the stories alters accordingly. The central question in the novels of the middle period is whether the hero will succeed in freeing himself from the limitations of his notions of innocence or "peace" and in arriving at a realistic solution of the human problems before him. Will Pinkie grow out of the petrified adolescence which he associates with the memory of Kite and his distorted ambition of priesthood, and succeed in establishing a true relationship with Rose? Will the Priest grow from a concept of priesthood based upon personal and moral security to a true priesthood based upon acceptance of his own humanity and the ultimate uncertainty of moral values in a corrupt world? Will Scobie and Rowe move from an inhibiting inability to contemplate suffering to an acceptance of its inevitability in the human situation? In each of these cases, since the initial limiting vision of moral simplicity is strongly associated with the hero's past, the impulse to reevaluate it is presented in terms of a symbolic "journey back," which forms an episode in each novel crucial to an understanding of the hero.

In the later novels we have a different situation in that the hero is not significantly inhibited by any longing for lost innocence but is already fully aware, usually from his own past experience, of the complex and imperfect nature of the human world. These are men who have already made the transition required of the middle heroes, a transition which is broadly from a false innocence to compromising experience. The past which concerns them is not one of lost childhood or youth but one in the course of which outstanding obligations have been incurred. The typical situation in these novels is that of world-weariness, the situation of a man who knows life too well and has had his fill. These heroes are men who have deliberately withdrawn to the sidelines, out of the conflict, to a position from which they may be spectators but which isolates them from involvement. Involvement is now the crucial issue, and the central question of these novels is whether the hero, already fully aware of the moral complexity of human action, will allow himself to be drawn back into the fray from which he has once withdrawn. There is no longer any need for a "journey back," but there are usually old debts to be paid to characters from the hero's past life before he can move forward.

In a broad sense, "involvement" may be said to be a crucial issue in the earlier novels. Will Czinner turn back, or will he go on with his journey and commit himself openly to the rising? Will Pinkie remain ascetically aloof, or will he involve himself with Rose? Will Rowe continue to live in isolated inactivity, or will he join with others in the war effort? On such a flexible and wide interpretation of the term, however, "involvement" might be said to be an issue in almost any story. In Greene's later novels it becomes a critical matter in two quite specific ways, one arising from the hero's initial position of withdrawal and the other as a subject of explicit discussion within the story.

These late heroes have removed themselves from the field of moral action by deliberate withdrawal into the role of spectator. Fowler is a reporter, Querry leaves civilization and becomes an observer in the leproserie, Brown runs a hotel from which he watches local affairs, Plarr sees the struggle in Paraguay from across the river, and Castle collects intelligence. In most cases the stance of observer is reinforced by physical removal to a geographically remote location. Fowler has settled in Saigon, Querry goes to the African jungle, Wormald is in Cuba, Brown in Haiti, and Plarr in Argentina. Among the serious heroes, only Castle remains on his native ground—but in his case the relevant scene of action is not in Europe but in South Africa, the country from which he previously fled. These men are Greene's hermit-heroes, men who have withdrawn from the conflict of life and who manifest an explicit reluctance to return to it.

Their reluctance to re-engage is usually a matter of open discussion within the story. Fowler talks of his disengagement with Vigot and Trouin, and his attitude is contrasted with Pyle's overenthusiastic wish to get involved. Querry's story is precisely the story of a man who takes the idea of withdrawal to its limit: he runs away until there is nowhere left to run to, and he explains himself at length, particularly to Colin and Parkinson. Henry Pulling is drawn only with reluctance and protests from his quiet and uneventful retirement into his aunt's lively world. Plarr is reluctant to help Leon and is only gradually, and in the course of much soul searching, persuaded to do so. Castle believes he has paid his debt and is on the point of ending his secret aid to Moscow when his conscience is stirred by Muller and he feels obliged to act openly.

The Conradian archetype behind the middle heroes is Marlow in *Heart of Darkness*, the man who must face unpleasant truth by looking into himself. The later heroes are modeled rather upon Heyst in *Victory*, the man who has looked into himself and, not altogether liking what he found, chosen isolation from action. In both cases the background is the same: a corrupt and morally complex world in which the hero is required to participate but which yields no simple or perfect solutions. An abstract of the typical plot of the middle period is as follows:

—The hero is placed in a situation with a background of violence and corruption.
—He reacts by maintaining a vision of "peace," of a world of lost innocence in which moral problems have satisfactory solutions.
—He is confronted by specific instances of suffering which require him to take action.
—In a symbolic "journey back" he confronts something representative of the lost innocence he envisions, which is shown to be false, dangerous, even deadly.
—In the end he accepts or fails to accept the necessity for compromise in the world of experience.

The order in which these elements occur in the sequence of events within the plot may vary—for instance, Rowe's confrontation with suffering takes place, in the matter of his wife's illness, before the main action opens—but all of these elements are essentially present in each of *BR*, *PG*, *MF*, and *HM*. On the other hand a different set of ingredients occur in the abstract which might be made from the plots of *QA*, *BC*, *TC*, *HC*, and *HF*:

—The hero is placed in a situation with a background of violence and corruption.
—His reaction is withdrawal to spectatorial role and usually also involves a removal to a location remote from the scene of his previous life.
—He is confronted by instances of suffering which require his intervention.
—He is required to confront one or more figures from his past life, to satisfy outstanding claims.
—In the end he accepts or fails to accept the necessity for compromise in the world of experience.

The differences, which represent the essential divergences between the middle novels and the serious novels of Greene's later work, arise from the factors we have observed. Because the later heroes are men of wider experience and awareness, their response to life consists not in a vain attempt to square experience with an ideal of innocence, but rather in a deliberate and somewhat embittered withdrawal. Because they do not yearn for the actual or imagined past they do not need to confront it; but because they have already lived for some time in the world of human affairs, making errors and contracting obligations, they need to settle old debts before they can go forward. Consequently in the later novels the "journey back" is replaced by the figure from the past who reappears in the hero's present.

QA employs the hero as first-person narrator and makes use of time-shift techniques, both features used experimentally in EA. Fowler, the hero, tells the story, which spans some six months, from September to the following February. The narrative opens with Pyle's death in February, but as events slowly move forward from that point Fowler embarks upon a series of protracted retrospections, covering his relationship with Pyle from their first meeting the previous September. The retrospection becomes in effect the main action, framed and only occasionally interrupted by the narrative present. In the final pages the past catches up to the point where the novel began, revealing only then the full extent of Fowler's part in Pyle's death.

Having cut himself off from his former life in England, Fowler is now a strictly disengaged spectator, as is reflected in his work as a reporter in Saigon for an English newspaper. He is an observer in a foreign country of a war in which his own nation has no part. Pyle, his antagonist, represents the contrary position, believing that involvement, personal commitment, and active participation are the proper course. Fowler states his position clearly:

> "I'm not involved. Not involved," I repeated. It had been an article of my creed. The human condition being what it was, let them fight, let them love, let them murder. My fellow journalists called themselves correspondents; I preferred the title of reporter. I wrote what I saw. I took no action—even an opinion is a kind of action. (1.2.2)

In the course of the story, after witnessing a number of scenes of cruelty and suffering, Fowler decides to compromise his principle of disengagement. He secretly gives information to one party involved in the struggle, which results in the elimination of another. The question of involvement as a moral issue is meanwhile kept before the reader in a number of discussions between Fowler and other characters, particularly Pyle, Vigot, and Trouin.

Closely related to the question of whether or not the hero should engage himself in the public domain, in the political struggle which is the background to the story, is the matter of his personal commitment in private life. Fowler has left his wife, Helen, and then a mistress, Anne, behind in England, and in Saigon he has found contentment with a Vietnamese mistress, Phuong. The hitherto unstable nature of Fowler's private life, his inability to bind himself in a lasting relationship, is the personal correlative of his public stance of detachment. Pyle, again, is different: he believes in "being involved" and consequently for him, in sexual matters, "the keyword was marriage" (1.2.2). Pyle thus challenges Fowler on two fronts, both as an advocate of involvement in public affairs and, with his offer of marriage, as a rival for Phuong.

Fowler's relationship with Phuong is inherently unstable. He cannot match Pyle's offer of marriage, and Phuong is already being urged by her forceful sister Miss Hei to find a man who can give her a more secure future. Fowler's past life, in England, comes into the story on this issue. If Fowler could marry Phuong he could preempt Pyle so that, even if he did then have to return to England, Phuong would remain with him. Fowler cannot offer Phuong marriage, however, because he remains legally married to Helen. On his return from Phat Diem he writes to Helen asking for a divorce, but he has little hope of her consent. Helen's first answer, a refusal, arrives after Fowler's return from Tanyin.

An apparently small point here throws light on the structural mechanism of the plot. Helen's refusal to agree to a divorce arises from religious belief that divorce is wrong. This we might reasonably expect to be a Catholic issue, but it is not. Helen is an Anglican, and her feelings about divorce stem more from personal conviction than from the rules of her church. The crucial point is that the decision is hers, so that it may remain a matter of uncertainty. Helen must be reluctant to divorce Fowler, but the possibility of her doing so must remain open. Helen is the figure from Fowler's past, to whom he is still bound in obligation. The question of his possible release, raised quite early in the course of events, when Pyle announces his rival interest in Phuong, is resolved only at the end of the novel.

The matter of Fowler's recall to London is an integral part of the business. Fowler learns of his promotion at the same time that Pyle becomes his rival, and just as he writes to Helen about the divorce, so at the same time he writes to his employers asking to be allowed to stay in his present post in Saigon. The eventual favorable response is as unexpected as that which, again at about the same time, finally comes from Helen. Apart from the structural symmetry—the private and professional aspects of Fowler's life running parallel in these exchanges of letters, much as they do over the issue of involvement throughout the story—there is a good logical reason for Fowler's double jeopardy. If he were summoned home but not married to Helen, he would be free to invite Phuong to accompany him as his wife. If he were free from the threat of recall, even though still married to Helen, he might ask Phuong to reject Pyle and remain with him permanently as his mistress. The point of combining both factors is to avoid leaving Phuong's reaction in doubt.

It would detract from the focal issue of the novel, namely Fowler's process of decision making, if Phuong's course of action were left to her own decision and not clearly foreseeable. Helen's decisions are entirely "offstage" and do not figure in the narrative; but Phuong is a prominent presence in the story, and if she is allowed to make crucial decisions her character will attract attention which needs to be kept upon the hero. This is also the purpose of Miss Hei: to ensure that the reader sees Phuong as simply responding to pressures. Once it is clear that Fowler will be recalled and that he cannot marry Phuong, her line of action is automatic. This has the further effect of keeping Fowler's attention firmly upon Pyle. There is no point in his attempting to influence Phuong herself: once he has written his appeals to Helen and to his editor, he has nothing left to do but concentrate upon his rival.

Again, once Pyle has been removed, Phuong's return to Fowler is equally automatic: he does not even have to ask her back.

Fowler's private struggle to keep Phuong is conducted both with the absent Helen, a figure from his past, and with the newcomer Pyle. Through the figure of Phuong, this struggle is connected with the public, political theme of the novel; for the taciturn, passive Phuong is representative of her people, silent victims of a war fought over them by global powers, and Fowler is not only Phuong's lover but also one of Greene's confirmed humanitarians, a successor of Rowe and Scobie. "I cannot be at ease," Fowler says, "(and to be at ease is my chief wish) if someone else is in pain, visibly or audibly, or tactually" (2.2.4).

Fowler's life in his room in Saigon, with his opium and his compliant mistress, is a place of refuge. Although we are given fewer details, it is clear that he is like Querry in having chosen to withdraw to a place geographically and culturally remote from the scene of an emotionally turbulent former life. Like Querry, Fowler sees no future for himself and desires only "ease" and isolation for the rest of his days. He does not expect to live long: "I came east to be killed," he shouts at Pyle (2.2.4). Fowler has chosen the Vietnam War, much as Querry chooses the leproserie, as a place where he may expect an empty life and perhaps a quick death; but paradoxically, again rather like Querry, he finds his sympathies engaged, and his sense of life reawakened, by the suffering he sees around him.

Fowler's attachment to Phuong goes along with a love of Vietnam and its people, and gradually through the novel he witnesses the suffering of the country made a battleground by political factions. He sees the casual slaughter of civilians at Phat Diem, he witnesses the comic unreality of Caodaism and realizes the futility of expecting anything realistic from a "third force," and in the bombing raid he sees again the great beauty of the country made a background for mindless killing. The final straw for Fowler is the big bomb in Saigon, which mutilates dozens of civilians and which would have caught Phuong had she not been warned away by Pyle. Fowler's decision to involve himself at this point, by giving the information which puts a stop to Pyle's activities, is an attempt at once to protect Phuong and to lessen the suffering of the Vietnamese people.

The novel, framed by the several interviews and events which follow Pyle's death, is the story of Fowler's gradual decision to get involved. The two poles between which Fowler has to negotiate a way in the process are represented by the two flanking characters Granger and Dominguez. Granger is at first simply a parody of Fowler, a fellow journalist, lazy and vulgar, who treats the local people as objects for his own amusement. Fowler, of course, is not really like this, but there is a superficial resemblance, such that a newcomer, like Pyle, would initially see them as alike.

> Pyle looked at me as though I were another Granger. I suddenly saw myself as he saw me, a man of middle age, with eyes a little bloodshot, beginning to put on weight, ungraceful in love, less noisy than Granger perhaps but more cynical, less innocent. (1.3.2)

Fowler dislikes Granger intensely, as his narrative makes clear, and Granger becomes the focus for Fowler's misanthropy, the embodiment of all that is coarse and uncaring in man. The likes of Granger, and the element of Granger in himself, are what Fowler has come to Vietnam to escape.

While Granger illuminates the cynical, self-critical aspect of Fowler, Dominguez represents his better self, particularly his honesty and capacity for sympathy. Dominguez is portrayed as a powerful vatic figure, reminiscent of "a rajah or a priest." He is characterized by "an absolute love of truth" (2.3.2), which is echoed in Fowler's own journalistic integrity and his "plain dealer" approach to human affairs. Dominguez is also credited with a respect for life in all forms, a quality which reflects, again in extreme form, Fowler's sensitivity to suffering.

Fowler's progress, the development of his character leading up to his decision to deliver Pyle up to Mr. Heng, is revealed through his changing relations with Granger and Dominguez. At his first appearance in the story, a little after Fowler's return from hospital, Dominguez is a sick man. It is tempting to read the illness of this lover of truth as a reflection of the lies which Fowler has just been telling about his expectation of obtaining a divorce. These lies, along with his attempt to conceal his recall to London, mark the beginning of Fowler's compromise with his own integrity and therefore invite comparison with Scobie's shielding of the Portuguese captain. The lies have no material consequences, any more than does Scobie's concealment of the captain's letter. In the end the recall is revoked, the divorce agreed, and Dominguez's illness, accordingly, disappears as inconsequentially as it came.

Dominguez's second and final appearance is noticeable for its oddity. Dominguez was first introduced at length and as a figure of some depth and importance. Now, when he suddenly reappears in Fowler's doorway, we expect something significant to occur, but the episode which follows is strangely brief and unrealistic. Fowler has, or says he has, forgotten that Dominguez customarily arrives at this hour to ask, as Fowler's assistant, for instructions. When Fowler opens the door on this occasion, however, he sees it is "only Dominguez" and asks him abruptly what he wants. Evidently surprised at this reception, Dominguez asks if there is anything he can do for Fowler. Fowler upsets Dominguez by killing a mosquito and tells him curtly to "leave me alone tonight" (4.2.2). Dominguez goes away and never reappears. The explanation for Fowler's odd behavior here can lie only in the fact that it follows immediately upon his second meeting with Mr. Heng and the arrangement for his betrayal of Pyle. Consciously or otherwise, Fowler finds that his contemplation of the taking of a life is not consistent with his relationship with the gentle Dominguez.

While Fowler moves away from Dominguez he is drawn closer to Granger. While he has to depart from the absolutes of Dominguez's veracity and respect for the sanctity of all life, he must also expand his humanity in practice to include Granger, the common man. On the night of Pyle's death Granger reappears in distress and confides to Fowler his concern for his son, who is suffering from polio. This is a new, human Granger, and Fowler listens with sympathy. While the two men agree that they do not like each other, Fowler admits his attitude to Granger has been wrong, and Granger acknowledges Fowler's sympathy

(4.2.3). This unexpected moment of human contact coincides almost precisely with the time of Pyle's death. The purpose can only be to underline that complicity in murder does not mean that Fowler has cut himself off from human feeling.

The complex course of Fowler's progress is thus revealed. His cynicism and sensibility make him, in his own eyes at least, unfit for the moral and emotional turmoil of life, and he withdraws to Saigon where he lives in isolation, except for an undemanding mistress and his opium pipe. He becomes on principle a disengaged spectator. Through the activities of Pyle, however, the events of the world around him impinge upon Fowler's personal sphere, and he finally decides to act. Action involves a movement away from the unrealistic ideals of truth and innocence ("innocence" in the etymological sense of "causing no harm") held by Dominguez, towards real human sympathy, towards an understanding of ordinary people like Granger and the nameless victims whose massacre Fowler has witnessed. The movement is a compromise: ideals are sacrificed and hands are dirtied, but as with the heroes of the middle period the motive, although not entirely pure, is in the end a large justification.

Much is lost in the process, not least Pyle himself, with whom Fowler had a genuine bond, and to whom he owed his life. For all the harm he does, Pyle remains in a kind of "innocent" (in a broader spiritual sense), and his death is a loss of innocence, both for a world in which Pyle's good intentions were perverted to evil ends, and for Fowler, whose personal integrity has been lost in Pyle's betrayal. Yet something is also gained. Phuong returns and seems likely to stay, and Fowler will stay in Vietnam. Most important is the sense that, by the end, Fowler has completed a cycle, returning to the fold of everyday corrupt humanity from which he had tried to isolate himself as a spectator.

Helen's change of mind, the granting of the divorce in the last pages of the novel, is the sign of this completion. Although there is no literal connection, since Helen has no knowledge of Fowler's activities in Saigon, the arrival of her unexpected acquiescence just as all is over is more than a glib happy ending. The question of the divorce, kept deliberately open, is resolved only now, after Pyle's death has rendered it, from a merely practical point of view, unimportant. Without Pyle's rivalry (and without the threat of recall) Fowler does not need to offer Phuong marriage. It is evident, however, that he will do so. In this novel, involvement in the public domain goes along with involvement in private life, and Fowler's marriage to Phuong is the logical counterpart to his compromising action on behalf of the innocent victims of the war. The divorce is a symbolic acknowledgment of Fowler's incipient re-engagement.

OM is Greene's first major comic work. The several novels he wrote which may be broadly classed as comedies—*OM*, *TA*, and *MQ*—differ widely from one another. *OM* belongs to the kind of comedy in which the sympathetically disruptive hero plays his tricks, causes trouble, and in the end manages to escape capture or punishment, but leaves the world to go on in its old way. He has had fun, aroused our merriment, but effected no lasting difference.[37] Wormold plays out his game, achieves his object, incidentally wins his lady, and, after a few knocks and close shaves, escapes with virtual impunity. On the other hand, the usual background of fear and violence is no less present here than in the serious novels, and is by no means exorcized by the comic spirit. Wormold leaves Cuba on the verge of revolution, the Cold War goes on, and the spies and secret police continue their deadly games. The stage is littered with innocent victims, of whom the most prominent in *OM* is the amiable Hasselbacher. This is comedy with bitter undertones.

Greene first conceived the story in the mid forties, after his own experience of intelligence work during the War. He wrote it down originally as a sketch for a film, a sketch which he published in 1985 as a twelve-page short story included with *The Tenth Man*. The sketch, entitled "Nobody to Blame," includes many of the ideas later used in *OM* but suggests a much more farcical, lighthearted approach to the material than finally emerged in the novel. The real source, of course, is Conrad's *Secret Agent*, the masterpiece of grim humor which Greene had already quarried for atmosphere and characters deployed in *IB*. From Conrad come the central ideas of the agent who lives by making up the secrets he sells but who falls victim to his own inventions.[38] Greene updates the setting: Conrad's revolutionary anarchists become wartime agents in the 1940s sketch and Cold War spies in the novel.

Although in terms of genre *OM* is a kind of comedy, the story it tells still has much in common with those of the serious novels. Wormold himself, as a middle-aged Englishman living an obscurely routine life in Cuba, is not unlike other expatriate heroes of Greene's later novels, particularly Fowler and Plarr. We do not know much about Wormold's past, except that he was once married, and we cannot therefore claim that his present life is in any specific way a withdrawal, such as Fowler and Querry make, from moral complexity or emotional stress: but the suggestion is latent, and Wormold's repatriation at the end, however somber, has the air of a cycle completed.

More specifically, Wormold's situation, as a man of limited means trying to secure the future and happiness of a loved one, is close to that of Scobie. Scobie borrows from Yusef to get Louise a passage to South Africa; Wormold enlists as Hawthorne's agent to get money for Milly's education and expensive tastes. Each man compromises his integrity for the whims of a woman. Wormold's action in becoming a spy is not only a moral compromise but also a dangerous "involvement" comparable to the crucial actions in their respective stories of Fowler, Plarr, and Castle. Wormold's story is a comedy, however, and the compromising action is not seriously intended, nor is it seen as completely serious in itself. Nonetheless, the compromise still provokes reaction: just as Scobie is suspected and tracked by Wilson, Fowler by Vigot, and Castle by Daintry, so Wormold is eventually found out by Segura, who luckily (again, since this is a comedy) turns out to be less vicious than at first suspected and allows Wormold's escape.

As in the cases of some of the other heroes, Wormold discovers that the first casualties of his compromise are innocent victims. Scobie's association with Yusef ends in the murder of Ali, Castle's espionage results in the killing of Davis, Brown's inheritance of his mother's hotel leads to Marcel's suicide, and Wormold's pretense of secret intelligence brings about the death of Hasselbacher. *OM* being a comedy, Wormold is much less morally responsible for Hasselbacher's death than is, for example, Scobie for the death of Ali, or even Brown for that of Marcel. Wormold remains largely an innocent, unaware until Hasselbacher is killed of the possible dangers of his line of conduct.

The love story element in *OM* also echoes that in some of the other late novels, particularly *QA* and *BC*. In all three of these cases the hero is initially bound, to some extent, to an unsatisfactory past relationship which subjects him to restraints from which, towards the end of the story, he is released. Just as Fowler is still, at the outset, married to Helen and secures a divorce from her only towards the end, so Wormold is initially still in love with his exwife and, as he finally leaves Cuba, transfers his affections from her to Beatrice. The business of Wormold's past is handled lightly, but the pattern of action, close to that of *QA*, remains clear. As Wormold and Beatrice are packing their things prior to deportation, Wormold finally discards old photographs and other oddments associated with his exwife (5.6.3). This leaves him free in the final pages, like Fowler with Phuong, to plan a new life with Beatrice.

Greene's newfound interest in comedy went through several permutations in the novels which followed *OM*. Of the next novel, *BC*, Greene wrote that "in the course of the blackest book I have written I had discovered comedy"(*WE* 8.3). The comedy in *BC* is very different from that of *OM*, being in reality irony of the grimmest kind. It consists in the apparently unbridgeable gap between the hero's intentions, his present conception of himself, on the one hand, and the way in which other characters persist in seeing him on the other. The irony arises from the way in which the hero's extreme efforts to put his past life behind him are persistently misinterpreted as further, more dramatic, manifestations of his old self. The hero's story in *BC* is therefore built upon a tension between past and present comparable to similar tensions in *QA*, *TC*, *HC*, and *HF*.

Querry is the most obvious of the hermit-heroes. His retreat is, in literal terms, the most extreme: from a European life of wealth and celebrity to the spartan obscurity of an African leper hospital. His story opens with his arrival at his chosen place of self-exile, and the novel covers precisely the tale of his attempt to maintain himself there. Like the other heroes of the late novels, therefore, Querry is established at the outset as a man who has withdrawn to a position of isolation, to a geographical remoteness from home reflecting a spiritual rejection of the world.

Querry's initial disengagement is evident. The imagery surrounding it is clear and, if anything, too heavy-handed. Querry's refuge among lepers is appropriate because leprosy entails loss of feeling in the parts of the body affected. This physical loss of sensation images Querry's spiritual apathy. "I haven't enough feeling left for human beings to do anything for them out of pity," he says (2.3.2); and in a dream he sees himself as a leper, unable to feel human contact (2.1.2). Querry's retreat to the leproserie thus stands for a kind of self-imposed emotional anaesthetic, an attempt to escape the harrowing demands of human feeling, such as is also the initial goal of Fowler and Plarr.

Querry is assigned as his "boy" a leper who has lost all his fingers and toes. In the course of the story a bond is formed between these two, and the suggestion is that the leper's mutilations mirror Querry's human deficiencies. The man's name, Deo Gratias, is ironic, like Pinkie's Paradise Piece, since the leper has evidently so little to be thankful for; but as the story develops the name seems also to hold out to Querry the possibility of the sort of "conversion," recounted in *JM*, to a view of life, however grim, as something to be gratefully treasured.

Querry has left unresolved problems behind him. Not only is there the matter of his old reputation, which still pursues him, but there is also at least one personal relationship from which he needs to feel free in order to complete his escape. Fowler had his marriage to Helen, which needed to be annulled if he was to commit himself fully to life with Phuong in Vietnam. Querry is still pursued by the lady he deserted when he embarked upon his sudden flight from Europe. She is only the last in a series of women whom he has loved and abandoned. One young woman, Marie Morel, even killed herself for Querry's sake. Querry can therefore expect to be held to account for outstanding moral debts.

The woman Querry last abandoned is known in the story only by the name she signs on her letters to him, Toute-à-toi, a name underlining the kind of close human involvement from which he is in flight and which he sees as a "phrase of immolation" (3.2). She manages to trace him and sends a letter which reaches him at the leproserie about two months after his arrival. He makes no response, and towards the end (appropriately on the morning after his innocent night in the hotel with Marie Rycker) he collects another batch of mail and, noting there is nothing more from her, feels safe in concluding she will trouble him no more (6.2.1). Toute-à-toi remains a shadowy figure, but she stands, as her name suggests, for the claims of humanity which Querry is trying to shake off. She occurs only twice in the narrative, each time in connection with the arrival of the mail and associated by coincidence with Marie Rycker, who is effectively her replacement. The letter from Toute-à-toi arrives just at the moment when Marie Rycker first comes to the hospital in search of Querry, the second reference occurs when he is with Marie in Luc. There is therefore a gradual replacement in the hero's awareness of the woman of the past by another of the present. Just as Phuong succeeds Helen and Beatrice succeeds Wormold's exwife, so Marie succeeds Toute-à-toi. This is not, however, a promising outcome for Querry, who observes that Marie's name, "like a warning," echoes that of the girl who killed herself on his account (6.1.1).

The general course of events, whereby Querry settles into isolation and then comes under some pressure to abandon his principle of noninvolvement, runs closely parallel to that of Fowler's career in QA:

1. Arrival and establishment in a location remote from home (Fowler in Saigon; Querry in leper hospital in West Africa)
2. The hero meets his antagonist (Pyle arrives in Saigon; Querry encounters Rycker in Luc)
3. An interval in which the hero achieves some feeling of sympathy for the local people (Fowler sees the dead at Phat Diem and the wounded soldier under the tower; Querry

agrees to help with hospital buildings and rescues Deo Gratias from the forest)
4. The bond with the old life is reasserted (Helen refuses divorce; Querry gets letter from Toute-à-toi)
5. An interval in which the activity of the antagonist becomes offensive (Pyle takes Phuong from Fowler and is responsible for the bicycle bombs; Rycker sends Parkinson after Querry)
6. The climactic offence which stirs the hero to action (Pyle's big bomb; Parkinson's article)
7. The hero compromises his principle of noninvolvement (Fowler betrays Pyle and reclaims Phuong; Querry confronts Rycker and takes Marie to Luc)
8. Conclusion (Helen releases Fowler to marry Phuong; Marie Rycker "avenges" Marie Morel by laying a claim on Querry, who is killed as a result)

The structural similarity of the two stories is clear: in both cases a hero settles into a withdrawn existence only to find himself increasingly troubled by the actions of his antagonist and, at the same time, subject to claims made upon him from the past. Beneath the resemblances, however, lies a fundamental moral difference, which has its effect in the divergent endings of the two novels. Whereas Fowler establishes a positive feeling towards his new environment, reflected in his feeling for Phuong, Querry remains detached and has no personal feeling at all for Marie. Consequently, whereas Fowler's rivalry with Pyle and love for Phuong are real, Querry's confrontation with Rycker and "affair" with Marie are unreal, based upon ironic misunderstandings and lies. Phuong, at the end of *QA*, is Fowler's "phoenix," his way to a new life; but Marie Rycker is Querry's nemesis, the avenging spirit of Marie Morel.

On his second trip to Luc, with Marie, Querry believes himself at last secure. He has confronted Rycker, he finds no further letters from Toute-à-toi, and he has as yet no worry over his visit to Marie's bedroom, which was indeed quite harmless. Viewed abstractly, his position appears to be coming to much the same sort of conclusion as is reached by Fowler in *QA*: his antagonist is eliminated, the heroine is by his side, and the claims of his old life upon him have been dropped. But the reality is otherwise. Rycker is not, like Pyle, dead, but only temporarily sick and already on Querry's trail. The silence of Toute-à-toi is misleading, for the vengeance of his old life is already being planned in the mind of Marie Rycker. When she claims publicly that Querry is the father of her unborn child, he observes bitterly: "The other Marie [i.e. Morel] had been properly avenged: as for *Toute-à-toi* the laugh was on her side now" (6.3.3).

The ending of *BC* is precipitated, in a fine stroke of comic irony, when Marie Rycker suddenly seizes the initiative and forces Querry into the position already implied by his unwitting actions. She claims falsely that he has been her lover, which makes his hostility towards Rycker now seem like sexual jealousy and his taking her to Luc like an abduction. She claims his protection, and thus reasserts the kind of personal bond he had come to Africa to escape. Rycker himself then becomes, like many earlier antagonists, convinced that the hero has deliberately and maliciously betrayed him. The irony lies, of course, in Querry's actual innocence of any designs upon Marie and, at the same time and more deeply, in the way Marie's false claims act as a vengeful reassertion of the old claims of his former mistresses.

In a limited sense Querry succeeds where Fowler fails, for Querry does not compromise what he sees as his integrity. Fowler survives, in possession of Phuong and of the field, but he is a sadder, if a wiser man, regretting the death of Pyle and feeling guilt over his own part in it. In a limited sense Querry remains innocent: nothing he does in Africa harms anyone, and Rycker in particular suffers nothing at Querry's hand. Yet in a larger sense Querry fails where Fowler achieves a measure of success. Fowler establishes a new personal relationship which seems likely to endure, and he survives in a kind of tranquillity, while Querry preserves his personal isolation and dies. The difference reflects the moral point at the heart of these stories: the necessity for compromise, the overriding need for the hero to accept a measure of involvement in human affairs, however imperfect the human world may be. Fowler shows himself, in the end, willing to compromise and accept involvement, even guilt, for a greater good (or at least to mitigate a great evil); whereas Querry remains inflexible in his repudiation of personal involvement and in the preservation of his artificially created innocence.

While Fowler changes, particularly in the ways marked by his altering relationships with Dominguez and Granger, and ultimately compromises his principle of disengagement by taking steps to eliminate Pyle, Querry remains committed to the personal isolation and noninvolvement for the sake of which he came to Africa. It is true that Querry helps build the new hospital and rescues Deo Gratias, but he continues to insist (for instance, in his interview with Parkinson and in his story told to Marie) that he remains meanwhile essentially unconcerned. The difference in attitude between Fowler and Querry is revealed particularly in the climactic actions of their respective stories.

Fowler finally decides to betray Pyle on general grounds of humanity after witnessing the carnage of the big bomb. The structurally equivalent action in *BC* is Querry's aggressive confrontation with Rycker following the appearance of Parkinson's article. Fowler's action against Pyle may have selfish undertones (his wish to win back Phuong, or at least to avenge her departure, may be contributory motivating factors) but the reality of Fowler's humanitarian concern for the victims of Pyle's activities remains undeniable. His concerns for the welfare of the people of his adopted country are well established early in the story. Querry, however, confronts Rycker in mere self-defense to protect his own privacy, and he has no claim to any higher altruistic aims. His motives remain personal, a point emphasized in his conversation with Father Thomas:

> "Can't you see, father, that I must silence him [Rycker]? This mustn't go on. I'm fighting for my life."
> "Your life?"
> "My life here. It's all I have." He sat down wearily on the bed. He said, "I've come a long way. There's nowhere else for me to go if I leave here.... I had no good motive in coming here. I am looking after myself as I have always done, but surely even a selfish man has the right to a little happiness." (5.2)

Of course, Querry is overstating the case here, and there is more to his withdrawal than mere selfishness; but the fact remains that the crucial issue upon which he takes his stand in the novel is his right to personal privacy.

The unusually self-centered nature of Querry's purposes come across also in the notion of "Pendélé," a place or state of simple tranquillity which comes to represent what Querry is seeking. Pendélé has much in common with the various visions of "peace" entertained by the heroes of the middle novels, except that it has no association with Querry's personal past and that to find it, in his view, he would have to go, not backwards into his youth, but somehow further into the jungle, in the direction indicated by Deo Gratias, from whom he first hears of it. Like Pinkie's nostalgic vision of childhood and Scobie's dream of peaceful treks, Pendélé is, in reality, a regressive and inhibiting idea. The point is made in Querry's conversation with the superior:

> "What's Pendélé?"
> "I don't know [Querry replies]—a dance at a friend's house, a young man with a shiny simple face going to Mass on Sunday with the family, falling asleep in a single bed perhaps."
> "People have to grow up. We are called to more complicated things than that." (3.2)

Querry's interest in the native concept of Pendélé again reveals his yearning for a world of childlike moral simplicity, the world also desired vainly by Rowe and Scobie. The superior's dismissal of the idea as immature carries weight and indicates the moral direction of the story. Querry needs to face the complexity of the real world. Pendélé, which is simply a continuation of the process of flight from life which has brought him to Africa, is symptomatic of his failure to achieve this confrontation.

We sympathize in *QA* with the reasons behind Fowler's cynical withdrawal. The world he observes, the world upon which it is his job to report, is a place of extreme cruelty, misery, and folly.

Nonetheless, the thoughtful reader here, as later in the cases of Plarr and Castle, will also appreciate the necessity for the hero's eventual re-engagement and return to the world upon which he has turned his back. Querry, however, refuses to complete the cycle and devotes his energies entirely to constructing for himself a new world which remains essentially idiosyncratic. Despite the examples of Doctor Colin and the superior, Querry will not admit to finding any value in serving others, and at the same time he rebuts the saint-like image held of him by Rycker and Parkinson. As Querry's world becomes increasingly divergent from that of the other characters he becomes, in a sense, quixotic in his maintaining it, particularly because, as in Fowler's case, he commands a certain sympathy in his assertion that reality is too grim or too absurd to be acceptable. "I found myself, in . . . *A Burnt-Out Case*, in that tragic-comic region of La Mancha where I expect to stay," Greene wrote in 1980 (*WE* 8.3). Wormold is the first of Greene's quixotic heroes, but Wormold never loses sight of the fact that he is playing a game. Querry engages his very life in an effort to enforce a different reality, an effort similarly made after him by Brown and then, with more success, by Aunt Augusta and by Monsignor Quixote himself.

The difference between Greene's serious heroes and the quixotic heroes of *OM*, *BC*, *TC*, *TA*, and *MQ* is broadly the difference between tragic irony and comic irony. Greene's grim view of the inescapable unhappiness of the human world is common to both types. In the serious novels the hero learns painfully through experience and either reconciles himself to reality or pays a heavy penalty. In the comic novels the same rules ultimately apply, but the focus of the narrative falls upon the hero's efforts to ignore them. As far as the heroes are concerned the difference can be explained in terms of the images of the priest and the clown. The serious heroes are priest-like in that for them the only true response to the human condition lies in compassion and sacrifice; the comic heroes, on the other hand, turn rather to roleplay, to the creation of an alternative world, to a quixotic disregard of hard facts, and to what Aunt Augusta calls "fun."

In most of Greene's novels from *MW* up to and including *HM*, the idea of the priest, the man through whose ministry grace may be obtained, hovers metaphorically behind the hero. All of the early heroes, Andrews, Czinner, Conrad, and Anthony, die trying to help or save others; and Raven, at the moment of his death, preserving as he is the peace of the world, is even compared to Christ. Pinkie, who wanted to be a priest, is Christ-like as an inverted image, a kind of innocence betrayed by a kind of disciple (Dallow) into the hands of an uncomprehending secular authority. In *PG* the hero is a priest, and his changing conception of his priesthood is central to his story. His death at the end is a kind of martyrdom. Scobie presents a secular approximation to priesthood, making himself responsible for the welfare of others to the point of ending his life rather than subject them to distress. Of course, this is "an almost monstrous pride" (*WE* 4.2), but it is also an emulation of the Christian sacrifice.

The element of self-deception in Scobie, however, brings us to a turning point. When the hero's sacrifice or unworldliness has at its root nothing more than a refusal to face facts, then the priest becomes a clown. Querry stands at this mid point. Although not a priest, he is widely credited with priestly qualities and admits to having had a kind of "vocation." His having abandoned this vocation, he tells Parkinson, makes him a "spoilt priest" (4.3.2). Querry's failure to live up to his vocation stemmed from the same self-centered failing which prevents him, in the story, from achieving true involvement with others. His particular calling was architectural, the design of great public buildings, especially churches. From the start, however, he designed more "for his own pleasure" than with a view to utility or public service (2.3.1). He is, in this respect, like the Priest in *PG* before the beginning of the persecution, finding his vocation a source of personal satisfaction but having little regard for its wider obligations. "What I have built, I have always built for myself [Querry writes], not for the glory of God or the pleasure of a purchaser. Don't talk to me of human beings. Human beings are not my country" (2.3.2). Querry is known, nonetheless, as a man with a vocation, and when he tries to escape this falsehood by withdrawing to the jungle it is assumed by almost everyone that his action has spiritual significance. That Querry has no spiritual object and wishes only to escape from the vocational image which he had once enjoyed becomes a source of ironic comedy. Querry is forced into the role of a pathetic clown, forever protesting that he is not really what all appearances indicate him to be.

The comedy deepens in *TC*, *TA*, and *MQ*, as the hero's perception of the world becomes more widely divorced from reality. Querry, with his vague dream of Pendélé, is merely self-obsessed and unable to see himself as others see him; but Brown, Pulling, and Monsignor Quixote, each in his own way, escape from dull or harsh reality into a world of fantasy. The hero becomes more dynamic in pursuit of his vision, even achieving some temporary success in its assertion. Lear-like heroes, such as the Priest and Scobie, tragically out of step with the world they live in, now give place to quixotic figures, like Wormold, Brown, and the Monsignor, whose unworldliness assumes a creative exuberance and establishes itself as a comic virtue.

The conceptual foundation of Greene's view of comedy[39] is set out in *OM* precisely in terms of this quixotic refusal to accept reality. Wormold is pondering the way in which the real world, dominated by the political gangsterism of the Cold War, threatens the fragility of his domestic peace and particularly Milly's future security.

> The cruel come and go like cities and thrones and powers, leaving their ruins behind them. They had no permanence. But the clown whom he had seen last year with Milly at the circus—that clown was permanent, for his act never changed....
>
> "... Do you remember the clown last year, Milly?"
>
> "He walked off the end of a ladder and fell in a bucket of whitewash."
>
> "He falls in it every night at ten o'clock. We should all be clowns, Milly. Don't ever learn from experience.... God doesn't learn from experience, does He, or how could he hope anything of man? It's the scientists who add the digits and make the same sum who cause the trouble. Newton discovering gravity—he learned from experience and after that.... It was only a matter of time before Lord Rutherford went and split the atom. He had learned from experience

too, and so did the men of Hiroshima. If only we had been clowns, nothing bad would happen to us except a few bruises and a smear of whitewash. Don't learn from experience, Milly. It ruins our peace and our lives." (1.3.3)

The real world is "cruel" and destructive of personal "peace." It is a world governed by laws, particularly physical laws, which are discoverable through "experience." The denizens of this world are those who learn by experience and accept the laws. The alternative is to reject experience, to persist in some personally selected line of conduct despite repeated failure to obtain practical results. To do this is to be a "clown" and to engage in comedy. The clown or comedian is unlikely to enjoy success in worldly terms, and indeed he may frequently be hurt by his failures, but he may nonetheless preserve his personal peace.

Particularly interesting is the suggestion that God is also a comedian. This remark not only lends fuel to those who like to speculate upon the theological implications of Greene's novels, but also indicates a measure of approval for the comic spirit. If God does not learn from experience (as indeed, being eternal, he cannot, since learning is an essentially temporal business) then, to this extent, the clown who persists in his folly is godlike. Seen in this light, the difference between the serious and the comic heroes is between men like Czinner and the Priest on the one hand, who imitate the sacrificial deity in accepting death for the betterment of others, and on the other hand men like Wormold, the Monsignor, and even Brown, who echo the jovial, creative aspect of deity in their efforts to fashion new and happier worlds.

The conceptual basis of this notion of comic creativity, the idea that the real is what you imagine rather than what you are given in experience, that reality is ideal rather than material, is again set out in *OM*. Hasselbacher says to Harry Morgan in the bar: "You would not exist if I didn't believe you existed, nor would those dollars. I believe, therefore you are. . . . You exist only in my thoughts, my friend" (1.4.1). Hasselbacher argues that reality is mental and that consequently he can remake the world simply by an act of imagination. This philosophy goes along with the character of Hasselbacher, who lives on the level of dream. In private he wears the uniform of an officer in the Kaiser's army, and he gives his spare time to the cultivation of molds from which he hopes to discover a drug comparable to penicillin by mere chance. He believes religiously in omens and subscribes to the lottery, and it is he who suggests to Wormold the idea of inventing the information to be passed on to Hawthorne.

In *TC* the clown's subjective view of reality, his tendency to recreate the world in a way ungoverned by experience, is associated with the idealism of George Berkeley. Martha says to Brown: "To you nothing exists except in your own thoughts. . . . You're a Berkeleyan. . . . My dear, try to believe we exist when you aren't there. We're independent of you" (3.2.1). What Martha has in mind here is probably not a strict interpretation of Berkeley but the popular misreading of idealism as a breaking down of boundaries between the real and the imagined. In this view a Berkeleyan could be said to be a comedian in the same sense as Wormold's clown: one who ignores the experientially real and constructs in imagination an alternative reality.

In this sense Wormold himself becomes a clown when he adopts Hasselbacher's suggestion and invents information. His temporary success in so doing is reflected when Carter calls Wormold a "clown" in the course of the gun duel which is the climax of the story (5.5.2). Brown in *TC* is chief among several such "comedians," people who assume a role and act out the part regardless of the objectively real situation. Brown does not at first see himself as a comedian, but he becomes one increasingly in his efforts to maintain his highly improbable way of life in the deteriorating environment of Haiti. As Martha points out, Brown's comic role includes the consistent misreading of other characters in the light of his own presuppositions. He sees Martha as a whore and Jones as a joke. Like Wormold, he creates what he believes to be a purely fantastical scenario and then finds himself caught up in its consequences. He thinks Jones's trip to join the rebels is mere farce, but when Jones's rebellion becomes a reality Brown is implicated and forced to abandon his hotel and his mistress.

In *TA* the comedy becomes more overtly quixotic, with the hero cast as Sancho alongside the extravagant figure of Aunt Augusta, who travels the world imposing her own extraordinary perception upon reality. Henry Pulling, a little like Brown, finds himself gradually drawn into the comedy until, in the end, he becomes himself part of the comic action. In *MQ* it is the hero who is the quixotic figure, supposedly a "descendant" of the original Don Quixote. Monsignor Quixote travels about Spain putting his own naively innocent interpretation upon what he sees. Towards the end, however, his unworldliness emerges more and more in the light of a leap of faith. We come back to Wormold's suggestion that the comic vision is also divine. The clown and the priest are ultimately united in Monsignor Quixote.

Brown is another failed priest, like Querry, a man who has turned his back upon a "vocation" (3.2.1), and who is finally seen as a "comedian." He is also, and most obviously, another in the line of disengaged heroes running from Fowler to Castle. Born in Monaco of mixed English-French parentage, Brown has no roots and regards himself as "a citizen of nowhere" (3.2.2). In Haiti, under Papa Doc, he is surrounded by corruption and violence as well as by incipient movements towards resistance, but his only concerns appear to be to enjoy his mistress and run his hotel. Although flanked by characters who represent a variety of different kinds of involvement (the Smiths, young Philipot, Doctor Magiot, his own mother, and even Martha) Brown remains strictly a spectator. He states his skeptical creed in the closing pages:

> We are the faithless; we admire the dedicated, the Doctor Magiots and the Mr. Smiths for their courage and their integrity, for their fidelity to a cause, but through timidity, or through lack of sufficient zest, we find ourselves the only ones truly committed—committed to the whole world of evil and of good, to the wise and to the foolish, to the indifferent and to the mistaken. We have chosen nothing except to go on living. . . . (3.4.3)

This claim to a broad and inclusive sympathy, while refusing subscription to any particular program of action, might also have been advanced by Fowler or Querry. It is the statement of the benevolent spectator, the skeptic who can find fault with each specific position, if only insofar as it excludes others, and who therefore excuses himself from engaging in any particular purposefully guided line of action in the public domain. This claim is answered in *TC*, not only implicitly in characters such as Magiot and the Smiths, who do engage in action and who, despite failures, emerge more honorably in the story than does Brown, but also overtly by the sermon preached for the fallen rebels. "The Church condemns violence," says the priest, "but it condemns indifference more harshly. Violence can be the expression of love, indifference never" (3.4.4). These words apply clearly to Brown (as admonition), but might equally be applied to Fowler (in justification) or to Querry (in explanation).

Like *BC*, *TC* uses a plot outline derived from *QA*.[40] Like Fowler, Brown settles himself comfortably, after a somewhat checkered life in Europe, in a remote corner of the world. There he feels initially contented, despite a background of increasing violence. Both men take mistresses and live as spectators of the passing scene. In each case this position is then upset by a newcomer, by Pyle and Jones respectively, who not only appears to be a sexual rival but also undertakes the kind of violent partisan activity which the hero deplores. Each of the heroes then betrays his rival, with fatal result: Fowler gives the information which allows the communists to waylay and murder Pyle, and Brown arranges Jones's trip to join the rebels, which results, predictably, in Jones's death soon afterwards. There are ironic twists in *TC* which depart from the pattern of *QA*. Jones's rivalry for Martha is imagined by Brown, whereas Pyle is a real and successful rival to Fowler for Phuong. Again, where Pyle's military activities are real and have horrific results, Jones is not really a soldier and his activities as a rebel, although winning the respect of his men, result only in defeat. In these respects *TC* is an ironic reworking of the story of *QA*.

Like most of the other heroes of this period, Brown is required in the course of his story to resolve an outstanding issue from his past. In the three preceding novels this issue is marital or quasi-marital: Fowler must obtain a divorce from his exwife, Wormold must transfer his love from his exwife to Beatrice, and Querry needs to gather the loose ends of his affairs with women in Europe. *TC* begins a run of novels in which the hero's bond with the past is represented in parental rather than marital or sexual imagery.[41] Brown's story concerns his position as the son of his mother and also offers him a number of surrogate fathers, most prominent among whom is Magiot. In the next novel, *TA*, the story is framed by the hero's discovery of the truth about his parentage. Plarr's search for his lost father is central to *HC*, as is Baxter's relationship with his real and adopted fathers in *CE*. The sinister father figure who dominates the story of *DF* should also be mentioned in this connection.

Brown's past is set out in a lengthy retrospective which occupies the third chapter of the novel. Brown never knew his father and was abandoned as a child by his mother, who left him in a Jesuit school in Monaco. His appetite for adventure, especially for sex and acquisition, asserted itself, however, and he defeated expectations that he might enter the priesthood by running away to London. He became in England a more ingenious, postwar Anthony Farrant, and pursued an unstable career in minor fraud and trickery, until an unexpected message from his mother called him to Haiti. By this time Brown is middle-aged and unattached, with nothing to hold him in Europe. The reappearance of his mother seems a golden opportunity, since she has fortuitously become owner of a hotel which she, dying soon after Brown's arrival, leaves to her only son. Here for the first time Brown has a place of his own and the possibility of an honest, steady living; and he sets to enthusiastically to make the hotel prosper. By a sad irony the hotel is in Haiti, where Duvalier becomes dictator.

Brown's task in *TC* may be said to be to establish himself as the true son and heir of his mother. Pulling has a closely comparable task in *TA*, and Plarr's challenge in *HC* is to prove himself a true son of his father. Brown's inheritance, however, comprises not only the hotel but also, more significantly, his mother's character and view of life. This consists chiefly in two elements: a strong capacity for love and for inspiring love in others on the one hand, as evinced in her relations with Marcel and Magiot respectively, and on the other hand a willingness to take risks and get involved, as shown by her reputed work for the Resistance in wartime France. Love and involvement are the grounds upon which Brown is tried and tested: love in his relations with Martha and Tin Tin, involvement in his dealings with Jones, Philipot, and Magiot. His success in both spheres is limited.

In electing to take over his mother's hotel Brown ignores strong warnings from Magiot on the dangers latent in the Haitian political situation. By the time the novel's main action opens these warnings are proving well founded, and Brown is attempting unsuccessfully to sell the property. Magiot is an impressive figure, a man of evident integrity, and his opinion that Brown should never have tried to take his mother's place as proprietor of the hotel carries much weight. Magiot issues Brown with the kind of warning traditionally given to heroes about to embark on dire adventures. The prospect of the hotel appears inviting, but to take it on will involve severe trials, and there is doubt that Brown will be man enough to face them.

A second indication that all is not well with his mother's inheritance is the fate of Marcel. In order to establish himself as sole proprietor of the hotel Brown has to displace Marcel, his late mother's black lover, to whom she left a third of the property. Brown treats Marcel fairly, even generously, paying him a good price for his share; but the incident nonetheless creates a sense of something amiss. Brown is embarrassed by Marcel's presence, and Marcel feels shame in facing Brown. Marcel feels deep grief for the old lady's loss, which Brown (who hardly knew her) does not. Marcel loses all his money at a casino, some of it in a game where Brown is also playing and winning. Marcel then hangs himself in a room in the hotel. Marcel is clearly a sketch for the character of Wordsworth in *TA*. In both cases there is some jealousy and embarrassment between the lover and the son, and in both cases the lover dies unnaturally at the point where the son establishes himself as his mother's heir. There is a hint of something almost sacrificial here, and though neither Brown nor Pulling has any responsibility, on a purely literal level, for the black man's death, there is also a sense of something very wrong in the steps they are taking over these dead bodies.

Marcel's is the first of a series of unnatural deaths in *TC*, and not the only suicide. He is followed by the elder Philipot and eventually also by Magiot and Jones as well as a number of minor characters. Death is the keynote of this story, set in the country presided over by Francois Duvalier, *alias* Papa Doc, *alias* Baron Samedi, the voodoo spirit who patrols graveyards and controls the dead. Of the several climactic scenes of the novel's main action, one is a funeral, another occurs in a graveyard, and another, the last, is a memorial service for the dead. Brown, who keeps a miniature coffin paperweight on his desk, is spectator to most of these deaths and appropriately ends the story working for an undertaker. Marcel's death is not only another warning to Brown, that in taking over the hotel he is taking a grave risk, but also the first note in a mortuary harmony which resounds throughout the story.

Most of the deaths within the main action, particularly those of Philipot, Magiot, and Jones, arise from the subject's involvement in the chaotic and violent affairs of Haiti. Marcel dies from a different kind of involvement, from his love for Brown's mother, which is such that he proves unable to face life without her. We are meant to contrast Brown, who shows little concern for his mother's passing and who can later contemplate abandoning his mistress in Haiti when he goes to America to sell the hotel. The love between Marcel and the old lady, despite its fantastic and comic aspects, is obviously intense and reciprocal. She dies in the act of love and leaves Marcel a share in her property, and he dies soon afterwards unable to face up to her loss. The love between them sets up, at the opening of the story, a standard of commitment and personal involvement which Brown finds himself unable to match. "I should never have come to this country," he later reflects. "My mother had taken a black lover, she had been involved, but somehow years ago I had forgotten how to be involved in anything. Somehow somewhere I had lost completely the capacity to be concerned" (2.2.1).

Marcel is not, of course, Brown's father, but as his mother's lover and companion his relation to Brown is anomalously stepfatherly. A symmetry is thus created between the novel's two hanged men: Brown's mother's lover and Martha's father. Morally the two are opposites, one a lover, the other a Nazi official executed for his crimes; yet the story makes a point of their common ground in commitment and involvement, contrasting with Brown's detachment. Seen in this light, the Nazi minister had at least the justification of acting for something in which, however mistakenly, he believed. Martha sees that such action may be preferable to the passivity of the spectator who sees evil all around him and does nothing (2.1.2).

A second symmetry arises between Martha's father, the Nazi, and Brown's mother, who was apparently active in the French Resistance. The facts are never finally clear: while Brown characteristically believes his mother might have "played the part" of a resistance heroine without actually being one, Magiot "has no doubt at all" that she had been in the Resistance and was "a great woman" (1.3.3). The allusions to the Second World War serve again to highlight the mother's action in opposing tyranny. Brown himself, as a young man in England, had served during the war in British Intelligence, an episode which he looks upon as a fortunate period of "security and employment" and of temporary "peace and respectability" (1.3.2). Brown's failure to see the war other than in terms of his personal comfort points again to his wish to remain a spectator in the warlike conditions of Haiti.

Far from being a mere prelude, the business between Brown and his mother lays down the conditions under which the story will be acted out. If Brown is to make himself his mother's heir he must face the trials and dangers of Haiti. He must also be prepared to emulate her in making a personal commitment both to individuals and to the humanitarian cause. As the novel moves on from the point of his mother's death, Brown is increasingly seen to be flanked by other characters also representative of various kinds of commitment. Chief among these are the people whom he brings with him, in a manner suggestive of some special symbolic association, when he returns to Haiti by boat, namely Jones and Mr. and Mrs. Smith. Other involved characters, already in place in Haiti, are Magiot (his mother's friend), Joseph (Brown's assistant), and Philipot.

Brown sees most of these characters as "comedians," fantastic or comical figures acting out parts which fail to connect with the real world. He views the Smiths as naive and suspects Jones of concealing doubtful motives beneath a facade of good fellowship. Brown is partially right in his judgements. The Smiths accomplish nothing in Haiti, and their vegetarian mission is comically unrealistic. Jones is something of a fraud, and his venture into armed rebellion ends in a military disaster. Philipot becomes a refugee housed in a lunatic asylum. Yet like Martha's father, and with much more moral justification, these characters have at least acted upon their beliefs, and in the end they each acquire a certain personal dignity from having done so, however ineffectual their actions have been.

As with all of Greene's hero-narrators, the reader must be wary of accepting as complete and final Brown's judgements either of other characters or of himself. By the end of *TC* Brown's judgements can be seen to have been incomplete in two particular ways. First, he is wrong in his implied view of comedy, in the assumption that being a "comedian," playing a part, is necessarily unworthy. There is an element in Brown, as in Fowler and Querry, of the "plain dealer," of the man who rates sincerity supreme among the virtues and who will not allow himself to do anything which he cannot do with complete conviction. As a result he does, for the most part, nothing very significant, and tends to spend his time judging adversely, as dishonest or impractical, the actions of others. Of course, the honesty of the plain dealer commands much sympathy, which is why we are so ready to go along with Fowler, Querry, and Brown (and why, incidentally, the plain dealer Hamlet, with his emphatic rejection of "seems,"[42] has become the most powerfully fascinating hero in English literature). In Greene's later novels, however, we have also to be aware of the contrary point of view. The plain dealer insists upon what is real and has no time for what merely seems, but the comedian, like Wormold's clown, rejects experience and tries to create a reality out of what seems. He may not succeed, but, as Wormold's argument (*OM* 1.3.3) shows, his course of action has at least the virtues of avoiding harm and generating positive emotion.

Accordingly, in the course of *TC* we see a succession of "comedians," whose actions are perceived by Brown to be absurd or pretentious, turn out to have heroic qualities. Jones is accepted as a leader, takes his men into an action, and wins himself a monument; the Smiths show outstanding personal courage, and their "heroism" is eventually acknowledged by Brown himself (2.2.3); and Brown's own mother, who appears at first to be simply grotesque, turns out to have been a lover, a humanitarian, and "a great woman." It is not that Brown is wrong in his initial assessments of these people, for they are "comedians," but he is reluctant to accept that their comedy, their qualities as "clowns" in Wormold's sense, may also be heroic.

Brown's other mistake is his failure to appreciate the extent to which he is himself a "comedian," and this despite his mother's last words to him: "You really are a son of mine. . . . What part are you playing now?" (1.2.3). "I am not sure to this day exactly what she meant," Brown adds, yet it should be obvious to the reader that Brown's idea of maintaining himself as a hotelier catering for tourists in Papa Doc's Haiti is no less fantastical than the Smiths' expectation of converting the country to vegetarianism, or Philipot's belief that he can outface the armed forces of the state with a Bren gun. Brown's true status as a "comedian" is developed through comparison between himself and Jones. Jones has a past history of fraud similar to that admitted by Brown, and Jones's ambition to run a golf club in the Caribbean is, if anything, less unrealistic than Brown's projected career as a Haitian hotelier.

Brown is like Fowler and Querry in that, by the end of his story, a considerable gap has opened between what he says about himself and what he does. Querry, for instance, continues to protest his spiritual and emotional disengagement, even after he has taken some risk to rescue Deo Gratias and worked with the fathers on their new buildings. Brown pretends to be selfish and disinterested while actually involving himself in numerous ways. He goes with Smith to visit Jones in prison, he confronts the police at Philipot's funeral, he helps Jones find asylum at the embassy. He shows considerable personal courage, not only in his last drive with Jones, where his motives might be selfish, but also in facing the police who come to beat him. Other activists in the story—the Smiths, Jones, and young Philipot—place confidence in Brown and take for granted his support. Magiot confides in him as his mother's son, and Martha calls him a "prêtre manqué." "How strangely we must appear to other people," is Brown's comment (3.4.4), but in the end the reader is more likely to accept Martha's and Magiot's view of Brown as a man of human sympathies than his own presentation of himself as a misanthropic cynic.

In the end Brown's attempt to take his place as his mother's heir in Haiti is a failure. Like Wormold from Cuba, he is finally driven out of the country. Wormold, however, has not played an entirely losing game: he has made some money, killed Carter, and outwitted Segura over the matter of the gun and the list of agents; and he has also found himself, in Beatrice, a new focus for life. Brown has achieved nothing: he leaves behind him whatever property he had in Haiti, he leaves his mistress, and his activities have been completely ineffectual. The story ends with Haiti left as it was, under Papa Doc, after a general exodus of the more enlightened characters (the Smiths, Luis, Martha, and Brown himself) leaving others (Magiot, Philipot Senior, and Jones) dead behind them. If this is still comedy it is of a bitterly ironic kind.

Greene's next novel, *TA*, is comedy of another kind altogether, belonging to a different genre. It is a kind of picaresque, being a series of apparently disjointed adventures befalling a hero who finds himself launched from quite inauspicious beginnings into extensive travels and a wide variety of new experiences. The classic instance of this kind of story in English is *Tom Jones*, which is like *TA* in also framing its adventures with the hero's search for and discovery of his true parentage. For *TA*, like *TC*, concerns a hero whose goal is to find and accept his mother, and at the end Henry Pulling, like Tom Jones, enters into his matriarchal inheritance. Greene's model, however, was not so much Fielding as Cervantes. Aunt Augusta is conceived as a sort of Don Quixote, roaming the world trying to impose upon mundane reality a coloring of antiquated romance, and Henry becomes, as he says himself, her Sancho Panza (1.10).

Because it is modeled generically upon the picaresque romance, rather than the Conradesque adventure—story or popular thriller, *TA* seems out of place among Greene's novels, although it was eventually to have a companion piece in *MQ*. Where Greene's mature plots are usually unified and tightly knit, *TA* is strung out and episodic. Henry Pulling, moreover, seems an unusually passive hero, allowing the pace and direction of the action to be dominated almost entirely by his aunt. (The trip to Boulogne is, indeed, initiated by Henry, but even there Augusta is his guide.) Beneath these differences of genre, however, *TA* has much the same set of essential elements that we have found in the other late novels from *QA* onwards. Henry Pulling is another hero who has, at the outset of his story, withdrawn himself from the world; and in the course of events, like Fowler and Brown, he finds himself increasingly involved and under pressure to commit himself to action. As in the cases of Brown and Plarr, Henry's eventual decision to reenter the human fray is taken along with a reappraisal of his past, and particularly of his parentage. On the other hand, since *TA* (unlike *OM* and *TC*) is a truly lighthearted kind of comedy, there is little sense here that the hero's action is required to alleviate human suffering. The sense of "the terror of life" is not entirely absent from *TA*, but it is much muted.

Despite its episodic form, and its heavy sprinkling of anecdotes from Augusta's past, *TA* is closely organized around the central theme of Henry's progress from paralytic retirement to active participation, and the series of adventures is framed by the matter of his parentage. The novel opens with the revelation that his supposed mother was not his true mother, and Part I leads, through a number of adventures and anecdotes, to the discovery of his father's grave. The climax of Part II, the end of the story, coincides with the revelation—long anticipated by the reader—that Henry's real mother is Augusta herself. Within this framework there are further symmetries, helping to bind together what might otherwise seem a rather rambling story. At the end of Part I Henry meets his father's lover, Miss Paterson, and at the end of Part II he meets his (real) mother's lover, Mr. Visconti. In Part I, going east, he travels with Tooley, and in Part II, going west, he travels with Tooley's father. Moreover, the several anecdotes scattered through the story can be seen in retrospect to give not only a cumulative picture of Augusta's past but also a series of illustration of her concept of "fun."

    TA is a comedy in the straightforward sense that it ends happily. More specifically, it is a story in which the central characters succeed in vindicating their comic vision of life against the repressive forces of an unsympathetic world. Henry, Augusta, and Mr. Visconti achieve a measure of success, establishing themselves in a small community where their dubious activities are tolerated—at least for the time being. Henry has emerged from dull withdrawal into a cheerful, even dynamic life of activity. The story ends, in the traditional comic manner, with marriages: Augusta and Mr. Visconti, Henry and the young daughter of a local official. Nothing significant in the mature fiction of Greene is unambiguous, and the comedy of *TA* has its dark underside. The comic world is perilous, full of risks and dangers. Mr. Visconti is not a very attractive figure and appears to have been involved with Nazis, dealing in looted works of art, during the War. In becoming a denizen of this new country Henry experiences a loss of innocence, marked by the murder of poor Wordsworth, a death reminiscent of that of Marcel in *TC* for its purpose in marking the fact that the hero is about to enter a dangerous and morally dubious world. Nonetheless, as in the cases of the other heroes, Henry's innocence is well lost, and the reader is in little doubt at the end that his new life is, on balance, preferable to the old.

    TA also has that hallmark of Greene's comedy, a deliberate erosion or confusion of the boundaries between the real and the imaginary, between what is factual and fictional within the story. In *OM* and *TC* the heroes engage in an attempt to impose an imaginary view of things upon an ultimately intractable reality. In *TA* much the same is done, rather more successfully, by Aunt Augusta, whose perception of reality gradually displaces Henry's as the story progresses. This gradual displacement is managed chiefly through the narrative technique, employing a first-person narrator observing a second character whose frequent anecdotes are inserted in her own words. The reader is aware, not only of the more obvious process whereby Henry's rather dull picture of life comes under increasing pressure from Augusta's very different idea of things, but also of the no less important process whereby Augusta's presentation of herself and her activities is constantly undercut and revealed to be eccentric, if not simply false.

Henry's incredulity in the face of his aunt is not without justification and maintains an effective underlying tension in the novel to the end. In each of the cases where we are given sufficient evidence to judge, there appears a wide and evident discrepancy between Augusta's account of things and the way they stand in terms of everyday reality. The romantic and mysterious Mr. Visconti,[43] for instance, is in the end revealed to be a smalltime confidence trickster of limited success and uninspiring appearance. The business involving General Abdul, which Augusta represents in terms of high adventure, turns out to be a crazy plot with no hope of thriving, in which she has been manipulated by others.

The contrast between dull reality and Augusta's romantic fantasy is particularly sharp in her confrontation with Miss Paterson. The antagonism which Augusta displays towards the inoffensive Dolly is not simply sexual jealousy but also a resentment that Henry's father, whom Augusta remembers as a man of unusual qualities, should have chosen so uninspiring a companion and such undistinguished surroundings. The antagonism has a further source: through Mr. Visconti Augusta once moved on the fringes of high Nazi circles, whereas Dolly Paterson worked for the allied cause during the War. Even so, and despite the evidently fantastical nature of many of his aunt's stories, Henry is attracted (as the reader should be) by the overall vitality of her vision. He begins to feel that, despite their failure to stand up to strict scrutiny in the cold light of day, his aunt's stories have nonetheless a kind of "life."

> Perhaps she did have reason to despise Miss Paterson. I thought of Curran and Monsieur Dambreuse and Mr. Visconti—they lived in my imagination as though she had actually created them: even poor Uncle Jo struggling towards the

> lavatory. She was one of the life-givers. Even Miss Paterson had come to life, stung by the cruelty of her question. Perhaps if she ever talked about me to another . . . even I would come to some sort of life, and the character she drew, I felt sure, would be much more vivid than the real I. (1.18)

In the end it is this vitality which wins the day in *TA*. With a kind of willing suspension of skepticism, Henry finally commits himself to his aunt's fairytale world of palatial splendor, easy money, old-world courtesy, and romance. He becomes part of his aunt's ongoing story. In this respect *TA* looks forward to *MQ*, where again the hero becomes increasingly remote from everyday reality and closer to the imaginative realm of the fictional character whose name he bears.

Greene returned from comedy to tragic irony in his next novel, *HC*. This was the novel which, writing in 1980, he was inclined to see as his best (*WE* 9.5), an estimate which need not be seriously challenged. He had, perhaps, been breaking newer ground in *BR* and *PG*, but *HC* has both a higher technical mastery and a wider breadth of humanity. It handles with easy understatement the great themes of love, humanity, faith, and evil, avoiding the touch of manipulative contrivance from which plots like those of *HM*, *EA*, and *TC* are not entirely free. The prose has the lean translucence which Greene had developed in his postwar writing and is enlivened by a light sardonic touch carried over from the recent comedies.

This masterpiece of late maturity (Greene was sixty-nine when the novel appeared in 1973) is a natural development from his previous work, superior in many qualities but not greatly different in kind. Plarr belongs to the line of reclusive heroes, initiated by Fowler and including Querry and Brown, all men of European background who have chosen to live quietly in remote places, hoping to avoid involvement in local conflicts. The central issue of personal betrayal (Plarr's of Fortnum) goes back to the early novels and echoes particularly Conrad's betrayal of the imprisoned Jim in *IB*. Leon's band of rebels, earnest and deadly but ultimately incompetent, owe something to Pinkie's gang; and the situation of Clara, a native girl from a local brothel disputed between two Anglo-Saxon males, replicates closely that of Phuong. The matter of parentage, which is a prominent issue in *HC*, is a theme continued from *TC* and *TA*.[44]

The dramatic device of the "key scene" recurs here, in the long hours during which the captives are held in the hut while the police gather in the night outside. Some critics object to this scene in *HC* as unduly long, static, and verbose,[45] but the issues discussed can at least be said to arise naturally from the situation and characters involved. The scene as a whole is an obvious echo of structurally comparable scenes of nocturnal encirclement in *ST*, *GS*, and *QA*. The theology which Leon expounds here (which owes more than a little to Teilhard de Chardin) has something in common with the idea of progressive evolution set out by Doctor Colin in *BC*. (Evolutionary theology is also parodied by Javitt in *UG* and by Mr. Visconti in *TA* 2.7.) Theological issues arise in *HC* chiefly because of the character of Leon, who is a priest; but he is also a man whose political views incline towards communism, and in Leon's attempt to reconcile his Catholic faith with his politics we have the conceptual germ of *MQ*.

The plot of *HC*, like those of *BC* and *TC*, is basically a version of that of *QA*. In *HC*, as in *QA*, the hero gives information to a local group of political activists enabling them to intercept his friend, a man who has just succeeded in attaching to himself the girl with whom the hero has become "obsessed." There are important differences: Fortnum's capture by the rebels is the result of a mistake and is not foreseen by Plarr, whereas Fowler well knows the likely outcome for Pyle of the information he gives to Mr. Heng. Again, it is Plarr, not Fortnum, who dies in *HC*—although it could very well have been the other way around, as the reader is for a good while led to expect it will be.

HC uses the structural techniques of *QA* in opening the narrative at a critical point in the course of events, in this case the moment of the kidnaping of Fortnum, and then recapitulating the past in a series of retrospective episodes until it catches up with the main action. The point of this device, beyond its obvious dramatic effectiveness, is to underline the bearing of Plarr's past upon the decisions he takes in the narrative present. Like the other heroes of Greene's late novels, Plarr finds that his present problems are reflections of unresolved issues from his past, issues which he has now to confront.

Chief among the factors in Plarr's past which have bearing upon his present action are matters of his birth, parentage, nationality, and childhood associations. Born in Paraguay to an expatriate English father, and having lived most of his life in Argentina, Plarr nonetheless retains British citizenship even although he has never visited his father's home country. This makes him, very like Brown, a rootless person, with no strong ties to any particular place or nation, a situation which reflects his personal disengagement. Plarr's father was a liberal, active in resistance against oppression in Paraguay. He disappeared when Plarr was still a boy, and the possibility remains, at the beginning of the story, that he is still alive in a Paraguayan prison. Plarr was raised by his mother, who now lives a meaningless life of comfortable self-indulgence in Buenos Aires. Leon Rivas, the priest who has joined the Paraguayan resistance movement, was among the friends of Plarr's schooldays.

Plarr's background sets out the terms upon which he has to take crucial decisions in the course of the story. On the one hand his view of himself as an Englishman living in a remote foreign country inclines him to disengagement, an attitude reinforced by the influence of his mother, who has effectively isolated herself from reality in a complacent world of priests and confectionery. On the other hand Plarr has separated himself from his mother and inclines more to his English father, whom he remembers favorably and who was involved in fighting for a cause. At the opening of the story Plarr is in a state of equilibrium between these rival influences. He has rejected his mother's way of life and moved back to the place where he last saw his father and where, he fancifully supposes, his father might one day reappear. Yet he has made no real effort to trace his father or to follow in his footsteps by involving himself in the political struggle. He has become a doctor, which might be seen as a humanitarian move, and he does indeed give time to the treatment of the poor; but his work is mostly with the bourgeoisie and habitually extends itself into meaningless affairs with his married female patients. Plarr is evidently marking time in border territory.

The artistry of *HC* consists largely in the way in which Plarr's equilibrium is upset only gradually by a cumulative succession of events. Plarr has given information to Leon to enable him to kidnap the American ambassador. It is clear that Plarr could reasonably suppose no great harm would come of this: the hostage would not be hurt, and a few Paraguayan prisoners, perhaps Plarr's father among them, would be released in return for his freedom. Plarr expects his action in passing on the necessary information to be the only such action required of him, and he does it in the hope of securing his father's release. But when the kidnapped man appears to be suffering ill effects from the drug supplied by Plarr, the doctor is obliged to visit the hut where he is being held. When he there discovers that the prisoner is Fortnum, he finds himself more deeply involved.

The problem is not so much that Fortnum recognizes Plarr in the hideout—an embarrassment which, given Fortnum's well-known alcoholism, could be countered with a flat denial—as the nature of the relationship which already exists between the two men. While not close friends, they have, as fellow Englishmen living in an isolated place, passed time together. Moreover, Plarr is currently having an affair with Fortnum's young wife. Fortnum's removal from the scene, should the kidnap result in his death, would in fact be highly inconvenient for Plarr since it would not only make him an object of suspicion to the perceptive Colonel Perez but would leave Clara and her child on his hands.

From this point Plarr devotes all his energy to resolving the problem and securing Fortnum's release. The obvious expedient of revealing the truth to the authorities is ruled out, for not only would this be a betrayal of Leon but it would also involve admission of Plarr's complicity in the plot. Hence Plarr's visit to the British ambassador and his attempts to enlist others in publicizing Fortnum's plight. Then Fortnum is shot and wounded while trying to escape, making it necessary for the doctor to return to the hut. He is very reluctant to go, knowing that the rebels are unlikely to take the risk of allowing him to leave a second time. He is apparently swayed by Leon's honesty in admitting that the promised effort to obtain the release of Plarr's father was a deception, as the old man is dead. Paradoxically the knowledge that his father is no longer alive, knowledge which releases him from any straightforward obligation to cooperate with the rebels, is the reason for his returning to the hideout in the step which effectually commits him to their cause.

In a sense, by returning to the side of the prisoner, Plarr accepts Fortnum in place of his father. It is important to note in this connection that, whereas Fortnum is an older man of about the age of retirement, Plarr is "still in his early thirties" (2.3). Plarr acted initially in the slender hope of achieving his father's release. Now he discovers his father is dead and that, as a result of his action, another man is a prisoner, another Englishman of about his father's age. In the final phase of the action, Part Five of the narrative, Plarr shares Fortnum's captivity and expects to share his fate. In his final effort to negotiate Fortnum's release, by stepping out of the hut as the police wait around it, Plarr is in a sense resolving the initial problem. He has engaged himself in action, taken his father's place as a prisoner, and meets the same end.

The concept of fatherhood is a unifying motif in *HC*.[46] The three central characters are bound together by actual and metaphorical fatherhood. Plarr's absent father is always in his mind, and it is his task in the course of the story to justify himself as his father's true son, much as Brown's task in *TC* is to assume his mother's inheritance. Plarr himself is the father of Fortnum's wife's unborn child. Leon has renounced the world of his father, a powerful conservative, and in becoming a priest has himself become a kind of "father," a style by which he is frequently addressed in the story. Fortnum also remembers his father, generally with fear and dislike. Fortnum believes himself to be the father of Clara's child, and by the time he discovers the truth he has been established in the story as a symbolic father, replacing the one of whose loss Plarr recently learned.

Fatherhood, whether natural, surrogate, or pastoral, is a human bond, and the formation of bonds, the acceptance of commitment in human relationships, is as important to *HC* as is its political theme. Here, much as in *QA* and *TC*, the issue of the hero's involvement is developed simultaneously in two spheres: the public or political, and the personal or human. Fowler arrives at a stable, marital relationship with Phuong only in the course of involving himself in the political affairs of Vietnam. In a similar way, Plarr is called to action on two fronts. The question of his intervention in political business runs through the novel alongside the matter of commitment in his personal life.

When the story opens Plarr is not only aloof from the political, humanitarian struggle in which his father had been engaged, but also emotionally detached from his succession of mistresses. " 'Love' was a claim which he wouldn't meet, a responsibility he would refuse to accept" (4.2). He exhibits a cynical suspicion of interpersonal emotion reminiscent of Querry. Even with Clara he has no thought of effecting any permanent union. His expectation remains that, when Fortnum is released, she will continue to live with her husband, and the true parentage of the child will be concealed. The two aspects of Plarr's challenge, the public and the personal, are connected by the concept of fatherhood. A true father, like the elder Plarr and "Father" Rivas, engages himself in the humanitarian struggle. This is required of Eduardo, who must also face his responsibility towards Clara and her child. He must himself become a father in both respects.

The stimulus which first moves the hero comes, in *HC* as in the other late novels, in the form of a character from his past. Plarr is already in place at the outset, awaiting his father; but the figure who arrives is a father of a different kind. Leon, however, comes from the country where Plarr's father is supposed be, actually has news of him, and urges action in the same cause as that to which the elder Plarr was committed. Leon's offer, which is deceptive on a literal level but which retains a certain metaphorical validity, is that by taking action to help the cause Plarr may secure his father's release. The imprisoned father, who reappears in Aquino's poem (seen "only through the bars" (3.3)), is the only person for whom Plarr has felt love, and his release is therefore an imperative if Eduardo is to be capable of love in adult life. Although the natural father is dead, two other imprisoned fathers at once take his place: Father Rivas and Fortnum. These are also men of love, in the public and private realms respectively: Leon is a humanitarian serving the people, and Fortnum is Clara's devoted protector. Their release now becomes Plarr's task. He joins them in prison, but his efforts are only partly successful. Leon is killed. Plarr's own death seems almost inevitable—on what terms could he have survived if Fortnum had been killed in this escapade, and yet how could the story be resolved if both Fortnum and Plarr emerged alive? Fortnum's survival, however, allows Plarr a measure of success: a father like his own has been released, and the newborn Eduardo will be his own son.

HF and *HC* form a pair among Greene's novels, particularly in that both focus upon the image of an imprisoned humanitarian, on whose account the hero commits what is technically an act of betrayal by passing confidential information to the official enemy. In fact the composition of *HF* spanned that of *HC*. Greene began *HF* in the early 1960s but put it aside after 1963 because of the similarities between the story outline and the business of Kim Philby, who defected in that year to the Soviet Union. Greene had known Philby personally and, although there was no real connection, was afraid that the novel would be received as in some way based upon the Philby affair (*WE* 9.5). The novel was put aside and completed only after the publication of *HC*.

The real roots of *HF* go back far beyond Philby. As a story about espionage *HF* looks back to *OM*. Like Wormold, Castle engages in spying initially for reasons of familial love. Both men believe their activities to be inconsequential, and both are surprised to find that this is not the case. In each case a victim (Hasselbacher and Davis) pays with his life for the hero's betrayal of trust. *HF* has also a point of contact with *EA*, particularly in its London setting, especially the clubs and restaurants, and in the names Sarah and Maurice for the central pair. The character of Castle, however, owes more to Scobie than to Bendrix. Both Scobie and Castle are men of integrity in the government service, both are approaching retirement without enthusiasm, and both are burdened with personal responsibilities. Like Scobie, Castle can "seldom resist a call of distress" (3.6.1) and experiences a compelling sympathy for the suffering and oppressed. Each man betrays his trust for reasons associated with his wife. Although not a Catholic, Castle echoes Scobie's abortive attempt at confession (5.1.1).

Although Castle is not, like Fowler, Querry, and Plarr, in a remote place far from his home, he nonetheless continues the line of hermit-heroes in Greene's late novels. Castle's settlement in Berkhamsted (his childhood home, as it was in fact the author's) is evidently as much, for him, a withdrawal as Fowler's removal to Saigon. For Castle the crucial scene of action, where he once worked, where he met his wife, and which he still observes from afar, is South Africa. His settlement in Berkhamsted after escaping from Africa is presented in the opening pages as a withdrawal to place of "security." "In a bizarre profession anything which belongs to an everyday routine gains great value—perhaps that was one reason why, when he came back from South Africa, he chose to return to his birthplace. . . . Living thus with the long familiar he felt the security that an old lag feels when he goes back to the prison he knows" (1.2). The epigraph to *HF*, a line from Conrad's *Victory*, reinforces the point, for the hero of *Victory*, Axel Heyst, is another who chooses to withdraw to remote isolation in an attempt to avoid involvement in compromising action.

Like Plarr, however, Castle is already compromisingly involved when the novel's main action opens. Just as Plarr has already passed information to Leon, so Castle has for some time been passing secrets on African affairs to Moscow. As he repeats several times, Castle is not a communist, any more than is Plarr. He supports the communists in South Africa partly out of gratitude to Carson for his help in getting Sarah out of that country, and partly out of personal sympathy for the oppressed black people whom the communists were promising to help. As in *HC*, therefore, the question is not so much whether the hero will involve himself as how far he will go and how he will face the almost inevitable consequences of his action.

The general pattern of action in *HF* again echoes that of *QA*. In both cases the hero's love for a native girl leads him to involve himself in political action in support of her people. In many details, however, *HF* is particularly close to *HC*. In both of these stories the hero is already engaged in action as the story opens. In each case a suspicious investigator (Perez and Daintry) is already asking questions and will eventually find the hero out. Both heroes at one stage decide to back out: Plarr, having done all he can to raise support for the hostage, has no intention of returning to the hut or giving the rebels any further help; Castle decides to stop sending information to Moscow. In each case the turning point of the story comes as the hero changes his mind and takes the decisive further step which commits him and ensures his eventual discovery. Plarr returns to the hut and shares the fate of the rebels, and Castle passes on Muller's notes knowing that his own exposure will soon follow.

In each case this pivotal decision follows from a complex of factors at the heart of which lies news of a death. Over the telephone, having asked Plarr to come back to the hut to treat the wounded Fortnum, Leon confirms the news Plarr has just received that his father is dead, a fact which Leon had hitherto concealed; and this honesty is largely what determines Plarr's return to the hideout. Castle hears of Carson's death from Muller, who subsequently leaves accidentally his secret notes in Castle's hands, the notes which Castle feels his debt to Carson's memory obliges him to pass on. Plarr's father and Carson have much in common. Both are political activists in a sympathetic cause, and each commands the hero's personal affection. Both have been lost for some time in hostile territory, and both are now revealed to have died, to have been murdered while in prison. The memory of Carson drives Castle onwards into further involvement and final commitment in much the same way as the memory of his father motivates Plarr.

The structural resemblance between the offstage roles of Carson and the elder Plarr draws attention to another similarity, this one between Muller and Leon. These are the figures from the past who burst unexpectedly into the present, disrupting the even tenor of life and raising new moral imperatives. Personally they are in most respects opposite, as they are in their widely different positions on the political spectrum. Leon remains sympathetic despite his descent into terrorism, while Muller remains despicable despite his suave manners. They nonetheless work to the same effect in the structures of their respective novels, revealing to the hero the fate of the figure he idealizes and confronting him with a situation demanding his involvement.

Carson, of course, is not Castle's father, and the pervasive father imagery of *HC* is not significantly continued into *HF*; but *HF* does return to childhood imagery similar in some ways to that used in *BR* and *PG*. Castle himself has a sense of "lost innocence": he is said to have "lost both audacity and innocence for ever in South Africa" (1.2), and his return to Berkhamsted is in some ways reflection of a nostalgia for childhood peace comparable to that felt by Pinkie. The boy Sam functions in a way reminiscent of the Priest's daughter in *PG*, as a token of the fragility of childhood and the innate tendency of humanity towards worldly corruption. Castle's efforts to see Sam in the light of a fantasy world of games and fairies is constantly thwarted by the boy's enthusiasm for spying. Spying, still a game for Sam, like hide-and-seek on the Common, is a reminder for Castle of grim realities in which espionage is a deadly sport and where the hidden man pays with his life for being caught. Castle's agony over Sam's lost innocence recalls the Priest's concern for Brigitta.

Castle's efforts to preserve Sam's innocence reflect his own sense of loss, a sense which surfaces at a number of points in the story. One such point is the matter of the "drop" in the hollow tree on the Common (3.8.2), an episode in which Greene recapitulates the essence of a short story he had written in about 1937, significantly entitled "The Innocent."[47] The story is of an innocent childhood love abruptly confronted with sexual obscenity. In *HF* this story becomes Castle's childhood memory associated with a particular tree on the Common. The adult Castle selects this same place as the depository for his illicit messages to Moscow, a choice which clearly underlines his association of his activities on behalf of communism with loss of innocence.

The Common figures also in the autobiographical story of the dragon which Castle tells to Sam and which (assuming he is not making it up) reflects another childhood memory. The dragon, his imaginary friend and protector, reveals Castle's need, even as a boy, for "security," and he tells how its proximity was a comfort to him. Of course, the dragon never actually did anything, but

Castle's need was served by the feeling that, in an extreme situation, he could call upon its aid: "I knew I had only to give a signal and he would leave his dug-out on the Common and come down and help me." The dragon is evidently, with respect to Castle, an emblem for communism. Not only does he live on the "Common," but "every man's hand was against him," and Castle communicates with him by means of "private signals, codes, ciphers"(2.2). As the dragon was to Castle as a child, so in some respects is communism to the man.

In later life, in the adult world of South African apartheid, and far away from the Common, Castle experiences extreme need when Sarah's life is threatened and he is himself unable to help her. He invokes the aid of a real "dragon," communism, which performs his bidding in this case, but which, not unlike Mephistopheles, exacts a heavy price in return. This is Castle's loss of innocence, his placing himself in a situation of mutual obligation with the communist dragon. In return for Sarah's safety he will continue to communicate with it, by means of "private signals, codes, ciphers," and it will always be at hand to "come down and help" if Castle should ever call. When he has sent the final message and exposed himself to imminent discovery Castle uses the agreed distress signal. He is indeed rescued, although not on the terms he had desired.

The communist dragon, as Castle's secret security, has an ironic counterpart in Buller, the supposed protector acquired to give a sense of safety to Sarah. Although the dog is actually a boxer, the name and the facial characteristics of the breed suggest the bulldog, the traditional symbol of British strength and courage. Yet Buller is completely ineffective as a protector, an irony which appears to reflect the novel's depiction of British pusillanimity in having dealings with the upholders of apartheid. The political reference is underlined by the name's allusion to Sir Redvers Buller, the British commander-in-chief during the opening phase of the Boer War.[48] Although he did eventually manage the relief of Ladysmith, Buller is remembered chiefly for the military disasters of his earlier campaign. "Buller" is therefore an appropriate name for an ineffectual dog assigned to protect Sarah, a black South African; however, despite his uselessness the dog becomes a loved pet for Sam. Castle's disposal of Buller is a precondition of his departure for Moscow, and the bungled shooting of the family pet is not only a rather heavy-handed emblem of Castle's rejection of his British heritage but also a final farewell to the innocence of childhood.

Castle is very like Scobie: a man of integrity whose capacity for "pity" or sympathy leads him into a compromising situation. Scobie's compromise is achieved gradually in the course of his story, whereas Castle's took place seven years before we see him, when he contracted a personal debt to the communist agent who helped him to free Sarah. Castle's guilt and the weight of problems unresolved from his past life are clearly in place from the start. He is a double agent in constant danger of discovery, and his life in Berkhamsted is not only an attempt to recapture childhood innocence but also, on a more practical level, a cover, an effort to be inconspicuous by being ordinary and regular. Like the other late heroes, he finds his hiding place invaded by the past.

Castle's past, and particularly his loss of innocence, is represented by Muller. It was in the context of the situation which Muller embodies that Castle compromised his integrity by becoming indebted to communism. Muller's arrival on Castle's doorstep in Berkhamsted is a nemesis as dramatic as any in Conrad. Apparently purely fortuitous, it coincides with crucial developments: Daintry's security check and the elimination of Davis have made it impossible for Castle to continue passing information without discovery. He feels, moreover, that his debt is now paid, and he takes the necessary steps to break contact with Moscow. Had he held to this decision and sent no more messages Castle would have achieved the security he desires. His fabricated life as an ordinary man living a quiet existence would have become the reality. Muller's appearance, however, and the information he brings about Carson and "Uncle Remus," tell Castle that the debt is not paid. Carson gave his life, and Castle must therefore himself face greater risks; the threat to Sarah's people is greater than ever, demanding Castle's continued action. As Castle sacrifices his security to send the content of Muller's notes to

Moscow he "identified himself truly for the first time with Carson" (4.2.4). The hero is committed and the debt to the past is finally paid.

After excursions, in *DF* and *MQ*, into related genres, Greene returned to the novel with *CE*, which was to be his last. With a symmetry which can hardly have been accidental, Greene here reworks the story of his first published novel. In *CE*, as in *MW*, an unhappy boy, son of an indifferent father, is rescued from his boarding school by an exciting, benevolent stranger. The stranger, an associate of the boy's father, proves to be adventurous and chivalrous, and he soon fires the young hero's imagination. Although he quickly realizes the man's activities are criminal and potentially dangerous, the boy grows up under his influence and in expectation of joining him in his enterprises. Later, however, when the going becomes hazardous and the hero's rather fragile sense of self-esteem is upset, the young man betrays his mentor, and the consequences are fatal.

CE is thus largely a retelling of *MW* in a modern setting, with arms replacing spirits as the smuggled commodity, and a crashed plane in place of a wrecked ship. There are, of course, many variations, the most important of which concerns the heroine's role. Elizabeth, in the traditionally patterned story of *MW*, is presented from the outset as the hero's ideal mate and moral inspiration. In *CE*, however, Liza remains the Captain's mistress, and the hero's failure to accept the values she represents is pivotal in the course of events. Whereas Andrews, inspired by Elizabeth, achieves an heroic end, Baxter, having deserted Liza and betrayed the Captain, remains a mean and self-centered figure whose death is no more than his just desert.

Baxter is probably the least attractive of Greene's heroes, both because of his own ungenerous nature and because of the appeal of the character of the man he betrays. It was perhaps for this reason, because there was so little that could be said on Baxter's behalf, that Greene reverted in *CE* to the first-person narrative. By letting Baxter tell his own story Greene ensures that whatever justifications can be found for his conduct are kept before the reader's mind. Baxter thus becomes another, and the last, of the articulate, self-examining heroes, a group which begins with Bendrix and includes most of the later heroes, and which contrasts with the heroes of the early and middle novels, men for whom detailed weighing of motives would be out of character. It is for this reason, in order that he should be able to narrate his own story, that Baxter, like Bendrix and Fowler, is made a writer by profession.

Not only is *CE*, for the most part, told in the first person, but it also adopts the method (perhaps inherited ultimately from the "epistolary" novels of the eighteenth century) of breaking the narrative into stages, into a series of relatively short documents supposedly produced by the narrator at intervals during the story. As an aspiring author, Baxter practices his skills by drafting autobiographical fragments. The text of *CE* is presented as a series of three such fragments, followed by a short coda—necessarily in the third person, since Baxter cannot be supposed to have written an account of his own death. This is a rather cumbrous device, which involves Baxter in twice rediscovering and extending a personal manuscript which he must finally abandon to be discovered by others. The gain is in dramatic immediacy: the narrator tells his story, stage by stage, as it happened and without benefit of significant hindsight.

The narrator's lack of hindsight is crucial in *CE*. Baxter tells of his early life with Liza and the Captain before he learns, from the Captain's letters, of their intimacy and before his own failure to care for her has contributed to Liza's death. Again, he recounts his decision to go to Panama without knowing what he will really find when he gets there. Thus the earlier stages of the narrative preserve a kind of innocence, which they could hardly do otherwise, since Baxter is evidently an unreliable witness.

The adult Baxter displays disregard for truth and a willingness to fabricate and manipulate information. He admits to a habit of writing for effect with little regard for sincerity. A cavalier attitude to truth is, indeed, something which Baxter learns from the Captain, a trait which no doubt helped him into a career in "cheap journalism." Baxter therefore lacks the integrity which makes Bendrix and Fowler sufficiently reliable as narrators of their own respective stories. We would expect Baxter, recounting the whole of his life in one continuous document (written, perhaps, in the hotel room after the news of the Captain's death), to color his earlier relations with Liza and the Captain a such a way as to conceal or minimize the betrayals of which he is guilty. The requirement that he write up each of the major stages of his life before embarking on the next is the reader's guarantee of a fair degree of truth in the narrative.[49]

The dislocation of the narrative of *CE* into Baxter's three autobiographical fragments and the "coda" emphasizes the way in which, uniquely among Greene's full-length novels, this story concentrates upon childhood and upon the contrast between childhood innocence and adult moral complexity. In the other novels in which the hero's childhood is a significant factor (as it is more often than not) it is covered in short retrospective glimpses. Here the story opens with the hero aged twelve, and more than a third of the novel is devoted to his boyhood. A typical Greene novel is the story of the final stages of the relationship between the hero and the man he betrays, illuminated only as necessary by retrospective glances at the past. Thus *MW* begins after Andrews has already betrayed Carlyon, *EM* covers essentially the few days of Anthony's association with Krogh, *MF* begins with the cake which leads Rowe rapidly to Hilfe, and *HC* starts at the point where Fortnum is kidnaped. In line with this pattern, we would expect *CE* to open at the point of Baxter's arrival in Panama, to cover his earlier life in retrospective digressions, and to go in detail through the events leading up to the Captain's death. The equal and independent narrative weight actually given to the hero's childhood in *CE* indicates a new approach to Greene's usual material.

The primary purpose of this approach would seem to be to underline the process of Baxter's loss of innocence by presenting him in a series of stages of maturation. (The process of change in the novel affects Baxter dramatically, but leaves the Captain largely untouched: the Captain ages physically, but his goals, methods, and personal loyalties are already established at the outset and remain unaltered through the years.) In Part I Baxter displays the innocence of childhood. He sees the Captain as the fulfilment of his own longing for adventure, as one who opens up exciting new worlds. In this spirit Baxter responds enthusiastically to the Captain's unorthodox methods of education, adapts himself to the domestic routine of the basement, and begins to model himself on the Captain, acting as Liza's protector in the older man's absence.

Much of this innocence has gone by the time we see Baxter as a young adult in Part II. He still takes money from the Captain, but no longer subscribes to the chivalric ethos of the basement home, which he has already abandoned. He has become something of a drifter, comparable to Anthony or the young Brown, engaging in occasional work of doubtful probity and indulging in loveless sexual affairs. Whereas he had accepted the Captain as a surrogate father in Part I, he now associates again with his natural father, a heartless character also known as "the Devil." The chief business of Part II, however, is Baxter's discovery of the Captain's letters to Liza, revealing to him the nature and depth of their love. Baxter's failure to comprehend this love, or to emulate it, is the key to his adult nature, and is instrumental in the disastrous failure of his Panamanian venture.

Now no longer the child who had responded to the Captain's tales of adventure, Baxter in Part III still wants the material rewards of the Captain's lifestyle—easy money, freedom of movement, a sense of self-esteem—but has shown himself unable or unwilling to accept the Captain's ethos of love and loyalty. When the Captain discovers this, when the truth about Liza's fate is finally revealed to him, their association is at an end. (It is Baxter's desertion of Liza, rather than any information he might have given to Quigly, which precipitates the rupture.) Baxter sets off to seek "Valparaiso" on his own, but predictably fails to reach his destination.

Like Querry, Baxter cuts himself off from his past and ignores its claims upon him, represented by Liza and her need for his protection. His failure in this respect may be compared also to Brown's failure to achieve the standards of love and compassion represented by his mother. While Plarr, belatedly, succeeds in identifying himself with his imprisoned humanitarian father, and while Castle pays his debt to Carson, Baxter acknowledges no claims; and although, in material terms, his fate may seem no worse than theirs, they achieve a moral victory which Baxter does not even approach.

This chapter has examined Greene's novels in terms of genre and structure, looking particularly at the nature of the hero and the way his story is told. Setting aside the exceptional cases of *EA* and *MQ*, the "fables" *Loser Takes All* and *DF*, and the shorter fiction, we have arrived at a view of Greene's work as a novelist as falling into three reasonably distinct stages: the first comprises the early novels prior to *BR*, and includes also *CA* and *TM*; the second comprises *BR*, *PG*, *MF*, and *HM*; the third, initiated by *QA*, includes all the subsequent novels not already set aside. The criteria for this classification are basically structural. The second phase is marked by Greene's progression from the tightly structured, fast-moving early stories to the much more expansive plots characterized essentially by the hero's reconsideration of his past and by the "journey back" motif which this entails. The third phase retains this expansiveness and the requirement that the hero confront his past, but here the "journey back" is replaced by claims from the past represented by particular characters.

Within this broad framework further distinctions have been observed. The early heroes (excepting D, who is closer in this respect to the middle heroes) are generally social misfits or outcasts whose places in society have always been uncertain or insecure. The middle heroes are men who formerly enjoyed the security of a definite position in life, but whose comfort, perhaps too easily achieved, has been recently upset by dramatic events beyond their control. (Pinkie fits less well here than do D, the Priest, Rowe, and Scobie; but even in his case we can find evidence that an easy life under the protective shadow of Kite has come to an abrupt end with Kite's death, leaving Pinkie the harried figure we see, vainly trying to hold his world together against mounting odds.) The later heroes, from Fowler onwards, are distinguished not only by their preference for withdrawn noninvolvement but also by an articulateness, unknown among their predecessors, which makes them either able tellers of their own stories or, at least, reflectively well aware of the moral issues which surround them.

Already present in the early novels are what may be regarded as the fundamental themes of Greene's fiction: a sense of the irreducible complexity of life and the consequent necessity for disloyalty or betrayal. Onto this thematic base, in the middle novels, Greene builds a tension between the hero's yearning for a supposed state of innocence and the demands of an intractable present. More specifically, the hero in these novels is caught between a false, humanly impossible vision of moral simplicity, which would have the practical effect of isolating him from sympathy, and acceptance of the morally ambivalent world within which alone human relationships are possible. The middle hero stands poised, as it were, between past and present, required to free himself from the enthralment of the one and to accommodate the inevitable moral discomfort of opening himself to the other.

In the third phase we find the hero already seeking what he sees as innocence, not in childhood now so much as in mere disengagement from morally compromising action. His past now represents, not a sterile innocence, but rather a human commitment, typically personified in a former wife or lover, a lost parent, or a protector. The claims of this figure from the past have now to be reconciled with the hero's wish to achieve or maintain his disengagement. The hero's task, in this final phase, is generally to abandon strict isolation and to respond to the call of the past by re-engaging in action and recovering human sympathy.

3. The Antagonists

There is a striking similarity, both in general outline and in a number of significant details, between the stories of *MW* and *CE*, Greene's first and last published novels. Both feature a young, callow, and not entirely sympathetic hero falling under the influence of a colorful older man who takes over his education with a view to making him a partner in profitable but illegal adventures. In both cases the hero betrays the other, and himself dies soon after. The most pronounced coincidence of detail is the scene which occurs, with minor variations, at the chronological beginning of each story, the scene in which the unhappy boy-hero is abducted from the school where he has been placed, after his mother's death, by an uncaring father. In each case the novel turns upon the relationship which develops between the hero and his mentor, and in each case the climax is a betrayal.

There is much more to this coincidence than mere economy of material, for what is recognizably the same situation, between the young hero and the charismatic older man who offers exciting but unconventional opportunities, recurs in a number of Greene's stories. It is clearly central, for instance, in what are probably the two best of his shorter pieces, "The Basement Room" and *UG*. In both of these the boy-hero's education is temporarily taken over by an older man, who presents himself as a role model in clear opposition to the values of the boy's parental home. Baines, in "The Basement Room," plays the part of a bold adventurer. He is a more swaggering version of the Captain. He is a man who has been involved in exciting escapades in other countries, and for whom, even in peacetime London, life remains a matter of conducting covert campaigns and dodging hostile pursuit. The soldier-of-fortune image, with trappings of guns and military discipline, is common to both.

Javitt, an adventurer of another kind, is similarly representative of unconventional values. Seated on his toilet-throne deep beneath the tree roots, he is part nature spirit, part gypsy king. He teaches Wilditch a complex of notions, which prominently include the duty of disloyalty, the importance of ugliness, and the law of survival; and we note that the adult Wilditch seems, in his wandering life, to have put at least some of Javitt's principles into practice. Philip betrays Baines to the law, much as Andrews betrays Carlyon. Wilditch does not quite "betray" Javitt, but he does run away from him, tying him up and (perhaps with his connivance) stealing from him the golden po.

The relationship between the impressionable hero, usually but not necessarily younger, and the charismatic mentor offering the possibility of a more attractive way of life is central to Greene's fiction. The relationship between the boy-heroes and their respective father substitutes in *MW*, "The Basement Room," *UG*, and *CE* is echoed, acted out between adults, in a number of the major novels. Krogh in *EM*, for instance, offers the feckless but basically honest Anthony a way of life which seems at first to suit his wishes, with easy work, status, and ready money. All Anthony has to do to reap these benefits is to subscribe to Krogh's ethos, which turns out to involve fraud and oppression practiced against weak, underprivileged victims. Yusef in *HM* is a similar would-be mentor to Scobie. He confronts Scobie at a succession of crucial points, offering easy solutions to immediate problems if only Scobie will deviate from his strict notion of duty and tacitly endorse Yusef's illegal activities.

Specific common threads emerge. Yusef is smuggler, as is Carlyon and, in his own way, the Captain. Baines brags about guns and eventually kills Mrs. Baines, Carlyon (or one of his men) kills an exciseman, Yusef kills Ali, and Krogh orders the assault on Andersson and later the murder of Anthony. The violence of the mentor, initially part of his attraction, is also dangerous and in several cases becomes the reason why the hero eventually betrays him.

It is a short step from the adventurer like Carlyon, who offers himself as a substitute father or mentor to the hero, to the amiable eccentric, the quixotic figure who acts as the hero's guide. This character occurs most obviously in *TA*, where an elderly, unworldly, and rather fantastic figure leads the younger, more pragmatic and mildly protesting hero, Sancho-like, across a broad landscape of anecdotes and escapades. In *MQ*, exceptionally, the quixotic figure is himself the hero, but in a number of the other late novels the hero plays Sancho to his antagonist. The Captain is quixotic, not only in his devotion to Liza but also in the way he lives on the level of fantasy. Just as the original Quixote had his books of chivalry, and his "descendant" in *MQ* has his books of devotion, so the Captain takes boys' adventure stories as the stuff of life: fantastic escapes across war-torn Europe and tales of Drake, pirates, and lost treasure in the jungles of Central America. Jones in *TC* is another example, living in a world of make believe, presenting himself as a trained fighter prepared, as it were, to tilt at windmills by leading an inept revolt against the armed forces of Haiti.

Just as the charismatic adventurer, first encountered in Carlyon, has echoes in a number of subsequent novels, even to the last, so the quixotic figure, prominent in the late novels, is anticipated in a number of the earlier stories. Thus Monsignor Quixote and his devotional books, an allusion to the original Don and his old romances, is anticipated by Rycker and his theologians, and by Pyle and his preposterous "York Harding." The appearance of the hero as Sancho Panza, as a more prosaic character reluctant to enter fully into the fantasies or enthusiasms of his mentor, is again not confined to the last novels, to cases such as Pulling and Baxter. Brown spends much of his time trying to convince others that the image presented by Jones is deceptive. Martins, having once been under the spell of Lime's charm, devotes himself now to exposure of the reality beneath the adventure and romance. Even Carlyon, with his strain of "chivalry," is a kind of Quixote, unwilling to face the drab reality behind his idealistic facade: "a romantic with his face in the clouds, who hated any who gave him contact with a grubby earth" (1.4). The skeptical

Andrews is unable to surrender to the illusion and eventually betrays his leader.

In the context of Greene's fiction these two images, the mentor-adventurer and the Quixotic eccentric, the former coming from Conradian tragedy[50] and the latter from Cervantes, are two aspects of the same central idea, embodied in the character who figures in almost all of Greene's novels and whom we will call the "antagonist." The antagonist is simply the character between whom and the hero the main action of the novel is played out. The antagonist is not necessarily the "villain," although there may be a sense in which it is helpful to see him as such. As we shall see later, the term "villain" is best reserved in Greene for another character who appears occasionally and acts more directly as the hero's opponent. In the serious novels, where the story tends towards tragedy, the antagonist has an intense, protective, and sometimes even paternal relationship with the hero. In the more lighthearted stories he may become comical or fantastical, and the outcome of his influence may even be beneficial. These are, however, two versions or aspects of what may be seen as the same central situation, in which the hero is disposed to fall under the influence of the antagonist, an influence which, whether it leads into tragedy or comedy, involves acceptance of something of a new way of life with different and distinctly unconventional values.

In *HC*, for example, the antagonist is Fortnum. This is a serious novel which ends (for the hero) in tragedy. Plarr's reluctant association with Fortnum draws him into activities from which he was inclined to remain aloof, and results finally in his violent death. In Plarr's mind Fortnum becomes associated with his dead father, and towards the end Fortnum's role towards Plarr becomes paternal. Plarr is bound to Fortnum in several ways: as his doctor, as his wife's lover, as the man whose information brought about his imprisonment, and as a metaphorical son. Their lives become entwined, and in the end Plarr dies effectively in Fortnum's place. Even in this grim story, however, the quixotic side of the antagonist is still apparent. Fortnum's comical, fantastical aspect shows itself, for instance, in his babble about "Fortnum's

Pride" (perhaps an allusion to Rozinante) and in the very artificiality of his position as an "honorary" (i.e. not real) consul. His chivalrous nature reveals itself in his marriage with Clara, and his roguery comes out in his drunkenness and disregard of regulations.

At the other extreme, in the comic novel *TA*, the antagonist is Aunt Augusta. She is the only female to assume the role, and even she, towards the end, hands over direction to her male partner, Mr. Visconti, and reveals that she has, for the most part, been acting on his behalf. Which of them we take to be Henry's antagonist does not matter. In this comic story the quixotic aspect of the role comes to the fore. The business, for instance, of recovering, under the antagonist's guidance, a sense of contact with a lost father, a process traumatic and ultimately fatal for Plarr, is accomplished by Henry Pulling quite lightheartedly. Whereas Plarr dies out of *HC* to give place to Fortnum, the ending of *TA* is indecisive, with Augusta, Henry, and Mr. Visconti uniting into one familial entrepreneurial partnership. Only the death of Wordsworth, and a few minor casualties along the way, remind us of the sinister underside to Augusta's world.

The mentor and the Quixote, represented respectively by Carlyon and Augusta, are essentially different aspects of the same character idea, which appears in many various guises. At the heart of Greene's fiction, as the structural backbone of almost all his major plots, stands the relationship between the hero and this antagonist. A typical Greene novel is precisely the story of the association between a relatively ordinary and uncertain central character, the hero, and this more dynamic, usually more exciting, less conventional antagonist. The action between them typically involves the formation of some kind of bond and the leading of the hero into a questionable line of conduct as a result. The association not infrequently ends in betrayal and the death of one or even both parties.

Greene treats the antagonist variously in his different novels, and it is better to approach the type through "family resemblances" among its exemplars rather than to attempt a single definition to be matched in every instance. Discussion of the antagonist role in terms of these resemblances is the central business of the present chapter. The full list of the antagonist characters to be discussed is given, along with their respective heroes, in the following table:

Text	Hero	Antagonist
MW	Andrews	Carlyon
IB	Conrad	Jim
EM	Anthony	Krogh
"The Basement Room"	Philip	Baines
GS	Raven	Sir Marcus
BR	Pinkie	Kite
CA	D	Lord Benditch
PG	Priest	Calver
MF	Rowe	Hilfe
HM	Scobie	Yusef
TM	Martins	Lime
Loser Takes All	Bertram	Dreuther
QA	Fowler	Pyle
OM	Wormold	Hasselbacher
BC	Querry	Rycker
"Under the Garden"	Wilditch	Javitt
TC	Brown	Jones
TA	Pulling	Augusta/Visconti
HC	Plarr	Fortnum
HF	Castle	Carson
DF	Jones	Doctor Fischer
CE	Baxter	Captain

In *ST* there is no antagonist. If anyone in particular was responsible for setting Czinner on the path he is following, he is not mentioned in the story. *EA* is, again, not a typical Greene novel, being essentially a love story in which the main action is between a hero and a heroine. There is no antagonist. Henry Miles might be supposed to be Bendrix's antagonist in the love triangle, but the relationship between Miles and Bendrix is distinctly secondary in the novel. It grows out of the relationship between Bendrix and Sarah and acquires independent interest only towards the end, after Sarah has been removed from the scene. *MQ* would at first glance appear to offer a clear example of the quixotic version of the antagonist, but it is, in reality, again a different type of story. Monsignor Quixote is indeed quixotic, but he is the hero of the narrative that bears his name, and Sancho, although his companion, is not at all like the other antagonists here considered in his relation to the hero. Monsignor Quixote has no antagonist in this sense, and his story does not follow the structure common to most of Greene's other novels. *Loser Takes All* and *DF* are fables rather than novels, but since the characters of Dreuther and Doctor Fischer nonetheless show some of the features of the antagonist type they will be discussed briefly in this chapter.

Carlyon begins his relationship with Andrews as a substitute father. On Andrews's father's death Carlyon inherits his boat and his place as leader of the smugglers. He also takes over supervision of the son, removing him from the school where his father had placed him and making him thereafter a companion, giving him protection and a place in the adult world. Andrews's admiration for his mentor makes him wish Carlyon was his true father (2.9), and he mentally associates the two, dreaming that "his father and Carlyon were dancing round him holding hands" (1.2). In this respect Carlyon anticipates several later antagonists who act similarly as substitute fathers of their respective heroes, particularly the Captain, Kite, Baines, and Javitt. He anticipates also, if a little more distantly, Fortnum and Mr. Visconti, who are in the end accepted as surrogate fathers by their heroes. Moreover, if we extend the paternal relationship into that of a protective elder brother, it encompasses also that of Jim to Conrad and becomes recognizably similar to that of Lime to Martins and of Krogh to Anthony.

Carlyon is a charismatic personality, "a spirit on tiptoe" (1.3). His leadership of men who are evidently willing to die under his command anticipates something which occurs in Kite, in Jones, and even in the Captain (who mysteriously acquires in Panama friends who will kill to preserve or avenge him). Krogh, Benditch,

Sir Marcus, Yusef, and Pyle are all men of power, with others operating, more or less covertly, at their bidding.

Twice in *MW* Carlyon is obliquely compared to Christ in relation to Andrews, who then becomes a penitent sinner or a Judas (1.4). Greene does not pursue this line of thought explicitly. Subsequent antagonists are not often compared openly to Christ, and the statement of the comparison in *MW* is perhaps a mark of the author's relative immaturity in that early work. Nonetheless, it is useful to adduce the Christian analogy in the cases of the antagonists who suffer for others or for a cause. Both Jim Drover and Fortnum are innocent sufferers condemned to death in the course of violent struggles to relieve the oppression of the poor. Plarr is another Judas, insofar as it is his information, albeit given unintentionally, that leads to Fortnum's capture. Several more antagonists, less innocent than Fortnum, are also subject to betrayals over which their respective heroes feel a Judas-like remorse, particularly Hilfe, Lime, and Pyle.

The antagonist's idealism is often part of his charm. It takes a variety of forms. Javitt preaches his own unconventional doctrines, Rycker parrots a garbled theology, while Carson represents the human face of communism. Carlyon's idealism is described as "romantic" (1.4) and "chivalrous" (1.3), his chivalry anticipating particularly Pyle's attitude towards Phuong and the Captain's protection of Liza. Carlyon, whose very name has Arthurian overtones, sees himself as a knight errant, rather as does Jones and, in a way, Pyle. Carlyon is even said to be "quixotic" (2.8) in his willingness to take risks for his friends' sake, a notion which at once glances again at Christian self-sacrifice and looks forward to the more genuine quixotism of Hasselbacher and Aunt Augusta.

Even the none-too-perceptive Andrews, however, is able to see before long that in Carlyon idealism and chivalry go along with pursuit of inherently cruel and wrongful lines of conduct. Like most of the antagonists, Carlyon is two-faced, concealing brutal self-interest beneath a benevolent exterior. He is at once a protector and a threat, a gentleman and a thug. Andrews comes to view him as "a chivalrous ape" (1.3), a combination of idealism and base instinct. For all his pretensions, Carlyon remains a smuggler, a criminal on the run who has already, when we first see him, killed at least once and who will be responsible in the end for the death of Elizabeth. (The fact that, like Krogh, Sir Marcus, Yusef, and Mr. Visconti, Carlyon allows others to do the killing on his behalf is immaterial.) Like most of the antagonists, Carlyon embodies a moral conflict arising from a dual nature. On the one hand he represents for the hero a strong sense of personal loyalty arising from benevolence and colored by a degree of enthusiasm for shared ideals. On the other hand he arouses fear and repugnance through conduct which is often criminal and brutal.

Comparable dualities are evident in most of the antagonists. On the one hand they display warmth towards the heroes, giving shelter and support in ways ranging from financial loans to personal protection from threatened harm. On the other hand they engage in covert activities, which are frequently both illegal and life-threatening. Jim Drover, however innocent his intentions, has taken part in a riot and killed a policeman. Krogh is engaged in fraud and uses violence and murder to avoid exposure. Sir Marcus is a cruder version of Krogh. Baines also commits murder. Kite, although we do not see him in action, was evidently a criminal. Hilfe is an enemy agent, working with those who kill Jones (the detective) and Major Stone. Yusef is a smuggler, who arranges the murder of Ali and is probably responsible as well for the suicide of Pemberton. Lime is a black marketeer who causes death and suffering by dealing in adulterated medical supplies. Pyle is an undercover agent, probably CIA, whose work results in many civilian deaths and injuries. Rycker does nothing covertly, but even he kills his man in the end. Jones has come to Haiti on some sort of devious mission, apparently with the object of selling arms to Papa Doc. Mr. Visconti, like Carlyon, is a smuggler who is prepared to kill to protect his interests. Even the Captain is a small-time crook beneath his chivalric mantle. Among the antagonists, only Fortnum and Carson emerge as largely blameless.

The criminal or violent activity of the antagonist, however, is rarely the chief reason why the hero wishes to distance himself. Personal factors, in most cases, operate more strongly than considerations of law or public morality. Andrews is motivated by his hatred of the smugglers' way of life and by a sense of personal inferiority when among them. His feelings for Carlyon include "jealousy" (1.3). In a similar way Baxter comes to feel "envy" (2.7.3) towards the Captain, and Anthony feels jealous of Krogh over Kate (2.3). Sexual jealousy is also a factor in Fowler's feeling towards Pyle, Brown's towards Jones, and Plarr's towards Fortnum.

At first sight it might seem that Conrad's antagonist in *IB* is not the passive and inarticulate Jim, who spends the entire novel in a cell, but the Assistant Commissioner. The Assistant Commissioner does indeed occupy more of the narrative than Conrad himself, and it is he who becomes the chief object of the hero's hatred, which culminates in the attempted murder on Lady Caroline's doorstep. The only relationship between these two characters, however, subsists in Conrad's disordered state of mind, based upon his entirely mistaken impression that the Assistant Commissioner shares responsibility for Jim's plight. In fact the Assistant Commissioner is a neutral character, even mildly sympathetic towards Jim, with no actual influence over the prisoner's situation. He does not even know who Conrad is until the latter lies dying in hospital. Conrad's real bond is with Jim, and it is this tie, involving feelings of obligation and, later, of guilt, which prompt his action in the story. There are a number of similarities between the relation of Conrad and Jim in *IB* and hero-antagonist relations in other novels. As the hero's former protector, Jim echoes Carlyon and anticipates Carson and the Captain. The school setting for this remembered protective influence (2) is echoed in Lime's care for the schoolboy Martins. On the other hand Jim is also a kind of sacrificial victim, at first "in a steel cage driving through the rain" (2) and later in a prison cell awaiting execution. The imprisoned, self-sacrificing antagonist reappears much later in Fortnum and Carson. Jim's air of naive devotion to Milly, his "stubbornness . . . reliability and gentle obtuseness" (1), are all echoed in the Captain's attitude to Liza.

With Jim away in prison, moreover, a situation develops which anticipates that of the first part of *CE*. Conrad moves into the basement flat and takes over Jim's role as Milly's protector. In *CE* the adolescent Baxter (whose assumption of the name "Jim" is perhaps not merely coincidental) is left by the Captain to help and look after Liza. There is a sexual element in the relationship between Conrad and Milly which does not occur in that of Baxter and Liza, but the end result is similar: in each case the young hero fails to live up to the chivalric duty of protection which falls to him in the absence of his own former protector. More generally, the scenario here, in which a young and impressionable hero is taken into the subterranean domain of a protective substitute father finds echoes also in "The Basement Room" and *UG*.

The basement flat scenes with Milly are crucial to Conrad's development in the story. His new relationship with his sister-in-law overlays and complicates his original feelings of love and obligation towards Jim. There is also now in Conrad's mind a feeling that he has to prove himself equal to Jim as Milly's protector. "He had never, while Jim was there, been quite real to her. . . . Now he was a man in the house, a fellow drop of human life . . . " (2). Once Conrad has slept with Milly, his need to emulate Jim is tinged with jealousy and guilt. There is something in common between Conrad's conduct with respect to Jim, the absent husband, and Andrews's resentment of Carlyon's captaincy of his father's boat. A similar conflicting sense of obligation and jealousy affects Fowler's relationship with Pyle.

Jim, perhaps along with Carson, is the most simply benign among the antagonists; yet even he has his negative, potentially dangerous aspect. Whatever his innocence and naivety, Jim is a communist, takes part in an organized riot in which he carries a knife, and, in the course of this, defending Milly, he kills a policeman. This policeman is no Concasseur but a married man who has a very ordinary wife and home and who dies in tears. Jim's act, because of the presence of the knife (presumably implying "malice aforethought") is technically murder. Everyone in the story, including the Assistant Commissioner, is inclined to view Jim's case sympathetically; but even here, in an exception which would seem to prove the rule, the benign antagonist who protects the hero is still, in pursuit of his chivalrous ideals, a killer.

Krogh is plainly Anthony's antagonist in *EM*. The main action of the story covers precisely the period of their acquaintance, framed by a brief prologue in which Kate arranges their meeting, and a short epilogue made up of reactions to Anthony's death. Krogh is, besides, an impressive figure in his own right, dominating much of the action. Everyone except Loo revolves around him: Kate is his fiancée; Anthony, Hall, and Andersson are his employees; and Minty makes a living observing him. Krogh is the first in a line of entrepreneurial giants among the antagonists, his successors in this respect being Sir Marcus, Lord Benditch, Yusef, Dreuther, and Doctor Fischer, all rich and powerful men who manipulate the lives of others.

In the case of Jim Drover, whose positive, sympathetic qualities are evident, the reader needs to be attentive to counterbalancing evidence suggesting his negative aspect, to the description of the policeman's death and the account of Milly's visit to the widowed Mrs. Coney, passages which underline the harmful effects of Jim's action. In Krogh's case it is his negative qualities which are evident: his fraudulent dealings, his violent repression of his workers, his employment of the murderous Hall. In *EM* we can observe Greene deliberately adding episodes to bring out the sympathetic side of Krogh, as in the account of the visit to Tivoli and in the encounter with the workmen building the bridge. To the same end are the several short passages in which Krogh reflects upon the relative innocence of his younger days (e.g., twice in 2.2).

Despite his general coldness and want of geniality, Krogh does have some appealing qualities. He has evidently been a brilliant engineer and financier. He receives Anthony readily, not only giving him employment but accepting him as a social companion. His aloofness seems the result more of shyness and inexperience than of pride or malice. Indeed, he has a kind of naive simplicity in matters unrelated to business, which makes it seem at first likely that he will fall easy prey to Anthony's confidence tricks. In his aura of inarticulate stolidity (which is never fractured, since his fraud is not, in the event, exposed) Krogh shows something of Jim Drover, all the more so in that the grim glass and steel edifice he has built for himself seems almost as much a cage as Jim's cell or cab. More generally, Krogh's iron fist within the velvet glove of acceptance and support echoes the dual nature of many of the antagonists, from Carlyon through Yusef to Mr. Visconti.

The course of Anthony's relationship with Krogh echoes the relationships of Andrews and Carlyon and of Conrad and Jim. Like Andrews, Anthony begins with the expectation of living comfortably under the shadow of his benefactor, either as his brother-in-law or by blackmail, but in time he becomes upset by the undercurrent of inhuman violence in his employer's operations. The assault on Andersson echoes the shooting of the exciseman in *MW*, marking the point at which the hero openly dissociates himself from the activities of the antagonist. Andrews takes flight, and Anthony announces his intention to return to England, but neither man escapes the consequent resentment and revenge of the antagonist. From *IB* comes an element of sexual jealousy: Krogh is about to marry Anthony's sister, for whom the hero has feelings more than brotherly, and on this account Anthony is jealous (e.g., 4.1 and 4.3). As in *IB*, and as later in *QA* and *TC*, sexual jealousy is a factor in the increasingly hostile feeling of the hero towards his antagonist.

In most of the "entertainments" the antagonist tends to remain little more than a straightforward villain, lacking the moral ambivalence and the close personal bond with the hero which characterize him in the major novels. This is true of *GS* and *CA*, and also largely true in *DF*. The antagonist in *GS* is Sir Marcus, because it is he who is the instigator of the action in which Raven becomes involved, and because the story reaches its climax when Raven finally confronts and kills him. (Davis, however active in the story, is only an under-agent in Sir Marcus's plot.) As a powerful industrialist engaging in criminal activity to further his own fortune, Sir Marcus has much in common with Krogh, but he lacks Krogh's personal depth (his recollections of the past, his simplicity in human relationships). Sir Marcus is simply evil, and no personal bond of any kind is ever formed between Raven and himself. Only the outline of the pattern remains, the pattern of a weak and gullible hero who at first accepts a job from the antagonist but later turns against him as he discovers the consequences of the work in its augmentation of human suffering. Raven's work for Sir Marcus is a more extreme version of Anthony's for Krogh. Anthony is hired as a "bodyguard" and expected to inflict violent punishment on men like Andersson. There is talk of his having a gun, and he shows himself to be a good shot, although in the end he remains unarmed. Raven does have a gun, highlighted in the novel's title, and he uses it to kill on Sir Marcus's behalf. Raven therefore stands to Sir Marcus rather as does Andrews to Carlyon, Pinkie to Kite, and even Scobie to Yusef, as a junior partner in crime.

If we think of an antagonist simply as a character who acts in opposition to the hero, we are likely, in *BR*, to see this role as taken by Ida, or perhaps even by Colleoni. Neither of these, however, is Pinkie's antagonist in the sense in which that term is applied here, since in neither case is there any personal bond with the hero, nor is the hero's course of action affected, other than in merely negative reactions, by his association with these characters. Colleoni remains simply Pinkie's rival, another criminal gangster moving into the same territory. He functions in *BR* much as does L in *CA*, being opposed to the hero in the action of the story, but very different and distinct from him on a personal level. Ida's role in *BR* is related to that of the detective figure who appears in several of the other novels: the Assistant Commissioner, Mather, Vigot, Daintry. She is an observer and investigator, activated by an almost compulsive need to resolve the mystery and achieve what she sees as justice. Again, however, and like these other detectives, she has little or no personal influence upon the hero, whom she meets only, as it were, after the fact, after his character has been formed and after the murder of Hale. If we look in *BR* for a figure whose influence—as surrogate father, protector, employer—is comparable to that of Carlyon upon Andrews, Jim upon Conrad, or Sir Marcus upon Raven, we find Kite.

Like Jim Drover, Kite is removed by circumstances from the action of the story: indeed, like Carson in *HF*, Kite is dead by the time the story opens. His influence upon the hero is nonetheless decisive. Pinkie's initial encounter with Kite, as he recalls it, is a clear echo of the way the young Andrews is taken up by Carlyon, and of the protection given to the weak Conrad by Jim.

> This was the place where he [Pinkie] had come to after Kite had picked him up—he had been coughing on the Palace Pier in the bitter cold, listening to the violin wailing behind the glass; Kite had given him a cup of hot coffee and brought him here—God knows why—perhaps because he was out and wasn't down, perhaps because man like Kite needed a little sentiment. (7.5)

We do not learn very much about Kite, but the essential features are clear. He has a touch of "sentiment" or personal warmth, which disposes him to befriend Pinkie. He becomes the boy's protector and initiates him into the life and activities of the gang, much as Carlyon does with Andrews.

We first see Pinkie acting as Kite's avenger, pursuing Hale, whom he eventually corners and kills. This is almost as if Anthony had followed orders and attacked Andersson in defense of Krogh. Hale is the victim in *BR*, corresponding to Rexall (the exciseman) in *MW* and Coney (the constable) in *IB*. Kite himself is dead, but Pinkie becomes his agent and successor: "when Kite died in the waiting-room at St. Pancras, it had been as if a father had died, leaving him an inheritance it was his duty never to leave for strange acres" (5.1). Thereafter Pinkie remembers Kite as a model, forming himself in the dead leader's image. Indeed, he sees himself not only as a successor but as a kind of reincarnation of his protector. "Kite had died, but he had prolonged Kite's existence—not touching liquor, biting his nails in the Kite way, until *she* came and altered everything"(7.5).[51] Rose's influence, in working against Pinkie's deliberate avoidance of maturity, is also working against the influence of Kite. The degree to which Pinkie is angered by her mere rearrangement of his room, the room to which Kite brought him and which he is trying to preserve unchanged, is indicative of the developing conflict in his mind between the values represented respectively by Kite and Rose (7.4–5).

In this way the hero's growing relationship with the heroine in *BR* entails a form of betrayal of the antagonist, a pattern also evident in several of the other novels. As Pinkie becomes closer to Rose, marries her, begins to alter his way of life on her account, and even feels occasional affection for her, he is moving further from Kite, abandoning the inheritance, failing in his obligation to keep the spirit of Kite alive. A comparable tension occurs in *MW* when, under the influence of Elizabeth, Andrews is persuaded to stand his ground and give evidence against the smugglers. In several of the novels (*IB*, *CA*, *MF*, and *HC*) the hero is not only opposing his antagonist by associating with the heroine but also, in a sense, stealing her away from him.

As in *BR*, so in *CA*, the antagonist is not the character who simply opposes the hero as his enemy in the context of the action, but another with whom the hero's connection is more complex. D's enemy in *CA* is his rival, the representative of the opposing political party, the agent known as L. L's role is comparable to that of Colleoni in *BR*, of Hartep in *ST*, and of Muller in *HF*. He represents a position directly opposite to that of the hero in the politics of the story, and for that reason, and because of his willingness to use illicit means to achieve his goals, he is effectively the "villain." The Lieutenant in *PG* is another, more rounded example of the same role. Greene portrays these men as generally suave, personally courteous, and even given to a kind of idealism; but whatever more positive qualities they exhibit are outweighed by their employment of violence and cruelty, a fundamental lack of humanity. This character has no personal bond with the hero and is readily distinguishable from the true "antagonist," with whom the hero has ties such as those between Andrews and Carlyon and between Pinkie and Kite.

In *CA*, admittedly, the personal ties between hero and antagonist are not very strong. In the more straightforwardly presented stories of the "entertainments," where characters often lack the complexity of their counterparts in the major novels, the antagonist may be a less ambivalent figure, superficially not very different from a plain villain. Even so, in *CA* Lord Benditch can be seen to be the antagonist, chiefly on the ground of his crucial role with respect to the hero's course of action. Although D has had no prior personal contact with Benditch, he comes to England especially to keep an appointment arranged between them. The papers he carries, concealment of which occupies much of his energy in the first third or so of the narrative, are simply the credentials he will need to gain Benditch's confidence. D spends the first half of the story struggling to make contact with Benditch, and when the meeting proves abortive he devotes the rest of his time to working against Benditch, trying to sabotage the mines and thus to ensure that no one else will succeed in carrying out the deal which he has failed to conclude. In this way *CA* follows pattern of an initial impulse towards collaboration succeeded by hostility and betrayal, such as can be seen between hero and antagonist in *MW*, *EM*, and *GS*.

Benditch is in many ways like Krogh. Both men employ numbers of relatively impoverished workers. In both stories the hero, turning against his antagonist, becomes involved in the violence of industrial politics. At the same time Benditch anticipates Doctor Fischer in his paternal relationship to the heroine. Fischer is another such powerful father, emotionally estranged from a daughter who unaccountably falls suddenly in love with the older, unattractive hero. The fact that Rose is Benditch's daughter lends an element of intricacy to the central relationships in what is otherwise one of Greene's simplest full-length stories.

Leaving aside the "entertainments" *GS* and *CA*, we can see clear common features among the hero-antagonist relationships of the early novels. In each case there is a sense of personal obligation undermined by betrayal. The betrayal, while having some moral justification (like Andrews's social duty to bring the smugglers to justice, and Anthony's humanitarian refusal to participate in the oppression of Krogh's workers), is clouded by personal feelings of envy or even sexual jealousy (such as Conrad's love for Milly and Anthony's bond with Kate). There is, besides, a certain sameness among the antagonists themselves in these novels—Carlyon, Jim, Krogh, and Kite—in that they are all powerful, protective, elder-brotherly figures with respect to the hero, as well as being men of violence. With the next novel, *PG*, comes a deeper conception of the antagonist role, the influence of which can be felt in most of the serious novels which follow. The figure becomes more mysterious, even mystical, with Mephistophelean undertones. At the same time his relationship with the hero becomes more than merely circumstantial, representing some kind of demand which the hero must face and satisfy.

In *PG* the antagonist is the mysterious Calver, the wanted robber. He is mysterious just because he has no active role in the story, nor indeed any apparent reason for being there at all except to act as bait—as any human being might have done—to lure the Priest to final capture. The shadowy figure of Calver, the gunman whose face appears on "wanted" posters in every town, wanders with a price on his head across the landscape of the novel, into which he might have strayed accidentally from a Hollywood western. Whatever significance he has lies chiefly on a metaphorical level.

Greene draws a series of parallels between Calver and the Priest so sharply that the most casual reader can hardly fail to spot the effect. Both men are outlaws, and their pictures hang side by side on the police station wall in the second chapter. The Lieutenant compares them in conversation (1.2), and the Priest's daughter mistakes him for the "gringo" (2.1). When the Priest is held by the police in the capital he sees his picture on the wall beside Calver's (2.2). He remembers this later and, in delirium, comes to think of the robber as his "brother" (2.4). The metaphorical association of the two men becomes inescapable and demands attention all the more because it seems to exist for its own sake: it points to nothing obvious beyond itself, since Calver, the man to whom the Priest is apparently being compared, is present, except for a few brief moments, in name only, a mere shadow who becomes substantial only in dying.

Just as the Priest sees himself as an infected man, bringing danger and death to those among whom he moves, so Calver brings trouble and murder in his wake. Both Coral and the Indian baby seem to have died as a result of Calver's passing by, much as Montez is shot in Concepción because the Priest rested there. It is significant that the narrative avoids details of the deaths of Coral and the baby. A careless reader may get the idea that Calver himself shot them. He may indeed have done so (although his motives would remain unclear) but the narrative does not say so. It remains more likely that both were killed, like Montez, by the police in their efforts to catch the outlaw. That Calver has killed and robbed in the past is not to be doubted, and his being a criminal serves to deepen his metaphorical identity with the Priest, who is himself not only guilty of "crimes" against the state but also, in his own eyes, an offender against the church and God. Nonetheless, it is important that Calver, although known to be a violent man, cannot be convicted of any specific brutality within the story, of any wanton cruelty which might hinder his association, in the reader's mind, with the Priest.

The two men become mirror images, the one of the other, the very vagueness of Calver's portrayal making it possible to see in him the Priest's reflection. Their mutual reflection is reinforced by their eventual convergence. The Priest accepts death, in the end, as he goes back to find Calver. What he finds is another dying man, like himself, whose only concern is for the safety of the other. "He was thinking of me, it was for my sake," says the Priest over Calver's body, in words which might just as well have been spoken by Calver of the Priest (3.2). Calver is dying, having been shot by the police, as the Priest knows he himself will be within a few hours.

We are already in high altitudes of metaphor, and Greene takes us yet higher. Calver dies trying to save the life of the Priest who has sacrificed himself to bring Calver salvation. Calver's name suggests "Calvary," and the Christian connotation is reinforced by his initials, his name being James. Both his death and the Priest's are in a sense sacrificial, perhaps even redemptive. We are looking here at the two great themes of Greene's mature fiction: the ultimate responsibility of every man for every other, and the potential presence of the divine (if, indeed, there be anything such) in the human spirit.

From the early antagonists Calver inherits his reputation as a violent man, a killer and a thief. In this he is not so far removed from Kite or Krogh. His absence from the greater part of the action echoes that of Jim Drover, with whom he also shares a sense of being hounded and trapped by the forces of public order.

Even the protective disposition towards the hero, seen in Carlyon and Kite, comes out in Calver's dying concern for the Priest's safety. Largely new in Calver, on the other hand, is the mystic element. Carlyon is twice compared to Christ in a rather perfunctory fashion, and there is something sacrificial about the figure of the condemned innocent, Jim. Perhaps even Kite has a Christian connotation in the wooden cross which traditionally forms the framework upon which kites are made—although, of course, a kite is also a bird of prey. These, however, remain scattered and fragmentary hints of which little is made. In Calver, for the first time, we find a strong current of mysticism, anticipating the satanic undertones of Yusef, the numinous figures of Dreuther and Doctor Fischer, and the pagan magic of Javitt.

Perhaps more important is the way this mysticism extends into the antagonist's relationship with the hero. Calver is the first of the antagonists with whom, in some way, the hero's task is to identify himself. Just as the Priest has finally to surrender himself by turning back to meet Calver, so Plarr has to take Fortnum's place as the sacrificial victim, and Castle must identify himself with Carson. There is an alter ego aspect to several of these relationships, following from the comparisons developed in *PG* between the unlikely pair, Calver and the Priest. Rycker is similarly a distorted image of Querry, much as Jones is of Brown. The very considerable intensification of the metaphorical significance of the antagonist figure is an important aspect of the growth and development of Greene's fictional world.

The antagonist in *MF* is Hilfe. The other opponents whom the hero encounters—Poole, Forrester, Mrs. Bellairs, and the rest—remain mere villains. Of these, only Forrester is given any distinct motivation (in the references to his Tolstoyan idealism); but Forrester's association with Rowe is confined to the sanatorium episode. His incipient relationship with the hero comes to nothing and is terminated abruptly well before the end of the story. It is Hilfe, although in the background much of the time, who is coordinating the plot, and it is with him that the hero's final confrontation takes place. He has the dual nature of the early antagonists. He is on the one hand personable and supportive (his name means "help" in German), and on the other hand very dangerous. Hilfe is a German agent who is not only attempting to undermine Britain's fighting capacity but is also responsible for several murders and for the bomb which was supposed to kill Rowe and Anna.

The personal bond between hero and antagonist is established when Hilfe initially presents himself as a friend and willing helper. He passes as Rowe's protector in the contrived business of the escape from Mrs. Bellairs's house. It is from Hilfe, at the end, that Rowe learns the truth which he has to face up to; and it is therefore through Hilfe that Rowe finally confronts the situation by which, at the beginning, he had been effectively paralyzed. (Suspension of disbelief is necessary here: the reader has to overlook the fact that, in a world of newspapers and public records, Rowe might easily have acquired the information Hilfe gives him from other sources.) Hilfe intends the revelation to be hurtful, but in fact it is his last act of "help," enabling Rowe to accept what is past and move forward into a new life with Anna.

The fact that Anna, who falls in love with Rowe almost as improbably as does Rose with D, is Hilfe's sister creates the kind of conflict of loyalties which recurs in other novels where, as here, the heroine has ties with both hero and antagonist. The situation among Anna, her brother, and Rowe is reminiscent of that among Kate, Krogh, and Anthony, and among Anna Schmidt, Lime, and Martins. Despite the fact that he has tried to kill her, Anna remains loyal to her brother and endeavors to secure his escape. Rowe, meanwhile, is anxious lest he should find that Anna has been accessory to Hilfe's conspiracy.

There is in *MF* something of the mirror image relationship between Hilfe and Rowe which is also discernable between Calver and the Priest in *PG*. Hilfe is presented as "nihilistic" (1.3.2), specifically in his freedom from moral constraints. His outline of life as he sees it, in which murder can be justified by the goals or ideals of the murderer (1.3.2) is a simplistic parody of Rowe's stance in the mercy killing of his wife. Hilfe is here echoing the wider argument for freedom from conventional norms voiced by Poole (1.1.3). There is a resemblance, albeit superficial, between

Hilfe's wish to be liberated from moral constraint and Rowe's policy, exemplified in the killing of Alice, that extreme circumstances may justify actions such as murder which remain technically criminal. This is why the figure of Hilfe presides in Rowe's dream of the killing of the rat (1.5). It also explains Rowe's feeling of "trust" (1.3.2) when he first meets Hilfe, and why, even when he knows Hilfe's real nature, he still finds him "beautiful" (4.1.2).[52]

In reality, however, Rowe's position is the opposite to Hilfe's. Far from wishing to justify killing or to abandon moral restraint, Rowe believes fundamentally in consideration for others, making care for others his imperative. In the extreme case of a painful terminal illness, Rowe's response is superficially similar to Hilfe's: the killing of another person in accordance with one's own beliefs. There is a world of difference, however, between the respective motives: while Rowe acts out of "pity," Hilfe and his associates are impelled by political or philosophical ideals. Whether the doctrines derive from Nazi propaganda or Tolstoyan teachings in the end does not matter: the issue is whether *any* body of law or doctrine can override the humanitarian imperative. This is Rowe's question, as it is Scobie's and Fowler's and Castle's. From the midpoint of the novel, as Rowe gradually recovers his identity after the explosion, he begins to establish his distance from the position represented by Hilfe. He realigns himself with the British war effort, from which he had formerly held aloof. He assists the agents of the law in tracking down the conspirators. His final confrontation with Hilfe enables him to reaffirm the humanitarian code by repeating, in effect, the act of mercy killing over which he had formerly felt a life-inhibiting guilt. Convinced now of the rightness of his moral decision, based as it is on "pity," not dogma, he allows the cornered Hilfe to die quickly, as he had before saved Alice from prolonged suffering before death, and as, in his dream, he had killed the injured rat. As in *PG*, therefore, the antagonist in *MF* serves as a figure in relation to whom the hero comprehends, defines, and finally acts out his moral position.

One of the most extraordinary passages in this original and evocative novel is the description of the sleeping Hilfe when

Rowe, now aware of the man's crimes, comes upon him. Not only is Hilfe "beautiful," but he embodies the deep-rooted attraction of what Rowe now sees as ultimately evil. "Watching the sleeping man he [Rowe] could realize a little of the force and the grace and the attraction of nihilism—of not caring for anything, of having no rules and feeling no love. Life became simple . . . " (4.1.2). Hilfe represents moral simplicity—or rather, the simplicity of a life from which moral complexity is removed, a position very close to the "peace" and "innocence" desired by Pinkie and Scobie. Rowe himself at the beginning of his story desired a state of childlike moral simplicity. It is this attractive but ultimately delusive vision of release from moral conflict that the heroes of Greene's mature novels have generally to face and overcome.

In the image of the sleeping Hilfe, the vision even becomes divine. The words of the "epitaph" in the open pages which Hilfe is holding represent him as Orpheus, the young hero endowed with great creative power who suffers a cruel death.[53] Here again, in these overtones of divinity, Hilfe echoes Calver. Just as the death of Calver alludes to Calvary, so the death of Hilfe is, in a sense, the mystical sacrifice of a superhuman creature. In this case what the god represents, the Orphic vision of youth and innocence, has to be rejected because it lacks compassion and fails to encompass the reality of human suffering. Even so, there is more than a hint of regret over the necessity for Hilfe's death, much as there is over the death of Pyle, another youthful "innocent," at the end of QA.

The character of Hilfe takes a step further toward the notion of freedom from moral constraint which is hinted at in Calver and which may, with hindsight, be discernable in some of the earlier antagonists. Hilfe's position develops logically into the anarchic pursuit of personal goals which we see in Yusef and Pyle. From them, in another step, we arrive at the blithe irresponsibilities of Jones and Fortnum, an attitude which, in the more tolerant context of the comic novels, becomes a creative capacity for adventure and fun such as is apparent in Hasselbacher and Aunt Augusta.

The hero and antagonist in *HM* are Scobie and Yusef. The two men are moral opposites: policeman and criminal, the just and the corrupt. The point of section 2.1.2, where Wilson and Father Rank meet over dinner with Tallit, is primarily to present the reader with the contrasting reputations of Scobie and Yusef, and with the idea of their mutual incompatibility. The reader has also been told that "to give help to a Syrian was only a degree less dangerous than to receive help" (1.1.1.5). Scobie ought clearly to stay away from Yusef, much as Anthony should have stayed away from Krogh. Yet the story of *HM* turns upon the gradual entanglement of these two.

Like other antagonists, Yusef conceals crime and violence beneath a friendly exterior. He is constantly professing strong feelings of friendship towards Scobie and offering him help. Sharing Scobie's cynicism, the reader is likely to begin by dismissing this as hypocrisy on Yusef's part, but as events unfold even Scobie is half inclined to credit Yusef's sincerity (1.2.1.4). There is genuine poignancy in the scene where Yusef regretfully forfeits Scobie's friendship by blackmailing him. His reference to himself as the "base Indian" of *Othello* emphasizes his apparent remorse, making him surprisingly human (2.3.2.1).

Scobie sees his relationship with Yusef at first as simply a matter of business, the agreement to borrow a sum of money at a certain rate of interest. Yet he soon finds himself in a kind of "conspiracy" with Yusef (1.3.1.4). The two men become bound together by knowledge of one another's guilt. "He couldn't feel any hatred of the man. He had trapped Yusef as consciously and as effectively as Yusef had trapped him." The bond is like a "marriage," and in Scobie's mind it becomes as inescapable and constricting as the other human tie he has formed, his marriage to Louise (2.1.2.4). Even after Yusef has exploited the relationship, first over the business of the parrot and then by blackmail, Scobie still sees him as a refuge, as a possible source of help. He returns to Yusef in need with an "odd yearning" for the company of "the only man he could trust." They are again "conspirators," and the outcome this time is Ali's death (3.1.4.1). Scobie's feeling for Yusef in this scene is of particular interest. It involves a kind of moral surrender to the will of the other, redolent, perhaps, of the confessional or the couch. In Yusef Scobie finds his "only companionship," and in relating his problem to Yusef he "had the odd sense of having for the first time in his life shifted a burden elsewhere." He has the feeling of "being looked after," and "a kind of nursery peace descended" around him.

The hero-antagonist relationship in the middle novels is colored with a mysticism which has no parallel in the early stories, a mysticism arising from the introduction of factors which lie beyond rational explanation. In *MF* there is the vision of Hilfe as Orpheus, and in *PG* there are the Christian allusions in Calver's name and the extraordinary way in which his career in the story is set in parallel with that of the Priest. In *HM* the antagonist's role becomes Satanic. Yusef's home "had an eternal air like the furnishings of hell" (2.1.2.4), and in dealing with him Scobie is selling himself to the devil. This might remain no more than a figure of speech were it not that Greene builds a strongly mystical element into their relationship, so much of which defies explanation. Why does Yusef court Scobie's friendship when, as we know, almost any other officer would be more readily corruptible? Why does Yusef at times seem to show genuine feeling for Scobie? Why does Scobie persist in a feeling of "trust" for Yusef, even after deception and blackmail? How is it that Yusef gives Scobie a sense of "peace"? The crucial question concerns Scobie's state of mind in his several approaches to Yusef, above all in the last. Did Scobie not understand, on this occasion, that in placing his problem in Yusef's hands he was condemning Ali to death? And if he did not see this, was not his ignorance willful and seriously culpable?

It is part of the mysticism of the relationship between Scobie and Yusef that there are no answers to these questions other than what the reader may conjecture. Scobie's state of mind is deliberately veiled in this scene under a lot of talk about "trust." When Scobie at last asks Yusef just how he intends to "look after" him, he amazingly rests content with Yusef's elusive reply that Scobie must "not ask questions." As Yusef then proceeds to arrange for the interception of Ali, borrowing Scobie's rosary to use as bait, it is incredible that Scobie, an experienced policeman who knows Yusef well, would not have anticipated foul play.

When he later discovers Ali's body Scobie accepts the responsibility at once: "I am the man. Didn't I know all the time in Yusef's room that something was planned? Couldn't I have pressed for an answer?" (3.1.4.1).

Greene mitigates Scobie's complicity in murder by lowering or confusing his consciousness in his dealings with Yusef. Scobie is "magnetized" by Yusef's office, and declares on entering that he does not know why he has come. He begins drinking Yusef's whisky and gradually succumbs to the hypnotic force of Yusef's repeated instructions: "You do not need to be ashamed. . . . You must leave everything to me. . . . Everything will be all right. . . . You must not worry." The whisky, the isolated location, the late hour, and the gentle, reassuring tones of Yusef all contribute to an atmosphere of lowered awareness as this scene unfolds, so as to make it at least plausible that Scobie might have placed his problem in Yusef's hands without clearly visualizing the consequences.

The same lowering of consciousness affects every significant encounter between Scobie and Yusef. They first meet in darkness on a lonely road. When Yusef visits Scobie at Bamba the policeman is feverish, bedridden, and only half awake. (Significantly, the transaction in which Scobie borrows money from Yusef is simply not narrated, perhaps because it would require both parties to be alert and explicit about what they were doing.) Later, when Yusef visits Scobie at home, it is again late at night and Scobie is "sleepy," dozing in a chair. When Scobie visits Yusef at home it is the Syrian who is asleep and drugged. On his second visit to Scobie's house, Yusef first falls asleep and then, awoken, talks to Scobie while the policeman's mind is preoccupied over the letter he has just received from Helen and which he is reading while Yusef speaks. In these ways the narrative represents the relationship of Scobie and Yusef as developing to a large extent outside the rational control or conscious volition of the two men. Questions of motives thus become obscured and incapable of precise answers. Exactly what Yusef has in mind in his pursuit of Scobie remains purposely vague, just as does Scobie's state of mind in accepting help from Yusef.

Scobie's visit to Yusef's office is the moral climax of the story. It takes place in "a little white two-storey building" which stands "on the edge of Africa" by a jetty on the quay (3.1.4.1). The scene corresponds structurally to the "key scenes" of the early novels—the night in the barn with Czinner, the night which Anne and Raven spend in the railway shed. Here, by surrendering himself to Yusef, Scobie finally obtains the "peace" he has long desired, the kind of calm glimpsed briefly on his trek to Bamba. Yusef thus continues the protective, quasi-paternal role of the earlier antagonists: the feeling of safety and security he gives Scobie is a more sophisticated version of the kind of protection given by Carlyon to Andrews, or the kind of freedom from financial worries offered by Krogh to Anthony. It echoes also Kite's rescue of Pinkie, allowing the hero to withdraw from the turmoil of life into protected security, but at the cost of becoming an accomplice in crime.

The price of this peace is in the end too high. The moral simplification offered by the antagonist entails the resolution of the hero's difficulties at someone else's expense. As in most of the other novels, so in *HM* the hero's surrender to, or cooperation with the antagonist requires a victim. Krogh commands Anthony to do violence against Andersson, Pulling shakes hands with Mr. Visconti over the body of Wordsworth, Pinkie avenges Kite by killing Hale, and Yusef guarantees Scobie's security by having Ali murdered. Consequently here, as in *BR*, *PG*, and *MF*, the hero's vision of peace turns out to be delusive.

In the course of the novel the just and incorruptible Scobie becomes Yusef's accomplice in the perversion of justice, in smuggling and murder. In one sense the two men are thus shown to live by the same anarchic code, to share a willingness to disregard laws and convention in obtaining their personal ends. There is a sense in which Scobie is shown to be a kind of Yusef, just as Rowe is a kind of Hilfe and the Priest a kind of Calver. Yet at a deeper level, in Scobie's case as with the others, there is a fundamental difference. Yusef's code is akin to Hilfe's nihilism in its deliberate exclusion of "pity." "The way is not to care a damn," Yusef says to Scobie in discussions of his relations with women (3.1.4.1). Scobie's problem is precisely that he cares too much, particularly in his dealings with women. Like Hilfe and (presumably) Calver, Yusef breaks the rules because he has no regard for the suffering of others. Scobie may find himself doing the same, but for the very opposite reason.

TM, because it is a short novel written as the basis for a film script, is much simpler than the great novels Greene was writing in the immediate postwar years. It goes back for its pattern to the early novels, and particularly to the story of friendship, crime, and betrayal first set out in *MW*. Like *MW*, *TM* presents a rather naive hero who has been befriended as a boy by a stronger, more adventurous character, the antagonist. Later—some years later in *TM*—the hero realizes that his former friend and protector is a criminal, a dangerous man, and eventually assists the authorities against him.

The tension in *TM*, as in *MW*, arises chiefly from the betrayal, from the conflict of feelings in the hero as he approaches the point of siding with the forces of law and order against his old friend. In both novels there is much the same combination of increasing moral repugnance towards the antagonist, in conflict with a dying remnant of love and admiration. *TM* does not go significantly beyond this. Greene does not try to work into this simpler story the kind of very complex relations between hero and antagonist which he had explored in *PG*, *HM*, and *MF*.

Lime, as the story's antagonist, has the usual features of overt personal charm and friendliness concealing criminal activity and the threat of deadly violence against those who oppose him. Not only does Lime kill several men in the attempt to cover his tracks, but he is also responsible for the death and suffering of many children. The child-victims in *TM* echo Coral and the baby in *PG* and anticipate the casualties of Pyle's terrorism. In two particular ways, however, *TM* departs from the pattern of *MW* in a manner which looks forward to *QA*. It introduces a heroine, Anna Schmidt, who passes, in the course of the story, between the hero and the antagonist. Martins's gradual appropriation of Anna, formerly Lime's girl, looks forward to the way in which Fowler in *QA* establishes his claim to Phuong, who is at one point betrothed to Pyle. There is, as it happens in *TM*, no jealousy: Lime resigns

Anna willingly, having previously, in a move echoing Hilfe's attempt to destroy his own sister (another Anna), betrayed her to the Russians. Nevertheless there lies in this situation the potential for the kind of sexual triangle developed more broadly in some of the later novels. Secondly, whereas Carlyon survives the ending of *MW*, Lime dies, betrayed and killed by Martins. The somber ending of *TM*, which leaves Martins haunted by guilt for his part in his friend's death, anticipates closely the ending of *QA*.

Before *QA* came *Loser Takes All*, a longish short story featuring three central characters who exhibit some of the features of the hero, heroine, and antagonist in the major novels. The story is primarily an uncomplicated moral tale with a few ironic twists and a clear, comfortable conclusion. It invites an allegorical reading because of the extremity of its circumstances, which approach the limit of the credible, and because of the terms in which Greene represents the key figures. In this respect *Loser Takes All* belongs generically with *DF*, another fable concerned with the hero's relations with an older man who has improbably great powers over the lives of those around him.

On an allegorical level the story echoes the Book of Job and glances at the legend of Faust. Dreuther takes the part of an Old Testament god. He is associated in Bertram's mind with "providence" (1.2) and is described as "grand" and "like the weather—unpredictable" (1.3). When Bertram solves a problem at the office Dreuther, one of the directors, insists on paying for his honeymoon, sending Bertram and his new bride Cary, to Monte Carlo, where he promises to settle their bills and collect them in his yacht. Dreuther's reason for doing this appears to have a lot to do with his rivalry with Blixon, the other director.

Bertram had planned a honeymoon in Bournemouth, but Dreuther sends him to Monte Carlo, the seat of high living and gambling. Bertram and Cary are thus placed in paradise, but a paradise sown with tempting, dangerous fruits. When Dreuther fails to appear, Bertram becomes worried about his hotel bill and turns to the casinos. At first he is unsuccessful, but then he acquires a "system" from a stranger, a "devil" (69) who is represented as a Mephisthophelean deceiver. The system works, but as a result Bertram's relationship with Cary deteriorates to the point where their marriage seems lost. All is well, however, when Dreuther arrives, and under his guidance Bertram regains Cary's affections by giving away his winnings and destroying the written rules of the system.

This sort of story, with its focus upon the way in which a relatively weak and untried hero reacts under the ambivalent patronage of an almost supernaturally powerful father figure, has a common ground with novels like *MW* and *EM*. In his actions towards the hero Dreuther is not unlike Carlyon, Krogh, and Yusef. Dreuther resolves immediate problems, opens new vistas, and places the hero in a situation of opportunity; but as in these other cases the benefits he confers are dubious. The protection and friendship originally offered by the antagonist dissolve into unexpected moral crises and penalties to be paid.

Loser Takes All, however, being a comic story, departs from the pattern of the novels in its cheerful ending. Dreuther turns out to be genuinely benign, although perhaps a little inclining to senility, and conceals no sinister intentions. No one dies as a result of his actions, and no one is permanently harmed. Consequently there is in the end no tension between hero and antagonist in *Loser Takes All*, no betrayal or bitter parting of the ways. The potential for such a development, rather interestingly, is included, but it remains an avenue unexplored. Bertram coincidentally acquires, with his new wealth, the means to end Dreuther's power by buying the shares through which he might end Dreuther's control of the company. By taking these shares and joining forces with Blixon, Bertram might, in effect, have betrayed Dreuther, ending his career much as Andrews ends Carlyon's and Fowler ends Pyle's. This does not happen, for when Dreuther makes good his promises Bertram no longer has any reason to act against him. The matter of the shares is quietly dropped, and Dreuther never even knows of Bertram's option to purchase. The happy relation between hero and antagonist places *Loser Takes All* in a much more lighthearted, comfortable world than that of the novels Greene was writing in these same years.

The story of *QA* turns straightforwardly upon the relationship between Fowler and Pyle, from their first meeting to Pyle's death.

Pyle is unaccountably anxious to befriend Fowler, much as Yusef cultivates Scobie. The friendship is surprising since the two are opposed in many ways. Fowler is middle-aged, cynical, English, and uninvolved, whereas Pyle is young, enthusiastic, American, and convinced of the necessity for intervention. Pyle is apparently an honest man, sincere in his wish "to do good" (1.1), and even when he becomes Fowler's rival over Phuong he is scrupulously open in his handling of the matter. He is also evidently brave and takes great personal risks, without any unnecessary show, in the pursuit of his mission and on the occasion when he saves Fowler's life. This rescue of Fowler comes at the midpoint of the action and follows immediately upon a "key scene" in which the hero and antagonist have been isolated together for some hours at night in a confined place. The rescue establishes Pyle as Fowler's protector in a manner reminiscent of Kite's rescue of Pinkie and Jim's preservation of Conrad.

Pyle is opposed to Fowler over the crucial issue of involvement. Unlike Fowler, he "believed in being involved" (1.2.2). This in itself is not condemned in the novel, and Fowler himself has accepted the necessity for a degree of involvement by the end of the story. What is wrong, in a way very reminiscent of *MF*, is that Pyle's actions are based upon a preconceived ideology, the political doctrines of "York Harding," and on inexperience, with blind disregard for the human consequences. To Fowler, whose views in this respect are justified by the events of the story, Pyle's "innocence" (1.2.2) rests upon "a psychological world of great simplicity" (2.2.2), and his idealism is tinged with a "fanatic gleam" (1.2.1). Fowler concludes that the naively innocent Pyle is "like a dumb leper who has lost his bell, wandering the world, meaning no harm"(1.3.1). Beneath his attractive exterior of friendship and sincerity Pyle conceals a deadly danger, and he is "responsible for at least fifty deaths" in the course of the story (1.1).

Fowler's relationship with Pyle exhibits very plainly the kind of ambivalence evident in the hero-antagonist relationships in many of the other novels. On the one hand Fowler cannot help responding to Pyle's personal charm, and after the incident on the road from Tanyin he also owes Pyle his life. On the other hand, he is rightly skeptical of Pyle's beliefs and suspicious of his activities. The real threat posed by Pyle grows in both personal and public spheres, as Pyle takes Phuong and begins organizing the terrorist attacks which kill innocent people.

There is in Pyle little or nothing of the mystical element which can be traced in Yusef and Calver, and even in Hilfe and Kite. Pyle remains a very real, humanly plausible figure. The emphasis in his portrait is upon false idealism, an idealism which manifests itself harmlessly in his honest personal dealings and in his courtesy towards women, but which is also displayed, on a wider scale, as his willingness to leap into action in pursuit of an ideological goal without pausing to weigh the consequences. In this respect Pyle picks up a thread which runs back, through the nihilistic suavity of Hilfe, through the communism of Jim, to the chivalry of Carlyon.

The portrait of Pyle emphasizes the relative immaturity of the antagonist, a feature which seems to have preoccupied Greene in his middle period. Along with Hilfe, Pyle is the only antagonist significantly younger than his hero. (Calver is probably younger than the Priest, but both are apparently mature men, and any difference in their ages is unimportant.) To Fowler, Pyle appears boyish, with "an unmistakably young and unused face" and his "wide campus gaze" (1.1). In his bravery Pyle is like "a hero in a boy's adventure-story, proud of his action like a Scout's badge" (2.2.4). His youth is reflected in the dangerous "simplicity" of his moral judgement (2.2.2). In this respect Pyle echoes Hilfe, a young man who advocates a comparable simplification of moral issues. He also echoes Lime's Peter Pan–like failure to grow up (*TM* 14). The youthful immaturity of these antagonists is associated with the deceptive attraction of childlike simplicity in *MF* and *BR*. The underlying idea connects with that of the illusion of innocence by which heroes like Scobie, Querry, and Plarr are misled.

Although the tone of *QA* is predominantly tragic, Pyle's idealism has also a comic, quixotic side. The exaggerated courtesy of his New England manners is amusingly related in Fowler's dry, cynical narrative. His sexual naivety and prudery are out of place

The Antagonists

against the background of nightlife in Saigon, and his fussy courtship of Phuong steadily ignores the hard realities of her situation and motives. There is a constant tension concerning Pyle, between the way he sees things and the way things are. "I was to see many times," says Fowler, "that look of pain and disappointment touch his eyes and mouth when reality didn't match the romantic ideas he cherished" (2.1). Pyle's chivalric romanticism echoes something of Carlyon and anticipates the more fully developed quixoticisms of Aunt Augusta and the Captain.

Pyle's immediate successor, however, is Hasselbacher in *OM*. Hasselbacher is a kindly man, a doctor by profession, and the hero's true friend. He is also, nonetheless, a very impractical man, a dreamer. He has absurd faith in omens supposedly foretelling the outcome of the lottery (1.4.1), although he never wins. Like the clown of which Wormold speaks (1.3.3), Hasselbacher refuses to learn from experience: even his science appears to consist in a largely random growing of molds in the hope that eventually he will find one with medicinal properties. He longs nostalgically for a lost world of prewar innocence, and he secretly wears his uniform, that of an officer in the army of the Kaiser.

All this is harmless until Hasselbacher's taste for fantasy is passed on to the hero. Hasselbacher propounds the philosophy that, since reality is ultimately ideal, one can create or re-create it by an act of imagination. In line with this train of thought, when Wormold tells Hasselbacher of his arrangement with Hawthorne, Hasselbacher naturally suggests the notion of fabricating agents and making up reports (2.1.2). Hasselbacher sees no problem in this suggestion, since for him the boundary between the real and the imaginary is of no importance. The trouble that Wormold subsequently gets himself into, when his fabricated agents come to life and his false reports are read as having real implications, is therefore due ultimately to Hasselbacher.

In this sense Hasselbacher is Wormold's mentor, leading him into a world of fantasy which, deceptively harmless, soon becomes sinister and eventually life threatening. Hasselbacher himself becomes a victim, first blackmailed and then killed by enemy agents who believe in the reality of Wormold's information. Hasselbacher is not "betrayed" by Wormold—as several earlier antagonists are betrayed by their heroes—but it is clearly as a direct result of Wormold's activities, and because of his known association with Wormold, that Hasselbacher dies. Very like Fortnum, Hasselbacher falls victim to his friend's casual and irresponsible venture into the dangerous domain of espionage and terrorism.

The usual dynamics of the hero-antagonist relationship are absent from *BC* because of the passivity of the hero. Querry is an extreme case of noninvolvement. Having decided on a complete and literal withdrawal from action before the story opens, he pursues this rigorously and remains throughout, in all other respects, inactive. In a typical Greene novel the hero makes some actual or symbolic gesture of commitment to his antagonist. Andrews joins Carlyon's crew, Anthony takes a job with Krogh, the Priest turns back to find the dying Calver, and Plarr joins Fortnum in the hut. In *BC*, however, Querry makes no move towards Rycker. Although Rycker forces his acquaintance upon Querry, the hero sees through him from the start and never responds with anything more than bare civility. The usual bond of friendship or obligation between the two characters is never really formed in *BC*.

Although Querry refuses to join in the usual game of association and betrayal, the irony of *BC* lies largely in the way that the pattern asserts itself nevertheless. Despite his scrupulous avoidance of any sort of planned action, Querry is forced by events into proximity and comparison with Rycker, and finds himself in the end, however groundlessly, cast as Rycker's betrayer.

Despite Querry's indifference, Rycker goes through the motions of effusive friendship and makes claims on Querry's society, drawing the reader's attention to latent similarities between them. Like Calver and Jones, Rycker is a kind of distorted mirror image of the hero, confronting him with unpleasant self-comparisons. It is true that Querry has largely renounced the way of life which he now sees parodied in Rycker, but no Greene hero—as was seen in the previous chapter—can simply turn his back on the past. Rycker is the kind of hollow man that Querry has been.

Like Querry in his former life, Rycker lays public claim to a "vocation." Querry designed cathedrals, but for his own "pleasure" rather than for "the glory of God" (2.3.1; 2.3.2). Rycker, with a similar profanation, is a failed priest who parades his spirituality as a means to impress and dominate others. Like Querry, Rycker has come to Africa to live in self-imposed exile from a world he has rejected with bitterness. "I have buried myself too," he says to Querry when they first meet (2.1.3). Rycker's marriage, moreover, his callous exploitation of Marie for his own ends, echoes what we know of Querry's dealings with women in Europe.

Rather like Jones in *TC* and Carson in *HF*, Rycker works to hinder the hero's efforts to put his past behind him. Rycker persists in seeing Querry in terms of his old reputation, and he works to spread this image around the region. His determination not to let the old Querry die culminates in Rycker's manipulation of Parkinson, the gutter journalist (a remote descendant of Mabel Warren) whom he sends after Querry and primes with false information. This leads to the appearance of the magazine article which precipitates Querry's final, and ultimately fatal attempt to free himself from the past. He goes to confront Rycker; but instead of settling the issue he picks up Rycker's wife. In the ensuing misunderstanding, exacerbated by Marie's opportunism, Rycker assumes he has been betrayed by the man he has befriended and becomes, like Carlyon pursuing Andrews, bent on vengeance.

The sexual triangle in *BC*, among Rycker, Marie, and Querry, echoes that among Pyle, Phuong, and Fowler in *QA*, and looks forward to the situation of Fortnum, Clara, and Plarr in *HC*. The pattern is the same, but again with the crucial difference that the hero in *BC* remains passive and does nothing. The sexual rivalry remains apparent, not real. Querry goes through the motions: he "abducts" Marie and spends a night in a hotel with her, visiting her room while she is in bed. But he does nothing in her bedroom except, in an episode which reveals more clearly than any other the depth of his self-involvement, tell her the thinly veiled story of his life.

UG appeared in 1963 in the collection entitled *A Sense of Reality*. Although quite long, it remains clearly a short story, rather than a novel, in its sharp focus upon a single event (Wilditch's encounter with Javitt), and because it is presented as essentially a dream or fantasy. The story belongs generically with the dream vision, the tradition of which runs in English from *The Dream of the Rood* and *Piers Plowman* through *Alice in Wonderland*. In this kind of story the narrator, perhaps under some initial stress, falls asleep and has a vivid dream which, while in some respects fantastical or even mystical, offers him new insight to help him face waking reality. The vision may even present a "higher" perspective, and so may be the truth of which waking experience is a distortion.

In *UG* the hero, Wilditch, knowing he has a terminal illness, returns to the scene of his childhood and relives a dream, or memory, associated with the place. The dream is of his encounter with Javitt, which occupies the heart of the story. Nothing much happens in the way of overt action. Wilditch is detained beneath the garden by Javitt for a period which seems like three days, during which they talk a great deal and explore a few tunnels. In the end Wilditch manages to escape, and sees nothing more of the tunnels or Javitt thereafter. The point of the story lies clearly in the business of the central episode, in the doctrines which Javitt expounds to the young Wilditch during his brief captivity "under the garden."

Javitt is an odd, numinous figure, but his role with respect to Wilditch echoes the paternal, mentor relationship discernable in a number of other cases. He is unnaturally ancient, and there is something mystical about him, a touch of Pluto as he sits upon his underground "throne." The boy accepts him as a surrogate father. "I . . . listened to Javitt as I would have listened to my own father if I had possessed one," says Wilditch (2.3). Like the Captain in the first Part of *CE*, Javitt becomes the hero's instructor: "Sometimes I think that I learned more from Javitt than from all my schoolmasters," Wilditch writes (2.5).

The situation among Javitt, Maria, and Wilditch in their underground room echoes that of Baines, Mrs. Baines, and Philip in "The Basement Room," and anticipates that of the Captain, Lisa, and Baxter in the first Part of *CE*. Like Kite, Carlyon, and the

Captain, Javitt introduces the young hero to a new and unconventional outlook on life. There are promises of great rewards, represented in *UG* by Javitt's treasure, which corresponds to Krogh's wealth, Benditch's coal, Yusef's diamonds, Mr. Visconti's art treasures, and the Captain's loaded mules. There is also a hint of sexual delight when Javitt shows Wilditch a picture of his daughter, Miss Ramsgate, with whom the boy, although only seven years old, at once "fell in love for life" (2.3). This is reminiscent of the several cases in which the hero takes an attractive daughter (as in *CA* and *DF*) or a young wife (as in *BC* and *HC*) from the household of his older antagonist.

Javitt's world, being an ontologically uncertain realm, perhaps dream, perhaps vague memory, exemplifies the principle developed by Hasselbacher and Aunt Augusta, that the boundary between fact and fantasy is not a sharp one. In Javitt's world old certainties dissolve as the passage of time itself is suspended and life becomes apparently endless. Values become unusually subjective: Javitt's treasure may be no more than paste and paint, but it has worth as it is estimated; and so many moral norms, like the virtue of loyalty, are reversed by Javitt's teaching. "Absolute reality belongs to dreams and not to life," concludes Wilditch. "The gold of dreams is not the diluted gold of even the best goldsmith, there are no diamonds in dreams made of paste—what seems is" (2.6). Javitt, like the other quixotic antagonists, creates reality from what we would normally call imagination. In *UG*, as in *TA* and *CE*, the hero is left, in the end, to decide whether to accept the dream and live on its terms, or to reject it and return to the dull security of everyday life.

The hero-antagonist relationship in *TC* echoes the fugitive hero's reluctance to associate with his counterpart. Here again, as in *BC*, the hero initially wants nothing to do with the antagonist, but finds himself inescapably coupled with him, even over a deceptive matter of sexual jealousy, by force of circumstance. Brown and Jones enter the story together, both passengers on the *Medea*. Brown is asked to keep an eye on Jones, whom he dislikes, and is later recruited by Smith to help in the effort to secure Jones's release from prison. Jones crosses Brown's path again at Mère

Catherine's, and it is subsequently with Brown's help that Jones finds refuge in the embassy. Finally they become accomplices, although with very different motives, in a plot to aid the rebels.

Like Rycker, Jones exudes good fellowship, which the hero does not reciprocate. Nonetheless Brown does eventually respond, although his intentions remain negative, by becoming Jones's associate in the plan to join the rebels. The general progression of their relationship, much as in *PG*, *HM*, and *HC*, may be compared to the gradual convergence of two lines on a point which precipitates the climax of the story. Brown is initially indifferent to, and even suspicious of Jones, but despite scepticism and personal dislike he finds himself unable to ignore him, and in the end unites with him in the action which brings the events of the story to a close.

Much like Calver and Rycker, Jones functions as a kind of parody or mirror image of his hero. Brown's early career, which is retrospectively narrated in some detail (1.3.1–2), is very similar to that which Jones is still pursuing: a nomadic life of gambling, petty fraud, and confidence trickery. Jones's ambition, to own and run a golf club in the Caribbean, is close to Brown's dream of himself as proprietor of a luxury hotel in Haiti. Jones even proposes a partnership (2.3.1). Brown has to admit the similarity between them: "I was reminded, when I talked to him, of a time when I was young. . . . I remember looking at him one night on the boat from America . . . and wondering are you and I both comedians?" (1.5.2). In the end, as they wait together in the cemetery where they are to make contact with the rebels, Brown accepts the closeness of his relationship with Jones:

> It was like meeting an unknown brother—Jones and Brown, the names were almost interchangeable, and so was our status. For all we knew we were both bastards. . . . We had both been thrown into the water to sink or swim, and swim we had—we had swum from very far apart to come together in a cemetery in Haiti. "I like you, Jones," I said. (3.3.3)

A bond is formed between them even as they are separated. Jones dies soon after, and the novel opens with Brown's words about

Jones's memorial. He admits that he now has "no reason to mock" the memory of the other, and even takes "a certain pride" in the memorial which he has helped to erect (1.1.1).

The sexual triangle in *TC* echoes that in *QA*: in each case the hero first introduces the energetically active newcomer to the heroine, begins to feel jealous, and plots to remove the antagonist by underhanded means. The difference is that, whereas both Fowler and Pyle have strong feelings for Phuong, there seems to be no very deep love among the characters in *TC*. Jones only pretends to have had any kind of affair with Martha, and she is lying when she leads Brown to believe otherwise. Brown himself has just returned reluctantly from an attempt to cut his ties with Haiti, and at the end of the story he parts from Martha with little apparent regret. His jealousy of Jones is an aspect of Brown's "Berkelian" tendency to see people and events in the light of his own imagining rather than as they are.

Like almost all the antagonists, Jones is dangerous and costs others their lives. His victims are the rebels whom he leads to their deaths in a hopeless campaign. It is, however, a considerable mitigation that these men die willingly, accepting his leadership, and that he dies with them, loyal to their common cause. Hence Brown's grudging respect for Jones's memorial. Again, although Jones at one stage seems inclined to join forces with the Haitian government, they soon reject him, and no harm follows from whatever proposals Jones has put to them. In these ways the evil, dangerous aspect of the antagonist is very much softened in Jones. What we see, instead of a sinister or violent figure such as Yusef or Calver, is an entertaining, likeable rascal with something in him of the Shakespearean clown. This is also the way in which the other characters—other than Brown—see him: "he makes us laugh," Martha tells Brown (3.2.1). Among the antagonists, Jones is more than halfway to the quixotic end of the spectrum. With his claim to military prowess and experience, his notion of defeating the government of Haiti with a few ill-armed men, and his boyish stories of extravagant exploits, Jones is something of a Don Quixote, especially when he really does take up arms in the end and set himself, however hopelessly, against the forces of evil.

It is no great step from the quixotic aspect of Jones to the eccentricities of Aunt Augusta. She is another odd figure, with a checkered and not entirely salubrious background, given to engagement in petty deception and the narration of extravagant adventures. *TA* is a comedy and, unlike Jones in the deeply ironic story of *TC*, Augusta emerges unscathed from her escapades, even though she usually falls short of her intended goals. Her philosophy of "fun" and her vitality, her apparently eternally youthful spirit, make her an attractive, sympathetic character; and those who oppose her, however justifiably in terms of law and common sense, appear dull and small-minded in comparison.

Aunt Augusta plays Don Quixote to Henry Pulling's Sancho Panza, leading him on a series of travels and adventures in which he is at first a reluctant participant, maintaining a foothold in mundane reality and refusing, until nearly the end, to surrender to his aunt's fantastic vision. Where a number of antagonists, like Carlyon, Kite, and Fortnum, become surrogate fathers to their heroes, Augusta is maternal, not only in the way she takes control of Henry's life but also, as the novel belatedly reveals to the suspecting reader, as a matter of fact. She as it were adopts her long-lost son and eventually, like Krogh and Kite, finds the hero a place in her organization, with the offer of easy money and a measure of personal security.

At the end Augusta hands Henry over to Mr. Visconti, and it is he who inducts the hero into their new world and who from that point is directing its affairs. Augusta announces her intention to marry Mr. Visconti, who will then be Henry's stepfather. Man and wife being one flesh, it doesn't matter whether we take Augusta or Visconti to be the antagonist in *TA*: it is a role they share between them.

The world into which they finally introduce Henry is typically ambivalent. On the one hand Henry has found his mother, a new and more interesting way of life, and the promise of a young bride. On the other hand, it becomes clear that Augusta and Mr. Visconti, like Carlyon, Yusef, and the Captain, are engaged in smuggling and that there are risks. Policemen have to be bribed, there are occasional gunfights, and planes may crash or be shot down. There is also, as always, a victim: Wordsworth is killed in rather mysterious circumstances, just as Henry surrenders himself to Mr. Visconti's direction. The episode is reminiscent of the death of Ali in *HM*, except that here, in a comic context, the hero is not responsible—indeed, no one seems particularly at fault in the matter of poor Wordsworth's demise. There is also an echo here of the death of Marcel in *TC*; and although, like Brown, Henry Pulling is not to blame, there remains a sense that what he is doing, the critical step he takes at the moment of this death, is not as safe or harmless as it may appear.

HC and *HF* form a pair by virtue of new departures Greene makes in them, chiefly in the treatment of the antagonist role. In each of these two novels this role, hitherto embodied in a single character, is split into two. In each case the antagonist proper—Fortnum and Carson—remains a paternal, protective figure with whom the hero's main task, much as in *PG*, *TC*, and *TA*, is to effect some kind of symbolic union. Fortnum and Carson, however, are largely divested of the moral ambivalence of the preceding antagonists, the involvement in underhand dealings and the proclivity to violence, even to murder, such as is seen in Calver, Yusef, Pyle, Rycker, and Mr. Visconti. Fortnum and Carson remain benign and largely passive figures. Neither does any harm, both are represented as humane, and both are, for the greater part of the time that they figure in the narrative, helpless prisoners, reminiscent of Jim Drover in *IB*. Carson, indeed, has died some time before the main action opens, but it is the image of his death in prison which haunts Castle's mind.

The violence and underhandedness is meanwhile channeled into a new figure, a more sinister, threatening character who has had significant dealings with the hero in the past and whose sudden reappearance is the main cause of action in the novel's present. In *HC* and *HF* this role is taken by Leon and Muller respectively. In purely moral terms these two are virtual opposites, Leon being a humanitarian who wishes to harm no one, while Muller is a sadistic agent of a cruel regime. Both, however, carry the threat of violence, both use underhanded means (there is an equivalence between Leon's terrorism and Muller's secret negotiations), and both act as jailers of the imprisoned antagonist. It is the appearance of this character, this reminder of unsettled questions from the past, that creates a morally critical situation in which the passively inclined hero is at last compelled to act, and to act in a manner specifically supportive of the incarcerated antagonist.

Greene began work on *HF* in the early sixties, but put it aside and did not return to it until after the publication of *HC*, which may therefore be regarded as the earlier novel of the two. The antagonist in *HC* is Fortnum, whose claims upon the indifferent hero's friendship echo similar protestations of comradeship from Yusef, Rycker, and Jones. Fortnum and Plarr are inevitably associated as fellow Englishmen, and Fortnum also becomes Plarr's patient. Although he is a harmless character, Fortnum has something of the disreputability of men like Yusef and Jones: he drinks far too much, he abuses his semiofficial position, and he is regarded with some doubt by his superiors in the hierarchy. Most important, however, is the way in which, in the web of father imagery which pervades *HC*, Fortnum becomes increasingly a symbolic representation of the lost father Plarr is seeking.

It is with Fortnum that Plarr becomes entangled in a sexual triangularity echoing those in *BC* and *TC*. It echoes more specifically the triangularity in *QA*, where hero and antagonist are rivals over a local girl who is effectively available to the highest bidder. The outcome in *HC* differs from that of *QA* in that it is Fortnum, not Plarr, who survives and marries the girl—a matter which surely has something to do with Fortnum's actual harmlessness, as opposed to the destructiveness of Pyle.

It is Fortnum whom Plarr betrays, albeit not by design, by passing to Leon information, obtained from Fortnum himself, about the movements of the ambassador's party. Through a comic mistake, the terrorists, acting upon this information, capture Fortnum instead of the ambassador. Again there is a close similarity with *QA*, where a comparable passing of information to terrorists leads to the interception of the antagonist for whose fate the hero is then morally responsible. There is even an echo of *MW*, where Andrews's letter to the authorities leads to the ambush of the smugglers. Unlike Pyle, Fortnum is not killed, but he is held under threat of death. Although he has no great personal liking for Fortnum, Plarr feels responsibility for his fate and obliged to do all he can to secure the prisoner's release. His situation is comparable to that of Conrad in *IB*, working to save the life of an imprisoned "brother" while at the same time sleeping with his wife.

For these reasons based on analogy Fortnum is the main antagonist figure in *HC*, but it remains true that some aspects of that role have been taken over by Leon. Like Lime, Leon is a schoolboy friend of the hero and draws upon their youthful companionship in his efforts to involve the hero in his current activities. Like Jones, he is a supporter of armed resistance against an oppressive government. Like Jim Drover, and anticipating Carson, he is a communist. Despite his priesthood, and like so many of the antagonists, he is also a potential killer, a desperate man prepared to use violence in defense of the position he has taken. Leon himself kills no one, but a number of deaths, including Plarr's, follow directly from his actions.

The most important aspect of the antagonist's role which Leon takes over is that of the incitement of the hero to participation in morally ambivalent action. While Fortnum remains a largely passive figure, it is Leon who represents the political activism formerly espoused by Plarr's father. Leon persuades Plarr to obtain the information necessary for the plan to kidnap the ambassador. Plarr does this reluctantly, and then finds himself unable to refuse Leon's further demands for active help with the plan.

Leon represents the call upon the hero to involve himself in the public domain, in the political conflict in which his father had been engaged. In *HC*, however, much as in *QA* and *TC*, the hero's position with respect to the public conflict is developed alongside the question of involvement or commitment in his private life. The relatively successful conclusion of Fowler's story is jointly dependent upon both his willingness to involve himself in public, political action, and his being free and prepared to make a commitment to Phuong. Much the same is the case in *HC*, where the issue of Plarr's involvement in the political struggle is developed in parallel with the matter of his sexual relationships, and particularly his relationship with Clara. Plarr's failure on this front, his inability to love, would seem to be the main reason why, in the logic of the story, he has to die and give place to Fortnum, whose love for Clara, whatever his other failings, is indisputable. While Leon stands clearly in *HC* for political activism, for involvement in public affairs, it is the uxorious Fortnum, who has recently married Clara in defiance of social prejudice, who represents commitment in private life.

The issue of the hero's commitment in private life is not important in *HF* for the simple reason that Castle is already happily married to Sarah at the outset and remains devoted to her, and to her son, throughout the action. As a result, although there is in *HF* a division of the antagonist role between two characters comparable to that in *HC*, this division is not made to embody any thematic distinction between public and private spheres of action. Castle's decisions, within the story, bear upon the single central question of his debt to Carson, which he pays through his activity as a spy supplying information to Moscow.

Carson is the principal antagonist. It was he who originally befriended Castle in South Africa, helped him in difficulties, and was instrumental in the escape of Sarah. This "rescue" of the distressed hero places Carson alongside such earlier antagonists as Carlyon, Pyle, and Yusef, who provide help and support in comparable circumstances. Carson also resembles Carlyon and Pyle in being something of an idealist, a man who lives by a high-minded code or doctrine. In Carson's case the doctrine is communism. Castle does not share his beliefs, but sees Carson as benign and communism as the only force realistically likely to help Sarah's people in South Africa. Out of personal gratitude Castle therefore engages in espionage for Moscow (but confines his information to matters pertaining to Africa). In this way the role assigned to Leon in *HC* and previously given to the antagonists, the role of recruiting the hero to take part in some new and morally ambivalent line of action, has already been undertaken by Carson in *HF* before the main action opens.

On the other hand, like Fortnum but unlike most of the earlier antagonists, Carson represents no immediate threat or danger.

He himself does not even appear in the main action, and his successors, the other communist agents with whom Castle has dealings in the story, are also personally harmless. One of them, Boris, even becomes a supportive friend. The communists claim no victims in *HF*. Here the murdered innocents are Carson himself, dead in a South African prison, and Davis, killed by Perceval. The threat of danger, as in *HC*, comes not from the antagonist but from a different quarter altogether.

The chief threat is Muller, whose role in *HF* corresponds structurally to that of Leon in *HC*. Each character comes from the hero's past, bursting unexpectedly into his present equilibrium with a flurry of menace and reminders of old fears and loyalties. Leon heads a band of armed terrorists; Muller brings plans for the infamous "Uncle Remus" project. Greene allows a measure of sympathy for Leon, insofar as he is motivated by feeling for the poor, while there is no sympathy whatever for Muller. Nonetheless, Leon and Muller work in the same way within the mechanics of the action, each of them presenting his hero with a situation demanding action.

The overall pattern in both *HF* and *HC* is that first seen in *PG* and echoed in most of the subsequent novels, a pattern of the gradual convergence of the two chief characters. Plarr and Fortnum, although united by circumstances of geography and nationality, are initially separated widely by age and temperament. Plarr originally has little or no sympathy for the rather weak and disreputable older man. The events of the story nonetheless draw them gradually together. Plarr becomes obsessed with Clara, whom Fortnum has married, and there is then the erroneous capture of Fortnum, for which Plarr is partly responsible. Plarr becomes preoccupied with efforts to obtain the prisoner's release, and when these come to nothing he joins him in captivity. Confined with him in the hut, Plarr learns something of Fortnum's human qualities and eventually dies trying to ensure his safety. By this time the two men are closely bound together by the story's imagery: Plarr sees Fortnum as a father, while Fortnum survives to become stepfather to Plarr's child. Fortnum forgives Clara's love for Plarr and calls the child Eduardo.

In *HF* Carson and Castle are initially separated geographically and ideologically. Carson has, indeed, died since Castle last saw him, but his influence lives on in Castle's gratitude. Castle is about to sever the connection with Moscow, feeling that his debt to Carson is by now fully paid (3.5.1), but at just this point the arrival of Muller makes it necessary for him to go on. His involvement deepens as he continues to pass information, even after the removal of Davis has made his discovery inevitable. As he takes this decisive step, "he identified himself truly for the first time with Carson" (4.2.4). To effect his escape, he has to invoke the "dragon," to activate the network of communist agents which will remove him from danger. He arrives in Moscow, in the heart of communism, where he discovers that he has unknowingly been serving the Soviet cause all along.

DF is generically different from the novels, being more of a fable with strong leanings towards allegory. Its closest companion among Greene's works is *Loser Takes All*. It does not exhibit the kind of psychological and situational complexity we find even in the "entertainments," but tells a simple albeit rather extravagant story, with more satire and caricature than realistic credibility. Nonetheless, the central relationship between the story's hero, Alfred Jones, and the eponymous Doctor Fischer has at least a superficial resemblance to the hero-antagonist relationship in the novels.

With his ordinariness, middle age, restricted circumstances, and injured hand, Jones is a typical Greene hero: an unexceptional man who has suffered misfortune and who is trying to lead a life of quiet obscurity. He is particularly reminiscent of Scobie and Castle. Like Rowe and D, he is a widower who lost his wife in traumatic circumstances over which he still feels remorse. His past experience of air raids reminds us of Bendrix. Like several of these quiet, middle-aged heroes, he rather surprisingly attracts the love of a young woman, who may see in him something of a father figure. The situation in this respect is particularly reminiscent of *CA*, where the young heroine has a powerful and dangerous father, like Doctor Fischer, from whom she has separated herself. Fischer echoes Lord Benditch as the heroine's rich father, and as a powerful industrialist he reminds us also of Krogh. He has great power and can be dangerous, as is shown not only in the "bomb party," which is a voluntary game, but more especially in what he has done to Steiner. Steiner, as Fischer's victim, corresponds to Andersson in *EM* and to Wordsworth in *TA*.

Beyond these rather superficial points of resemblance, however, the relationship of Jones and Fischer fails to develop in the way the hero-antagonist relationship develops in a typical Greene novel. Fischer shows no personal warmth or protective inclination towards Jones, and Jones incurs no obligation towards Fischer. Jones takes a certain interest in Fischer and attends some of his parties, but he does nothing along the lines of the typical hero, who surrenders himself in some way to the antagonist or accepts a measure of symbolic identification with him. Jones maintains a strict distance. Even his marriage to Fischer's daughter creates no personal bond between the two men. Nor can Jones in any useful sense be said to "betray" Fischer. His participation in Fischer's parties is halfhearted, and his success in effectively sabotaging the last one (by failing to be blown up) is largely a matter of chance.

The story of *DF* has much in common with *Loser Takes All*, particularly in its presentation of Fischer as a god-like figure observing and testing common mortals. His calm acceptance of Jones's marriage to his daughter, and his subsequent invitation of Jones to parties where games are played for high stakes, reflect Dreuther's offhand transportation of Bertram and his new bride to Monte Carlo. In each case there are hints of a rather cold-hearted deity observing Adam and Eve in an Eden littered with snares. In Fischer, however, there is also much that is diabolical, vengeful, and cruel. Jones is fascinated by him, being generally repelled but also, at moments, pitiful. Perhaps here, as in *Loser Takes All*, Greene is rather impressionistically exploring a collection of images intended to reflect the relation between man and God.

DF suggests allegory but defies overall interpretation. It points several diverse morals. There is the very obvious matter of the greed of the "toadies," which gives Fischer his power over them.

They remain, however, mere caricatures, almost painfully cruel, and Fischer's easy triumph over them gives the reader little cause for thought. Only the Divisionnaire, at the very end, becomes for a moment human. There is also the moral explicitly drawn in the closing pages, that hate dies but love lives on—a point rather muted in the story by the fact that the loved ones are by this time no less dead than the hated Doctor Fischer.

More interesting (and less trite) is the doctrine of "souls" expounded in *DF* by Jones. The human soul, he says, is not innate and fully formed in every individual but has to be nurtured. Some people manage to develop souls, while others do not. He goes on to explain that the caricature-people surrounding Fischer, the "toadies," have not developed souls because they lack the necessary qualities, which include a "private life" and a capacity for suffering. The business at the end where the Divisionnaire suddenly becomes human is evidently meant to be an illustration of this doctrine. The ideas of the necessity of suffering and the importance of the private or inner life can also be traced in some of the novels, although they are not taken very far within the rather cryptic confines of *DF*.

CE presents us with the last of the antagonists in the figure of the Captain. In a clear echo of Carlyon, he rescues the young hero from school and takes over the role of his father. In due course, like Carlyon, he offers the hero a place at his side, a place which involves at once both the chance of adventure and romance and the risk of danger and confrontation with the law. Like Carlyon, Yusef, and Mr. Visconti, the Captain is involved in smuggling. As between Andrews and Carlyon, so between Baxter and the Captain differences of temperament lead in the end to rivalry and betrayal. Baxter betrays his protector by failing to take care of Liza and by consorting with his enemies in Panama.

The Captain is an attractive figure, chiefly because of his chivalric, selfless efforts to protect Liza, and also because of his anarchic tendency to see life in terms of adventure stories. In this last respect, in his continual blurring of the boundaries between truth and wish fulfilment, he continues the tradition of Hasselbacher, Jones, and Aunt Augusta. Both his chivalry and his imagination, however, have their negative aspects. His devotion to Liza is single-minded, and he has no scruples as to the methods he employs in what he sees as her interests. He commits violent robberies for her sake, and it was for her also that he abducted Baxter. Once Liza is dead, the Captain abandons Baxter with no sense of responsibility towards him. The Captain's tendency towards fantasy not only limits Baxter's education, but condemns both Liza and Baxter to a life of constant anticipation, living—in Baxter's case—upon dreams and promises which lie, for the most part, beyond the Captain's power of fulfilment.

The hero-antagonist relationship varies considerably from novel to novel, but a small number of interrelated features can be distinguished as each occurring in most cases. In his dealings with the hero the antagonist commonly exhibits one or more of these features:

1. His role is parental or quasi-parental, that of a father, mother, elder brother, or adoptive surrogate parent. (Clear examples are Carlyon, Kite, the Captain, Jim Drover, Javitt, and Aunt Augusta and Mr. Visconti. In addition, Fortnum becomes a symbolic father figure, while Benditch and Doctor Fischer are fathers-in-law.)
2. His role is protective. (This is plainly true in most cases, particularly Carlyon, Jim, Kite, Yusef, Pyle, Lime, Carson, and the Captain. Hilfe's protection is largely a sham, but its real nature is exposed only towards the end of the story. Even Calver, in the few words he utters, is primarily concerned to protect the Priest from capture.)
3. He offers the hero a place or station in life. (This may be in the form of employment, as Krogh employs Anthony, but it is more often a matter of induction into some criminal or underground organization. Carlyon, Sir Marcus, Kite, Mr. Visconti, and the Captain are all men operating outside the law, who give work to their respective heroes. Jones in *TC* very similarly contrives to get Brown involved in armed rebellion, and Carson recruits Castle as a Soviet agent. A

comparable case is that of Hasselbacher, who gives Wormold the idea upon which his covert activity is built.)
4. He offers friendship. (Even when he is not the hero's parent or natural protector, the antagonist may still come forward with pressing offers of friendship, as do Yusef, Pyle, Rycker, and Fortnum. Jones, with his efforts to take on Brown as a kind of partner, is a similar case.)
5. Despite the several kinds of bonds between hero and antagonist, there is also in many cases an element of sexual rivalry between them. (This occurs straightforwardly in *IB*, *TM*, *QA*, and *HC*. In *BC* and *TC* it is present ironically, in that the rivalry is more imagined than actual. There are also what might be called sublimated cases, in which the heroine is a sister and where the jealousy involved is not overtly sexual, as in *EM* and *MF*. Similar again are the cases in which the heroine is the antagonist's daughter, "stolen" from him by the hero, as in *CA* and *DF*, and potentially in *UG*.)
6. The antagonist may be presented, in the context of the story, as a kind of alter ego, a figure for the hero's self-comparison. (This occurs notably in *IB*, *BR*, *PG*, *BC*, *TC*, and *HF*.)

Quite apart from their relationship with the heroes, the antagonists themselves tend to exhibit salient common features:

1. The antagonist is usually a powerful man with control over others. (Several are leaders or employers. Others, like Yusef, Pyle, Carson, and the Captain, exert power behind the scenes by means of secret or underground organizations.)
2. He is often in some sense an idealist. (Carlyon is chivalrous in his dealings with women, as are Pyle and the Captain. Jim also commits his criminal act in protection of Milly, and Fortnum is comparably chivalrous in his concern for Clara. In other cases the antagonist's idealism shows itself not so much in pursuit of high personal standards of conduct as in the adoption of a rigorous public code or ideology. Thus Pyle practices the political teachings of York Harding, and Carson is a follower of Marx. Ironic cases of

the same kind are Javitt with his fantastic doctrines and Rycker with a parody of dogmatic Catholicism.)
3. In some cases the element of idealism is taken so far that the antagonist becomes a sacrificial figure, a man who accepts suffering for the sake of others. (The extreme instance is Calver, a symbolic Christ, but there are also the innocent prisoners, Jim, Fortnum, and Carson, expiating some kind of collective guilt. Jones also, in the end, gives his life for a cause. Carlyon is once or twice represented as a victim of a Judas-like betrayal, and echoes of the same idea can be traced in Hilfe, Pyle, and Lime.)
4. The antagonist's tendency towards some kind of idealism may also be extended into creative fantasy. (In the novels inclined to irony or comedy the antagonist's tendency to idealize or dogmatize over his activities turns into a leaning towards the fantastic. The archetype behind these cases is Don Quixote. The antagonists chiefly concerned are Hasselbacher, Jones, Aunt Augusta, and the Captain.)
5. At the same time, however, the antagonist is one who exists on the "dangerous edge," in that his line of activity is unconventional, usually underhanded, and in a number of cases simply criminal. (Jim and Carson are communists; Carlyon, Yusef, and the Captain are smugglers; Sir Marcus, Lord Benditch, and Mr. Visconti are profiteers; Krogh is guilty of large-scale fraud; Calver is a robber and an outlaw; Lime is a heartless crook; Jones is an illegal arms dealer; Hilfe is an enemy agent; and Pyle apparently works for the CIA.)
6. Despite the personal charm and affability towards the hero, most of the antagonists are very dangerous when crossed or thwarted in their pursuits. (A number of them are killers, not always with their own hands, but frequently as a direct result of their illicit actions or their attempts to keep these actions concealed. The novels are strewn with the corpses of their victims: Rexall, Coney, the minister and his secretary, Hale, Else, Coral Fellows, Jones [the detective] and Major Stone, Ali, the sick children in *TM*, the dead civilians in *QA*, Querry, the dead rebels in *TC*, and Wordsworth.)

Much as Greene's conception of the hero and his role broadened and developed as the author gained experience and evolved new insights, so the antagonist also changed and grew in the succession of Greene's novels. The antagonists of the early work—Carlyon, Jim, Krogh, Sir Marcus, and Lord Benditch—tend to be predominantly either protective or hostile towards the hero, occasionally (like Carlyon and Krogh) shifting from the one attitude to the other as the hero alters his ground. The relationship remains a relatively simple one, with its values largely on the surface. As in the case of the hero's role, however, a great step forward is made in *BR*. The significance of Kite lies hardly at all in what he does, and almost entirely in the effect he has upon the thought and conduct of the hero. This turn to the psychology of the relationship, and proportionally away from its embodiment in overt action, is already implicit in *IB*, where Jim, held throughout in isolation from the events of the story, nonetheless exerts great influence upon them. With *BR* Greene begins to discover ways of developing the metaphorical and symbolic potential of the hero-antagonist relationship.

Whereas in the early novels the business between the hero and antagonist is essentially a tense and highly wrought, but in the end quite simple matter of friendship, obligation, disillusion, betrayal, and perhaps revenge, in *BR* and in most of the subsequent novels what matters much more than whatever may survive of this pattern of action is the symbolic value which the relationship assumes. Thus Kite represents for Pinkie an entire way of life, and the central issue of the novel is how far Pinkie will be able to maintain this in the face of various pressures to abandon it. The issue is not simply material, for Pinkie identifies himself with Kite and assumes Kite's values. Some sort of comparable identification becomes frequent in Greene's subsequent major novels. Sometimes, as with Calver and the Priest, and with Rycker and Querry, the relationship is between the hero and an alter ego; in other cases, as with Fowler and Pyle, Brown and Jones, Plarr and Fortnum, and Castle and Carson, the hero confronts his antagonist as a self-comparison, as one with or against whom his own outlook on life must be measured.

In the late novels the antagonist role develops along two divergent lines. On the one hand, in a number of novels in which irony or comedy takes over from Greene's usual tragic vision, the antagonist tends to become a quixotic figure. In the cases of Hasselbacher, Jones, Augusta, and the Captain the antagonist's usual propensity to idealism becomes fantasy, and the lighter mood of these stories allows him a measure of success in living out his dreams. While the destructive, nihilistic visions of Hilfe and Lime are now turned towards "fun," the element of danger, of evil, in the antagonist is muted. The harm he does is less dramatic, more accidental, or else, like the murder of Wordsworth, simply overlooked in the story's rush towards an ending. On the other hand, in *HC* and *HF*, Greene's two last major novels, another new approach is developed in which the antagonist is largely divested of his negative qualities. He becomes, in Carson and Fortnum, a passive, benignly disposed figure towards whom the hero feels obligation which impels him to action. The danger, the fist in the velvet glove, the threat concealed under the cover of friendship, comes in these two novels from another character altogether, a character who in both cases acts as the jailer of the innocent antagonist.

Despite these developments, however, the antagonist role is well defined and can be traced as a single major strand throughout Greene's longer fiction, from Carlyon to the Captain. (The only full-length novels without the antagonist role are the structurally exceptional cases of *ST*, *EA*, and *MQ*.) The relationship between the hero and the antagonist is the backbone of the plot. Broadly speaking, the hero discovers his moral identity as he approaches and then withdraws from involvement with the antagonist, and it is in the light of this relationship that he takes (if at all) the morally crucial action which precipitates the story's climax. In every case the hero's dealings with his antagonist take him through a process of revaluation to a point of decision. The central issue of every novel in which an antagonist figures can be formulated in terms of the hero's determination as to how far he will allow himself to travel along the road indicated by him, and at what point he will either break free from the antagonist's influence (and probably in some sense betray him) or surrender himself to it unreservedly (and in so doing probably betray some wider public duty).

The role of the antagonist is to offer the hero, or to represent for his consideration. the possibility of a new and different way of life or course of action. The hero's chief business is to decide how far he is prepared to go, if at all, along the lines the antagonist indicates. It remains to look at the moral values involved, and to examine the ways in which this business between the hero and antagonist fits into the pattern of action outlined in Chapter 2. In particular, it remains to see how the antagonist's offer of an alternative view of life relates to the hero's yearning for innocence and his reluctance to face up to morally complex situations. This will be the burden of Chapter 4.

4. Greeneland

Greene's reviewers came to refer to the world delineated in his fiction as "Greeneland," suggesting a uniformity of background and something of an arctic bleakness in the pervasive atmosphere.[54] Greene was understandably irritated by this rather glib punning and its implications, to which he responded sharply:

> Some critics have referred to a strange violent "seedy" region of the mind ... which they call Greeneland, and I have sometimes wondered whether they go round the world blinkered! "This is Indo-China," I want to exclaim, "this is Mexico, this is Sierra Leone carefully and accurately described. I have been a newspaper correspondent as well as a novelist. I assure you that the dead child lay in the ditch in just that attitude. In the canal of Phat Diem the bodies stuck out of the water...." (*WE* 2.4)

The settings of Greene's works, despite a tendency to poeticize occasionally in passages of such early works as *MW*, *IB*, and *BR*, are generally convincingly realistic. It has even been said that one of the factors likely to make Greene a writer of enduring importance is his ability to capture in fiction the distinctive atmospheres of such crucial twentieth-century events as the London Blitz and the Vietnam War.[55] On the other hand, in matters of plot construction Greene is realistic only within clearly marked boundaries, and it is worth pausing here to see how these limits are drawn.

Greene's realism is limited by his frequent and sometimes quite blatant authorial contrivance. The thoughtful reader will be struck by the many coincidences and ironic turns of events upon which the stories rely.[56] Even more obvious, and occasionally intrusive, is Greene's predilection for episodes of uncannily accurate prediction or fortune-telling.[57] Greene's employment of chance and irony, however, are symptomatic of a more fundamental authorial crafting, as he shapes material closely drawn from the modern world into the timeless patterns of romance.

A number of Greene's heroes undertake recognizable "quests" and, Orpheus-like, pursue courses involving confrontation with underworld powers of darkness. Seen in this light, Greeneland becomes the devastated "waste land" of romance which it is the hero's task to restore. In a typical situation the Greene hero is prompted to action by the sufferings of others (imprisonment, persecution, or victimization) in an environment of political violence and physical deprivation. In an effort to alleviate this situation he embarks upon a series of activities, often involving a metaphorical descent into a kind of underworld, a place of darkness and despair, where there is a significant threat of death. Here he undergoes a critical confrontation and perhaps makes a crucial decision as to further action. He rarely emerges unscathed and, in a number of cases, he does not emerge at all but dies. Even so, his effort is not often completely vain, and some benefit to others follows from his adventure.

The journey to the underworld is self-evident in *UG*. In the novels, where it occurs, it is generally subject to a degree of "displacement." The quest pattern is nonetheless clear in *PG*. Here, in a devastated province, the spiritual wasteland from which the church has been banned, the Priest takes on the task of ministering to the suffering inhabitants. He is pursued by enemies who seek his death as he journeys "deeper" into the country and into his own past. He is eventually captured by the forces of evil and shut in a cell, a metaphorical hell where tormented souls are crowded in darkness. He survives this, however, and emerges a new man, with renewed confidence in his priesthood. He is rewarded with the vision of the crosses in the Indian cemetery, and with a period of material comfort from the Lehrs. Now, refreshed and restored, he can complete his mission by absolving

Calver, the "wounded king," the representative of suffering, sinful humanity. It then remains only for him to engage in a debate (which he clearly wins) with the Lieutenant, and to accept martyrdom.

In simply material terms, on the level of narrative realism, the Priest has achieved very little: he dies in a corner while the persecution goes on as before. In terms of the romance archetype, however, of the metaphorical quest, he has achieved everything: he has passed through all the terrors which evil could create to deter him, outfaced his arch enemy, and brought redemption to the archetypal sinner. He has opened the door through which healing may come to the stricken land, and even as he dies the next priest is welcomed.

In *HC* this waste land, the country of imprisoned and oppressed people, is Paraguay. Fortnum is the "wounded king," held hostage against the release of at least some of the Paraguayan victims. Plarr is given the task of helping him and, after a number of false starts, eventually journeys into the depressed and insalubrious region of the "barrio" and there enters the dark hut where, in an inner room with a single guarded door, he finds the wounded Fortnum lying on a coffin. This is again a type of hell. Plarr's eventual agreement to remain there, to make himself voluntarily a prisoner, is the crucial act of the story. Although Plarr does not emerge alive, Fortnum does. Like the Priest, on the literal level Plarr has accomplished little; but symbolically, in terms of the romance archetype, he has taken the place of Fortnum who then becomes free, and the story ends with a token of new life in the anticipated birth of Plarr's son to whom Fortnum will act as father.

Taking a hint from the reference to Orpheus in *MF*, we can find a number of episodes in the novels where the hero penetrates a subterranean or secluded and dangerous place to rescue a heroine who is being held or threatened by the occupants, a demonic pair who preside in this "underworld." Wilditch's confrontation with Javitt and Maria, where he states his claim to "Miss Ramsgate," is a plain case. There is also Pinkie's encounter with Rose's parents, and Raven's rescue of Anne from the bedroom of the house where Acky and Tiny keep guard from behind the stairway.

D's ineffectual attempt to rescue Else from K and the manageress probably belongs here too, as perhaps does Philip's dealing with Mr. and Mrs. Baines over the contentious presence of Emmy in the basement.

The search for romance archetypes can be productively pursued in most of Greene's middle and late novels.[58] This is not the business of the present study, however, which is concerned with more literal levels of character and plot structure. Nonetheless, the interested reader who seeks out the romance archetypes should find it a straightforward matter, where they occur, to map onto them the pattern of action and character that is emerging here. The hero, of course, remains the same figure on both levels of reading. The task or quest he undertakes in the romance pattern is normally to correct or alleviate an evil which arises from the background of conflict on the literal level, the "Greeneland" aspect of the fictional world. The strife-torn settings which Greene preferred for his stories provide the archetypal waste land of the typical quest pattern. Of the female characters, who will be the subject of Chapter 5, some (like Elizabeth, Pinkie's Rose, and Phuong) function as potential brides whom the successful hero may win, while others (like Else, Coral Fellows, Rose Cullen, and Anne Crowder) are more important as "helpers" who simply aid the hero on his way. A few of the women (like Lucy, Kate, and Señora Escobar) can be seen as negative influences, whose purpose is to lure or distract the hero from pursuit of his quest. The most important figure, after the hero, on both levels of reading, is the antagonist. He may be (like Jim Drover, Calver, Fortnum, and Carson) a figure like the wounded king, whom it is the hero's mission to help or heal, and maybe even to succeed; or he may (like Kite, Yusef, and Javitt) be a demonic figure, the lord of an underworld, who attempts to corrupt the hero and prevent his return to the upper regions. Most of the antagonists combine something of each of these roles, although one aspect, either the satanic or that of the suffering king, usually predominates.

The "Greeneland" label suggests that there is in Greene's fiction a uniformity of atmosphere, psychological as well as physical, and that the tenor of this cast of thought is generally depressed, like the unrelieved gloom of an arctic winter. So many of Greene's major, most perceptive characters, it is claimed, move in a world of grim despair, believing that the best they can achieve is some temporary avoidance of the misery which is the inevitable lot of humanity.[59] In almost every case the novels are written against a background of conflict, oppression, or (as in *BC*) disease, and in such a way that the morally crucial decisions which the hero is obliged to take arise from this conflict, from the human problems to which it gives rise.

The conflict situation in Greene's fiction is also responsible for the prominence of imagery relating to borders, a prominence commented upon by many of his critics. The borders are often political boundaries between countries or states, but they may also be rivers or oceans, or even simply partitions, the walls and doors of houses or gardens. Some of the novels, like *HM* and *HC*, are set beside political boundaries. The crossing of such borders may be a turning point, as in *ST* and *TA*, or a new beginning, as in *EM* and *CA*, or even a final exile, as in *TC* and *HF*. A border may also hold out the promise of safety, as in *PG*, or of adventure, as in *CE*. Domestic boundaries can play comparable parts, as do the garden wall and the green baize door in *MF*. There are also, on the other hand, some novels in which border imagery finds little or no place, as in *BR* and *IB*.

In earlier novels, such as *ST* and *CA*, borders function primarily as elements of plot, contributing to John Buchan–like adventures in a manner that has become the stock in trade of spy novelists. Already in *EM*, however, the boundary between Anthony's provincial but cheerful England and the sinister internationalism of Krogh has a symbolic significance, to which the title draws attention. In *PG* the border which the Priest is constantly seeking to cross provides not only a framework for the story but also a powerful image; and with Scobie in *HM* we reach the first of a line of heroes whose geographical position on a "dangerous edge" is a carefully crafted embodiment of their moral and spiritual situation.

By the time of the middle novels the border has ceased to be simply part of the mechanism of an adventure story plot, as it largely remains in *ST* and *CA*, and has become an image relating to the hero's situation, poised on a moral edge, in a kind of no man's land between two incompatible states. The physical border is often used, in the middle and later novels, to embody what Greene called, in a phrase borrowed from Browning, the "dangerous edge of things." The passage from which this phrase is taken, Greene says, might serve as an epigraph for all of his novels:

> Our interest's in the dangerous edge of things.
> The honest thief, the tender murderer,
> The superstitious atheist, demi-rep
> That loves and saves her soul in new French books—
> We watch while these in equilibrium keep
> The giddy line midway.[60]

The "edge" is the moral position occupied by most of Greene's heroes, men attempting to find a safe "line midway" between conflicting codes or duties. Thus Andrews hesitates between personal obligation to Carlyon and revulsion against the life and actions of the smugglers; Scobie tries to maintain his integrity as a police officer in the face of demands for active sympathy which he can meet only by compromising dealings with Yusef; the Priest is caught between church and state, between the ministry which is his vocation and the revolutionary ethos which forbids him to exercise it. The crucial problem facing virtually every one of the heroes can be formulated in this way, in terms of an irresolvable moral tension which, on the one hand, typically arises from the background situation of conflict and, on the other, is often embodied in imagery depicting a border or boundary between two incompatible conditions, be they warring nations or opposed points of view.

In moral terms the border is likely to represent the "dangerous edge" along or beside which the hero attempts to maintain an equilibrium between the different sets of conditions on either side. So many of Greene's heroes begin in this way, in a state of poised inactivity, living close to a critical boundary or else simply in neutral territory, thinly separated from the field of conflict. Such is Czinner, living as a schoolmaster in England; Scobie in Liberia, immersed in his work, before he yields to the demands of Louise and Helen; Fowler before Pyle's arrival, a spectator of a war in which he is not involved; Plarr watching for his father's return from the other side of the river dividing Paraguay from Argentina; Castle observing African affairs from his London office. From this point of view, the eventual crossing of a border involves entering an area in which the equilibrium of passivity is no longer possible, a place where the hitherto latent tensions and contradictions of his position become manifest and demand resolution. Thus Czinner precipitates the crisis in *ST* by crossing the border at Subotica; Anthony finds himself forced into a moral decision when he leaves his native England and enlists with Krogh in Sweden; D's problems begin, as the story opens, with his entry into England; Rowe abandons blissful ignorance and plunges into deliberate action when he penetrates the sickbay; the Priest faces his fate by returning across the border at the end of *PG*; and Brown is acting similarly in returning from the safety of America to Haiti at the beginning of *TC*.

In several of the stories, however, it is not the hero who crosses the border but others who come over, bringing the conflict to him. Scobie's compromises with Yusef and the Portuguese captain remain merely symptomatic of contradiction between public duty and personal sympathy, until Helen comes to him from across the river, precipitating an insoluble dilemma. Plarr is secure, living an unproductive and self-indulgent life while his father (so far as he knows) is a political prisoner, until Leon and his companions come from over the frontier to invoke Plarr's aid. Castle is securely under cover until Muller arrives from South Africa with a preposterous plan which forces Castle to show his hand.

Again, the crossing may be from conflict to security. This occurs at the end of *OM* and *TC*, where the hero leaves the embattled zone for another country where he will be relatively safe and quiet. It must be added, however, that this kind of safety, one which may be attained by staying on the quieter side of the critical boundary, is not highly valued in Greene's world. Brown's settlement in the Dominican Republic is an exile involving not only acceptance of a rather lugubrious way of life but also loss of his property and his mistress. Wormold, at the end of *OM*, keeps his mistress, but his removal from colorful Cuba to drab London, and again into a ludicrous job, certainly involves some loss and creates a somber mood. The crucial case here, however, is that of the Priest, who having reached safety decides finally to re-cross the frontier back into the conflict zone.

Greeneland is therefore a world of conflicts and, more significantly, of the moral contradictions and dilemmas which the conflicts create and reflect. It is also a world divided by borders, by literal frontiers the crossing of which usually entails confrontation with the consequences of some hitherto latent ambiguity. The option of remaining safely behind such a border, of avoiding the crucial crossing, exists in principle, but means denial of human obligation and is not open to the hero.

The conflict which underlies the action of Greene's fiction represents an irreducible moral complexity confronting the hero. The hero himself, as we have seen in Chapter 2, frequently longs for a condition of moral simplicity, one such as that of Rowe's remembered childhood, in which the distinction between good and evil is invariably clear, and the proper course of action unambiguously apparent. The actual moral situations faced by Greene's heroes, however, are very different. They are irresolvable in that they present no clear path, no way forward which will not involve good mixed with harm. They are irreducible in that it is beyond human powers to find a solution which will end the conflict or otherwise avoid the moral problem. And the option of mere passivity or noninvolvement, although perhaps theoretically available, is morally untenable and generally open only to dubious or second-rate characters.

It is sometimes suggested that the universe of Greene's fiction is fundamentally dualistic, a conflict of distinct forces of good and evil.[61] This conclusion is often based upon Greene's own remarks about his discovery of evil in human nature from his early reading of Marjorie Bowen's *Viper of Milan*, or of Henry James, whom he credits with belief in "supernatural evil."[62] Whatever Greene may have implied in such remarks, his novels do not reflect a dualistic view of the moral world. On the contrary, the simple dualistic view, in which good is regarded as practically separable from evil, is precisely the naive and stultifying picture which Greene's heroes have to reject. Greene's universe, the moral reality which has to be faced in his novels, is one in which good and evil are not separable, and where there are no obviously right answers to moral problems.[63]

The complexity of moral issues in Greene's fiction is well illustrated by *PG*. A superficial glance at the story might lead one to expect here a tale of a good priest and an evil police officer, of a good church persecuted by an evil political system. This view, of course, dissolves as soon as we read the book. The church, as in *HC*, turns out to be kindly in theory but materialistic and ineffectual in practice. The priesthood in the old pre-revolutionary days, exemplified in the hero's own former self, was more concerned with parish accounts than the salvation of souls. Come the revolution and the hierarchy flees to safety across the border, abandoning the poor and a few lowly priests. The state cares for the welfare of the people, but it deals with collectives and practices great cruelty against individuals. The Lieutenant is the agent of the state's oppression, hostile to the church and brutal towards its supporters. Yet he is also responsible for the two most conspicuous acts of pure charity in the story, giving money to the Priest as he leaves prison, and trying, in disregard of law and his own beliefs, to find a confessor for the condemned man; and he is called a "good man" by his opponent (2.3.3 and 3.4). The Priest himself certainly progresses, but he has been a weak man, neglectful and despairing. His goodness, like Pinkie's and Scobie's, grows out of his weakness—beauty coming from ugliness, as in Javitt's account of evolution. His alter ego is Calver, a common criminal, and in the climactic scene of the story, in a clear reference to the Crucifixion, the condemned Priest offers salvation to the dying thief. Evil is real, but not independently real; it is an inescapable part of the human condition; it cannot be put aside, but may, in the end, be transcended.

Another clear illustration is the plight of Andrews. He is bound to Carlyon by a debt of personal gratitude, as well as by respect for Carlyon's leadership and sympathy with his values. He owes loyalty, more grudgingly, to the smugglers, of whose band he has been a member. On the other hand, Carlyon's actions are both dangerous and illegal, and Andrews has not been treated kindly by other members of the crew. Their life of crime and violence is distasteful to Andrews. He betrays them to the law, but his motives are mixed, as much a matter of personal resentment and frustration as of conscience and public duty. Moreover, the outcome is indecisive. An officer is killed, and Carlyon and several of the smugglers escape. Andrews has to decide again, between making good his own escape or giving evidence against his captured shipmates. He has more or less decided to escape when his meeting with Elizabeth gives a new dimension to the question. He goes to Lewes and gives his evidence, but whether this counts as an act for Elizabeth or for Lucy never becomes clear. Again the outcome is indecisive, since the smugglers are acquitted and then re-arrested on another charge.

None of Andrews's decisions is a clear matter of right or wrong. He lives in the real, complex world, not in the simple world of Rowe's dreams of childhood or the Captain's adventure stories. It is simply not possible, at most points, to say categorically that this or that would be the right course for the hero to adopt. The initial situation, Andrews's life with the smugglers, is not tolerable, but as soon as the hero moves to end or alter it he finds that he has created a new set of no less pressing problems.

Very often in Greeneland there is simply no right course of action for the conscientious man. The law forbids the Priest to pursue his calling, but the church teaches that souls may suffer if he neglects his ministry. Yet because he is a "whisky priest," a notoriously weak man, his example may do more harm than good; and then the soldiers begin shooting men from the villages where the Priest has stayed. In a rather similar way Scobie cannot ignore the plight of others. To find the means to help them (the Portuguese captain, Louise, Helen) he compromises his integrity, and then finds himself drawn into an illicit affair. Whatever he does thereafter will hurt one of his women, if not both; and the problem of Communion adds another dimension to the issue, effectively closing the theoretical option of continual concealment.

In the generally simpler worlds of the "entertainments" the moral dilemmas confronting the heroes remain largely on the level of personal loyalties. Raven has committed a crime which, it turns out, betrays the interests of his own class. He is in turn betrayed by his employers, upon whom he then seeks vengeance. The option of giving himself up to the law is open to Raven, but to do so would leave unresolved the matter of the conspiracy and the threat of war. In pursuing his vengeance, however, Raven brings Anne into danger, and his final act, however just, is still another murder. *CA* is similar, with D caught between the two sides in his country's civil war and driven into a situation where he opposes the material interests not only of Rose's father but also of the unemployed miners. To do nothing would permit an unpleasant enemy to gain a significant advantage, but the only course of action he can take to prevent this involves him in murder and sabotage. In *TM* Martins is repelled by Lime's actions and their consequences, but he still feels that, in assisting the police, he has betrayed a friend.

In most of the later novels the hero's dilemma is quite plain. He has the option of remaining an uninvolved spectator, but if he does so an evil, which it may be in his power to end or to mitigate, will continue with disastrous effects. Pyle will continue to organize terrorist attacks, Papa Doc will face no effective opposition in Haiti, the Paraguayan government will continue to hold its political prisoners, and Muller will win backing for "Uncle Remus." By taking action, however, the hero not only compromises his principles and incurs personal risks, but he also imperils innocent bystanders or betrays a friend. (Fowler betrays Pyle, Brown leads Jones to his death, Henry Pulling becomes involved in criminal activities which include the murder of Wordsworth, Plarr causes the capture of Fortnum, and Castle's activities as a Russian agent lead to the killing of Davis.) To remain inactive is to sink to the level of purely self-involved characters, like Plarr's mother or Castle's mother; but action usually entails breach of some trust or law, and may well put other lives at risk.

The world of Greene's fiction is not a Manichean or dualistic world, in which good and evil are independent, separable, transcendent forces, but a world in which good and evil are inextricably bound together in the moral nexus of human action. This is true as regards the world in which the hero operates, but there are nonetheless other characters in the novels who are (more or less) purely good or evil. Such characters achieve their moral status, however, by self-limitation: they are secondary figures in the action, and persons of clearly limited vision.

The purely "good" characters are found usually among the heroines, of whom more will be said in Chapter 5. Such, for example, are Elizabeth, Else, Pinkie's Rose, Sarah Castle, and perhaps Coral Musker and Coral Fellows. They achieve and maintain their goodness, however, in one or both of two ways: by a degree of naivety or simple ignorance, which prevents them from seeing the whole situation which the hero has to confront, or by the mere fact of passivity, of being removed from any situation in which morally crucial decisions are required of them. Even Pinkie's Rose, probably the strongest and most fully drawn of Greene's purely good characters, is kept on the sidelines of the action. By the end she does seem to have a reasonably comprehensive general idea of what Pinkie is up to, although just how much she really understands of this is kept deliberately unclear. Her role remains subordinate, her task being to exert a general personal influence from a position following Pinkie's lead. She offers comments, and in the end begins to dig her heels in and resist his suggestions, but she never initiates action or suggests to him any realistic alternative courses.

The more or less purely evil characters are those who might be called the "villains." There are surprisingly few of them, and a number of the novels are wholly free of them. The group clearly includes Muller, Concasseur, and Hartep, and probably Davis in *GS* and L in *CA*. They are men of very limited vision, who do not see, or will not take account of, the moral implications of their actions. There is no point in including here minor agents of mindless prejudice, such as the smuggler Joe, Poole, or Captain Van Donck—men who act only under the direction of others.

The actual moral complexity of the human situation is not only a fact in Greene's fiction but a fact which must be faced, and the facing of it, the issue of involvement, becomes his central subject. Indeed, in a world where perhaps every other need or duty the hero feels is balanced by a contrary impulse or negative effect, the one constant imperative is that the complexity of reality must be taken into account. Characters who somehow avoid this recognition are seen to be, for that reason, correspondingly limited. The task of facing up to the moral complexity of the world falls squarely upon the shoulders of the hero, who sometimes receives support in this from a heroine. Most of the secondary characters (those other than the heroes and their female partners) can be grouped broadly in terms of their various strategies for avoiding complex reality, or dealing with it in terms of false and ultimately untenable simplifications.

First, there is the group of relatively minor figures who, whether by their good fortune or simply by a resolute refusal to look out at the world about them, contrive to cushion themselves from reality and live in calm comfort. The Lehrs in *PG* are probably the best example. Miss Lehr's horror of newspapers is symptomatic of her mental isolation (3.1). The mothers, Mrs. Castle and Mrs. Plarr, form a pair of much the same kind, each living securely the sheltered life she has chosen, in which there is no comprehension of the problems her son is facing. In the early novels Myatt is a similar case, sheltered by his wealth from the hardships which affect others, and able to shroud his mind in matters of business, the trivial business of currants, and to forget such matters as Coral's disappearance. Captain Fellows and Mr. Surrogate probably belong here too. These people can, if directly appealed to, be protective and helpful in the short term; but they lack real sympathy with the sufferers and have no understanding of the ills inherent in ordinary life outside their own enclosed spheres. Consequently they exercise little or no lasting influence on events.

Second, there is the group who may be said to face reality, but who deal with its problems in terms of a predetermined dogmatic framework. The dogmas or ideologies invoked in the course of Greene's fiction include communism and Catholicism, Tolstoyan mysticism, and vegetarianism. The exponents of these doctrines may be personally amiable, and even, like the Smiths, sincerely inclined to be helpful, but in the end their humanity is limited, and in some cases perverted, by their adherence to rigidly dogmatic principles. At their most sympathetic such characters become mildly comic, but the less humane examples, like the

Lieutenant in *PG*, can be at times hard to distinguish from mere villains. In this group belong the Smiths from *TC*, with their liberalism based upon vegetarian principles—all very well, but obviously absurd in the context of Haiti under Papa Doc. They are friendly, and even momentarily "heroic," but they give up and go away halfway through the action. The problems of Haiti are simply incalculable in the terms of their very limited theoretical framework. Forrester in *MF* is an idealist of a more harmful kind. His Tolstoyan beliefs not only alienate him from the British war effort but make him easy prey for Hilfe's "ministry of fear." One might also include here Ida, with her firm but not very penetrating notion of "right and wrong."

Greene is well known for his treatment of Catholicism and communism in his novels, and a number of the characters who make up this group subscribe to one or other of these doctrines. Not all Greene's Catholics and communists belong in this category, but only those who hold their beliefs dogmatically. We would *not* place here Carson, Monsignor Quixote, or the priest who speaks with Rose at the end of *BR*. The Lieutenant in *PG* is an obvious case, a man of humane impulses who nevertheless allows his belief in revolutionary socialism to excuse acts of injustice and brutality. Some of the less sympathetic priests also belong here, men like Father Crompton (*EA*), Father Thomas (*BC*), and perhaps Father Rank (*HM*), men who tend to resort to dogma rather than face up to the complexity of life's problems.

A dogma, doctrine, or ideology may embody fine and noble principles and propose admirable goals, but Greene has no time for it once it is turned into an excuse for inhumanity or a barrier behind which intellectual timidity takes shelter from inconvenient problems. To make this point is the chief purpose of *MQ*, a story which involves a sustained satirical attack on the two most nearly global ideologies of the twentieth century. As in some of the major novels, Catholicism is here treated quite harshly, while communism shows at times a more human face. Against the more repellent official doctrines of communism and a sprinkling of the more absurd, less widely known ruminations of Marx, Greene presents the good-natured pragmatism of Sancho. Against the dogmatic aspects of Catholicism—ably represented by the local bishop, Father Herrera, the Opus Dei, and the writings of Heribert Jone—we are given the delightful Monsignor. The two men at first appear as representatives of opposing ideologies, but what they come to stand for, as their relationship unfolds, are humane and highly unorthodox interpretations of their respective doctrines. And what they discover, in the course of their travels, is their common fundamental humanity. *MQ* is above all anti-dogmatic, a satiric attack on those who put ideology of any kind above humanity and so ignore the real complexity of the human situation.[64]

The antagonists, whom we have already brought together in Chapter 3, form another character group, some of whose members may appear to belong among the dogmatists. The antagonists may indeed be men of ideals and may even subscribe nominally to particular doctrines, but it is fundamental to their nature and role in Greene's fictional patterns that no set of rules or principles can govern or confine their exuberant, unretrainable energy. Carlyon preaches chivalry, but he is responsible for murder and brutality. Pyle's activities go far beyond whatever may have been advocated in the respectably published pages of York Harding. Carson's communism does not prevent his aiding a British agent. Typically the antagonist follows idiosyncratic and unconventional courses. Like Krogh or Yusef, he sets himself above the law and beyond moral restrictions, pursuing his own goals and propagating a limited, private code of values among a small inner circle—Kite's gang, Pyle's "third force," Krogh's personal supporters (Hall and Kate), Hilfe's fellow agents, Leon's band of terrorists. From the public point of view their conduct, when exposed, usually appears immoral or criminal, and is only counterbalanced, for the reader, by a degree of personal charm and the attraction of the creative energy which the character often displays.

The essential role of the antagonist is to offer the hero a radical solution to the problematic complexity of his situation. The antagonist suggests or exemplifies a course of action which promises the hero a way out of his difficulties. The offer is attractive, usually because it appears to guarantee security and a prospect of easily won material rewards. The personal charm or affability of its advocate is frequently a factor in the attraction. On the other hand, the course of action proposed is unconventional, usually disreputable, and not without its own risks. It is not infrequently criminal and tends to disregard the welfare, and even the lives, of others. In short, the alternative course of action represented by the antagonist consists in a refusal to recognize the moral constraints within which problems arise. Inevitably, therefore, the hero rarely finds any long-term solution by taking the antagonist's path. Usually there is a reaction. Either the hero himself sees the unacceptability of the course he is following, or else it leads him into deeper waters and often to an untimely end. Only in the comedies, *OM* and *TA*, is the antagonist's line of action allowed a measure of vindication or success.

Often, as with Carlyon, Krogh, Benditch, Kite, and Yusef, what the antagonist offers is simply criminal. It may solve the hero's immediate problems, but only at the cost of loss of integrity and of increasing social isolation. Other cases may be more complex but still follow the same basic moral pattern. In *IB*, for instance, Jim's solution to the social and economic ills of the "battlefield" situation is riot and violence. He may not have intended harm, but he causes it nonetheless. Conrad tries to follow Jim, to take his place. He too turns to violence and attacks a supposed upholder of the oppressive social order. The gesture is ineffective and Conrad dies. In *QA* Fowler is watching a destructive war with increasing disgust. Pyle arrives with an idea for a solution, but this involves terrorism and an intensification of the slaughter. In the end Fowler adopts Pyle's methods but turns them against Pyle himself. Fowler achieves his immediate object, the stopping of Pyle, but at the cost of dirtying his hands and betraying the man who had saved his life. *TM* is very similar in this respect to *QA*. In *HF* Castle's problem lies in South Africa and involves his love for Sarah. To achieve marriage and safety with Sarah he turns to Carson. Carson provides a solution, but in accepting Carson's help Castle incurs a debt and becomes Carson's fellow agent in the communist spy network. Years later the debt is called in, and Castle, accepting the obligation, becomes from the British point of view a criminal traitor.

The most complex cases are *PG* and *HC*, where the antagonist's role is played on a level of some metaphorical abstraction. The

Priest does not follow Calver in taking to robbery or murder, but he does, like Calver, elect to become an outlaw, living as a hunted fugitive pursued by the Lieutenant. Just as Calver seems to have been indirectly responsible for the deaths of Coral and the Indian baby, so the Priest is responsible for that of Montez. Although the Priest is never seeking *only* his own safety, as Calver presumably is, there is a sense in which his flight, the merely fugitive aspect of his life in the story, is wrong. When he recognizes this at the end, by turning back just as safety is reached, he goes back to face Calver, who is dying. Calver's dying causes the Priest to turn back, but at the same time the Priest's turning back, abandoning the role of a fugitive, is the metaphorical correlative of Calver's death. The fugitive (Calver) dies when the Priest (the fugitive) ends his flight from pursuit. Seen in this way, *PG* is another story in which the hero adopts the antagonist's course, follows it a fair way, but in the end rejects it, with the usual fatal outcome.

In *HC* we have an odd case of virtual inversion, as the antagonist's course is innocuous and perhaps even the right one to follow. The initial problems here focus upon the oppression of the poor, particularly of Clara's people and Leon's men. Fortnum, the antagonist, offers no solution—indeed, he remains generally passive—but he becomes unwillingly part of Leon's solution when he is made a hostage. Plarr, initially a detached observer, follows Fortnum's lead, first in becoming involved with Clara and then in taking his place beside Fortnum as a fellow hostage in the hut. Terrorism and armed revolt, however, here as in *QA* and *TC*, are two-edged weapons, and hostage taking does not in the end achieve any real solutions. Plarr himself does not survive, but what does emerge positively from the closing pages is Fortnum's care for Clara and the hope which this offers for the next generation.

The world of Greene's fiction, then, is one of importunate complexity. The task of confronting the moral tangle falls (of course) upon the hero, who is usually reluctant and, indeed, in several of late novels goes to extreme lengths to avoid this necessity. In the end, however, for whatever reasons, the hero cannot leave the world to go on as it is but is obliged to interfere. His course of action when he does so is invariably that laid down by the antagonist, whom the hero may follow as a leader or adopt as a model. The antagonist's course, however, involves some dodge or illegitimacy, some shortcut to an easy solution, and fails to face up to the complexity of the problem at issue, or refuses to accept the moral constraints within which the problems arise. The antagonist is therefore, along with the hero, a key figure in the dynamics of Greene's fiction, and it remains to look more closely at his principles of action.

The chief theoretical exponent of the antagonist's position is Javitt. While the others of the type simply go about their business, Javitt is a kind of philosopher who has abstracted the general principles behind his role. He is, besides, a teacher, and treats the impressionable Wilditch to a short course on the essential principles of "antagonism." This he does not in any systematic way, which would be contrary to the anarchic spirit of his message, but in a highly erratic and metaphorical series of disjointed precepts and allusions. Javitt's lessons to Wilditch provide the best starting point for a general appreciation of the antagonist's role.

At the center of Javitt's philosophy is a kind of parody of Darwinism.[65] In particular, he develops a notion of the "rogue" factor in the evolutionary chain, a factor which he uses as an explanation, and even a justification, for the vital and attractive but ultimately deviant ways of the typical antagonist. Evolution, according to Javitt, is a process of aesthetic and, by implication, moral degeneration. "Beauty diminishes all the time," he says; "it is the law of diminishing returns." The remedy comes about through the "rogue" factor, a kind of inverted natural selection whereby oddities and deformities are gradually intensified until a "zero" point is reached, a critical point from which a new beauty may be born. Javitt and Maria apparently represent such a "zero" point, the result of "generations of rogues," and the new beauty is embodied in their daughter, "Miss Ramsgate" (2.4).

Javitt's position is moral inversion of the kind of orthodox Christian Darwinism propounded by Doctor Colin: "All the same through trial and error the amoeba did become the ape. There were blind starts and wrong turnings even then, I suppose.... I think of Christ as an amoeba who took the right turning" (*BC* 5.1). Colin is a morally straightforward character who accepts the usual framework of human values and sees evolution as progressively "upwards" towards the higher forms. Javitt, arguing from the antagonist's essentially unorthodox position, sees evolution in terms of Colin's "wrong turnings." It is also significant that while Colin talks in moral terms, Javitt is thinking is terms primarily aesthetic. The antagonists in the novels exemplify Javitt's view in that they seek an attractive (rather than simply "good") end by means of odd, unconventional, and often illicit behavior. They do not set themselves to further the moral advance of humanity, but rather, by deliberate deviancy, seek a kind of "zero" point in the hope that something fine will emerge.

Javitt elaborates his point in a paragraph often quoted in commentaries on Greene.[66] This is a crucial passage which, expressive of the moral independence and idiosyncrasy of the antagonist's position, also encapsulates the quality in the antagonist which commands a kind of admiration.

> "Be disloyal. It's your duty to the human race. The human race needs to survive and it's the loyal man who dies first from anxiety or a bullet or overwork. If you have to earn a living, boy, and the price they make you pay is loyalty, be a double agent—and never let either of the two sides know your real name. The same applies to women and God. They both respect a man they don't own, and they'll go on raising the price they are willing to offer. Didn't Christ say that very thing? Was the prodigal son loyal or the lost shilling or the strayed sheep? The obedient flock didn't give the shepherd any satisfaction or the loyal son interest his father." (2.5)

Here, in deliberately provocative terms, is the justification for the spirit of independence, even of selfishness, which directs Jim to defy the law, Krogh to build his empire in defiance of both unions and governments, and Pyle to accept whatever allegiance offers itself to gain mastery of the field. Many of the antagonists are "double agents" in the sense that they profit from operating in situations of conflict but without commitment to either side; and hence the fact that several of them are profiteers or smugglers. It is just this refusal to be bound by ties, laws, or moral constraints that gives the antagonist his special powers, which he then uses to entice the distracted hero.

Javitt presents his philosophy of disloyalty with another glance at Darwinism. Whereas the generally accepted Darwinian picture would represent the human capacity for cooperation, for social cohesion, as a positive factor in the development of the species, Javitt takes a radically different view. The socially oriented man, the "loyal" man, is weak and less likely to survive. It is, again, the "rogue" factor of disloyalty which ensures the survival of the species by promoting the advantages of individuals.

The several Biblical references in Javitt's lesson take us a step further. The loyal man is of less value than the "lost sheep" or reclaimed sinner. The man who is constantly loyal, it is suggested, is of less "interest" because he is wholly predictable and can therefore be taken for granted. The point may be related to the doctrine of "souls" and of the "private life" outlined by Jones in *DF*. The loyal man commits himself in advance, while the disloyal withholds commitment and makes his decisions as events unfold. It is perhaps this capacity for continuing self-determination which constitutes a "private life" and so gives rise to a true "soul." The same argument relates also to the idea of the necessity for doubt, expounded by the Monsignor in *MQ*. The man of unshakeable faith is simply a special case of the loyal man, one whose allegiance may be counted upon and whose position in this respect is fixed by a prior commitment. Just as the loyal man is less "interesting" than the unpredictable, potentially fickle, so the doggedly faithful man becomes spiritually inert. Faith, like human relations, needs continuous reaffirmation, and this can occur only where there is also the real possibility of infidelity, of loss of faith or change of loyalties (*MQ* 1.4.2; 1.5.1; and 2.2.2.).

Underlying these arguments is the simple point that the exercise of any virtue depends in practice upon the real possibility of an alternative course. In a context in which everyone is invariably loyal and has nothing to gain by being otherwise, it is no special virtue in me to show loyalty. Loyalty becomes a virtue only among those who are, and who may be expected to be, occasionally disloyal. The same is true of faith. Faith would have no value—indeed, no meaning at all—in a world where the truths in question were so plainly and completely revealed that no sane person could doubt or be unaware of them. This is the Monsignor's nightmare. Faith depends upon the real possibility of doubt.

The antagonist's quality of "disloyalty," and more generally his pursuit of unpredictable and unconventional courses, are the root of his attraction in a dull Greeneland world. They are also the reason why, despite his often criminal tendencies and the serious harm he may do, the antagonist in the major novels is never merely a "villain" (although he is sometimes little more in the "entertainments"). The antagonist's disloyalty, his independence from conventional restraints, represents a vital human quality: the capacity for innovative action and the willingness to strive for personal goals. These very positive qualities distinguish the antagonists on the one hand from the initially inert heroes (such as Fowler, Conrad, and Plarr, men who have been cowed by the problems of life into submissive withdrawal), and on the other from the numerous minor characters who find shelter from the vicissitudes of life behind dogma or complacency.

Although the antagonist usually embodies the virtues of purposive action and self-determination, what he offers is not, in the end, satisfactory. In almost every novel the course of action taken by the antagonist leads the hero into serious trouble, not infrequently to death. And the landscapes are littered with innocent victims, from Rexall, Elizabeth, and Coney, to Wordsworth, Joseph, and Davis. The point is clear even in *UG*, although Javitt's remarks are sometimes taken out of context as expressing Greene's personal code, or ideas which have the author's unreserved endorsement. Javitt is, after all, himself an antagonist and therefore pleading his own cause. The effect of his teachings upon Wilditch, the central character of the story, is far from beneficial. The reader must treat Javitt with some scepticism.

The older Wilditch is evidently a man who has, in the course of his life, taken Javitt's teachings to heart. "If it had not been for his dreams of the tunnel and the bearded man and the hidden treasure, couldn't he have made a less restless life for himself? . . . [H]e had never taken his various professions seriously: he had been loyal to no one—not even to the girl in Africa (Javitt would have approved his disloyalty)" (3.2). He has lived as a wanderer, driven by his vow to find "Miss Ramsgate" in the upper world (2.5). It is clear that Wilditch's life has been neither happy nor particularly successful. He now has no further desire to live (1.2), and his own brother sees him as "unhappy" (1.3). Wilditch feels now that "his whole life had been wasted" (3.2). There is no evidence in all of this that Javitt's influence, for all its promise and impressive vitality, has been at all beneficial. At the end of the story, as Wilditch sits on the island by the spot where he supposedly found the tunnel years before, he experiences a revival of the feelings he had on that occasion. But the "curiosity" which now grows in him once again is compared to the "cancer" which threatens his life (3.3). Javitt's influence upon Wilditch turns out, in its way, to have been as negative as Kite's on Pinkie or Yusef's on Scobie.

For all his vitality and charm, the antagonist is like the dogmatists and other characters of limited vision in that he fails to face up to the moral complexity of his world. He does indeed, unlike the Lehrs and self-centered figures such as Mrs. Castle, involve himself in a wide field of action, and unlike the Lieutenant and Father Crompton he is not bound in his actions by any predetermined code or doctrine. Even so, mere dynamism and lack of constraint still fall short of an adequate response to moral problems, which the antagonists characteristically bypass, usually by means of deception, bravado, or plain brute force. The antagonist does not untie the moral knot, but simply slices through it.

In other words, the antagonist aims at a radical simplification of the issues he confronts. This he achieves, typically, by a disregard of crucial aspects of the situation—perhaps a failure to look to the longer term, or a ready willingness to subject arbitrarily the interests of some parties to those of others. In the few cases where the antagonist is largely innocuous and genuinely benevolent, as with Jim and Fortnum, he becomes something of a naive innocent and himself one of the story's victims. In the comic antagonists (Hasselbacher, Jones, and Augusta) simplification of reality becomes creative, a deliberate reduction of life to the level of adventure story. The delusions of these more overtly quixotic antagonists remain ultimately sympathetic, but they are illusions nonetheless.

The negative aspect of the antagonist is often represented in imagery of childhood and by suggestions of relative immaturity. His wilful determination to have his own way regardless of prohibitions and consequences is seen as a childlike trait, reflecting the character's inability to operate successfully within the rules and constraints of the adult world. Obvious cases are Pyle, with his youthful naivety and his air of being "a hero in a boy's adventure-story" (*QA* 2.2.4). In a similar way, Lime has "never grown up" (*TM* 14). Martins's comment about Lime, that "evil was like Peter Pan—it carried with it the horrifying and horrible gift of eternal youth" (*TM* 14), reminds us inevitably of Pinkie, the focal image in Greene's depiction of arrested development. Pinkie fights long and viciously to preserve his adolescent status and to maintain his freedom from the restrictions of adult situations such as marriage, parenthood, and moral responsibility.

It is not only the boys among the antagonists who betray immaturity. The Captain, with his view of life modeled on stories of adventure and escapes, pirates and treasure, is another such case despite his age. He does indeed show a kind of love for Liza and accepts responsibility for her welfare, but his way of showing his love and carrying out this responsibility, involving long absences in pursuit of fantastical and generally criminal projects, is not a very realistic response to the demands of the situation. Seeing himself as a kind of Francis Drake or Robin Hood, the Captain lives in a dream, free from the domestic and economic drudgery which is, for most of us, the daily round. He appears to send Liza funds just sufficient for her support, but in the end he allows his household to disintegrate. Baxter inherits his stepfather's taste for adventure and personal freedom, and soon abandons Liza to pursue his own life, leaving her to die poor and alone during the Captain's prolonged absence in Panama. The Captain may be likeable and well intentioned, but he remains a limited character whose effect upon the lives of others is not generally beneficial.

Krogh is basically similar. Although he clearly has abilities as an engineer and financier, he remains evidently immature in personal dealings with others. This is reflected in his reliance on Kate and in the readiness with which he accepts the more extrovert Anthony as his protector and guide. Krogh is led like a child, for a time, by Anthony and Kate—to Tivoli, for instance, and to the dinner at Saltsjöbaden—until the arrival of Hall. Krogh is amiable until he is crossed, but when difficulties arise his solutions are deception and violence. For all the opulence and urbanity of his environment, he is not essentially different from Pinkie, living by lies and brutality. Hall is only a better-dressed version of Cubitt and Dallow. When his schemes are threatened, like Pinkie, Krogh responds with force and does not hesitate to kill.

This is also reminiscent of Jim, normally powerful and protective but nonetheless capable of murder. Jim's aura of personal strength and power, combined with a childlike willingness to be led, results in an act of violence not really intended. Krogh gets away with his killing, while Jim is shut in a cell.

A number of the antagonists who are themselves of mature age are remarkable for their selection of children or immature young men to play Horatio, to be companions and recipients of confidence. The implication is clearly that the outlook on life which the antagonist accepts and wishes to confide may be acceptable to a child of as yet unformed intelligence, but would probably be rejected by an adult. Once again *UG* offers a clear case, with its sharp distinction between the seven-year-old Wilditch who was once impressed by Javitt, and the adult, many years on, who is not even sure whether the experience was real, dreamed, or imagined.

The story of *UG* tells of the hero's return to a childhood scene, where he systematically recalls the crucial "memory" and revisits the very spot of its supposed occurrence. The memory involves an introductory passage through a narrow tunnel into a subterranean enclosure, an image suggesting return to the womb. There Wilditch found Javitt, whom he accepted as a surrogate father; and his eventual return to the surface, back through the narrow opening, is suggestive of a rebirth. In the interim Wilditch was for a few days Javitt's pupil, and it is clear that the capacity to learn from Javitt depends upon the seven-year-old hero's boyish receptivity. The adult Wilditch finds the tunnel closed, and he remembers that his original account of the adventure was disapprovingly censured by his mother. The vision gained in Javitt's underworld does not translate into adult reality.

Very similar, but in a more realistic mode, is the way in which Baines, who also lives in a "basement room" with a fearsome wife, makes a confidant of Philip, another seven-year-old boy. The pattern, in which the adult antagonist deliberately selects a younger, potentially impressionable person to be his companion and, in a sense, his pupil, echoes throughout Greene's fiction, from the earliest to the last. Carlyon takes Andrews from school and makes him a friend and associate. Jim Drover is protector of his younger brother. Kite adopts the boy Pinkie. Krogh accepts the fatherless Anthony as an employee and companion. Lime befriends the not much younger but less worldly-wise Martins in their schooldays. Aunt Augusta takes her younger "nephew" along on her travels, and in this special case the image of the parent introducing a child into the adult world turns out to be the story's literal truth. The Captain takes young Baxter from school and educates him as an adopted child.

Even when the hero is not literally a child the antagonist frequently behaves towards him as if he were. Mr. Visconti tells Henry that he feels "very like a father" to him, and on the next page Augusta, who has just announced her impending marriage to Visconti, makes Henry feel "like a child pretending interest in a story to delay bedtime" (2.7). Augusta has, indeed, treated the middle-aged Henry throughout as if he were a child and subject to her direction, and now, at the end, he is recognized as her son and as the heir to the family business. Rather similarly Scobie, another middle-aged hero, confronting Yusef in the climactic scene of *HM*, has a feeling of "being looked after," as "a kind of nursery peace descended" on him (3.1.4.1). Again, in *MF*, by means of the bomb in the hotel, Hilfe causes Rowe to regress temporarily to a childlike mental state of dependance and innocence. Several of the antagonists—Benditch, Dreuther, Fischer, Fortnum—assume roles as fathers or potential fathers-in-law towards the heroes.

In relation to the antagonists, then, the hero, if not actually a child or distinctly younger person, tends to be maneuvered into such a position, into the place of a pupil, a son, or a junior protégé. The point of this is clear from the more developed instances, as in *UG* and *CE*. What the antagonist seeks to teach or pass on to the hero, as his chosen associate, disciple, or successor, is a view of life similar to his own, a view colored by attractive but superficial benefits, and one which does not probe too deeply into long-term consequences or moral implications. It is a view of life, in short, likely to appeal to a childish or unformed intelligence; and in teaching such an outlook the antagonist is himself childlike, a kind of philosophical Peter Pan, a man of essentially adolescent thinking who fails to encompass the complexities and limitations of adult experience. In Greene's novels, therefore, this kind of childhood innocence is essentially inadequate, representing a simplified moral perspective which, while perhaps comforting and liberating, fails to address reality.

The "terror of life," the sense of reality as oppressive, demanding, and unyielding, is basic to Greene's fiction. Against this background unfolds the dynamic situation outlined in Chapter 2. The hero is caught between, on the one hand, the moral imperatives that require his involvement, his active participation in life, and on the other hand his yearning for a state of "peace" or "innocence," which can be realized only by denying or withdrawing from the conflicts which dominate the real world. While this tension remains latent in the early novels, it is expressed in the middle novels in terms of the hero's "journey back" to past innocence which he undertakes at the same time as he is considering his position with respect to pressing moral problems. In most of the late novels the same tension asserts itself as between the hero's wish for retreat or noninvolvement and the increasing demands of life, calling for his commitment and action.

The central dynamism of a Greene novel may therefore be expressed in terms of this tension between, on the one hand, the moral imperative to confront reality and, on the other, the natural yearning to find instead a condition of "peace" untroubled by moral and emotional conflicts. The role of the antagonist is, very generally, to act upon a hero caught in this dilemma in such a way as to tip the balance and to induce the hesitant hero to plunge into action. The antagonist's role is Mephisthophelean in that he presents himself as the hero's guide, offering him attractive benefits in line with his inner yearnings, but with hidden consequences and at the cost of personal obligation.

The antagonist frequently offers the hero something akin to a return to childhood, a retreat from moral complexity into a kind of innocence. The hero is already disposed to rediscover a lost paradise of childlike simplicity, such as is imaged, for example, in Pinkie's memories of the church, Rowe's "Arcady" and dream-garden, Quarry's "Pendélé," Plarr's recollections of security within his father's bolted doors, and Castle's protective dragon. The antagonist offers a way of life which promises to bypass the moral complexities of experience and to give the hero the peace he desires. In seeming to offer what the hero so deeply wants, the antagonist appears as a friend and is readily accepted as a guide and protector, a surrogate father, and even (like Hilfe and Calver) a metaphorical savior. But the innocence offered is not genuine, and it comes at a price which is, in the end, too high. The price is represented chiefly by the victims—Rexall, Coney, Andersson, Mrs. Baines, Else, Major Stone, Ali, Wordsworth, Joseph, Davis. When all is revealed the antagonist is seen to have been a tempter, morally dissolute, often criminal, even (like Yusef) Satanic.

Here is the very center of Greene's fictional world, the general principle upon which all of the mature, serious novels (excepting *EA*) are written. The hero embodies, perhaps rather extremely, the distress and reluctance of intelligent, sensitive humanity facing the commonplace ills and confusions of life. He naturally desires a world without suffering, a world where he would be free from feelings of moral guilt and uncertainty. He remembers, or thinks he remembers, such a world in his own youth or childhood. The antagonist seems to offer him something very similar, a way to bypass immediate problems and achieve peace of mind. As the hero begins to follow or copy his antagonist, however, new contradictions begin to emerge.

5. Heroines

The central situation in a typical Greene novel is that between the hero and his antagonist. Almost all of the novels also involve a love story of the traditional kind, in which the hero either wins or loses his lady. Only in *EA*, however, is the love story central. In other cases, where it occurs, it is clearly subordinate to the hero-antagonist business, and the "heroine's" role is correspondingly secondary and frequently passive. For this reason the term "heroine" is not finally very helpful in discussion of Greene's novels. A better starting point than the notion of the love story heroine, in discussion of the female roles in Greene's fiction, is the view of these characters as moral influences, influences exerted on the heroes and bearing directly upon the crucial decision he has to make as a result of his dealings with the antagonist.

Early writers on Greene observed the tendency of several of his leading female characters to conform to a type, being young, frail, socially disadvantaged, and not overly attractive.[67] Such are what might be called Greene's "working girls," as most of them are of low social status and obliged to work hard for a slender living, usually in menial or demeaning jobs and sometimes on the verges of prostitution. Anne Crowder is a chorus girl, not above accepting free meals from wealthy patrons. She is only a slightly more robust version of Coral Musker, another chorus girl; and Anna Schmidt in *TM* makes a third. Both Anna Hilfe and Helen Rolt are displaced persons, thrown into positions of dependency by the events of war. Helen Rolt, little more than a girl, is reminiscent in her naivety of Pinkie's Rose, another young female turned out early in life to make her own way.

Despite her married status, Marie Rycker belongs in the same group. She is immature and is treated like a servant by her husband. She is unhappy and, like Rose, turns all too readily to the first man who speaks kindly to her for a means of escape. She has not actually been guilty of loose conduct, but cheerfully pretends to it. Her absorption in a collection of romantic fiction looks back to Helen's stamp album and Phuong's glossy magazines. Phuong is equally opportunistic, looking to sell herself, in effect, to the highest bidder. A more blatant prostitution is practiced by Clara, until Fortnum takes her as his wife. All of these are young women, still in many ways girlish and very much at the mercy of circumstances. The group is characterized chiefly by their dependence and vulnerability, qualities which they use, sometimes none too scrupulously, to engage the sympathies and support of men.

But not all of Greene's women are like this. Kate Farrant, for instance, and Ida Arnold, are plainly not members of this group but women of a very different type. These are women of mature character, capable managers of affairs, usually in easy circumstances and endowed with some social standing and personal sophistication. As well as Kate and Ida, Rose Cullen belongs here, the daughter of a peer and able to give the hero considerable help in his adventures and eventual escape. Martha in *TC* is another, and Sarah Miles probably belongs here too, along with Louise Scobie.

A broad contrast emerges between two female types, defined principally in relation to the hero: the one weaker and inclined to be dependent, the other a stronger, independent, more dominating character. The weaker woman is additionally often young, even childlike, living in restricted circumstances, demanding sympathy and sometimes actually in need of a kind of rescue. The stronger, more mature woman is able to make her own decisions, and is sometimes also inclined to make decisions affecting the hero. She usually has resources, often as the wife, daughter, or mistress of a powerful man. She does not need rescue, but may be able to offer help or protection to the embattled hero. The importance of this contrast of types is underlined by the way in which, in many of the novels, they are paired, and the hero placed between two women, one weaker, one stronger.

The first such pair, a very clear case of two morally and personally contrasting women each exercising influence upon the hero, occurs in *MW* in the persons of Elizabeth and Lucy. Elizabeth is young, about the hero's own age, and despite her apparent self-assurance and moral wisdom, she is, as events reveal, very vulnerable and isolated. The death of Jennings (who has been, in any case, a far from ideal guardian) has left her all the more unprotected, and she faces only hostility from her neighbors. Andrews tries to protect her but fails, and she dies. Lucy, on the other hand, lives safely and comfortably as a rich man's mistress. She enjoys considerable influence and freedom—she has no difficulty in arranging to spend a night with Andrews and evidently leads poor Sir Henry a merry dance. The narrative treats her quite harshly on moral grounds, but she is allowed some humanity. She shows genuine concern for Sir Henry, and would doubtless have been more sympathetic towards Andrews if he had not parted from her with such rudeness. She does provide him, at least, with a place to spend one night in safety.

A number of similarly contrasting pairs succeed Elizabeth and Lucy. In *ST* there are Coral Musker and Janet Pardoe, two very different creatures who become, unwittingly, rivals for the attentions of Myatt. Coral, a working girl, is described as not especially attractive and is clearly very much a victim of hard circumstances. She is in poor health, but nevertheless rushes across Europe to take up a job she desperately needs in a chorus line. Janet, on the other hand, is steering her own course, leaving Mabel in order to travel on the lookout for a rich man, whom she soon finds in Myatt. She is an overtly attractive woman and has powerful connections: Mr. Stein is her "guardian" and looks out for her interests. In the symmetry of the story, lucky Janet takes poor Coral's place as Myatt's potential bride, while Coral is captured in Janet's place by the horrible Mabel.

The same sort of pairing is apparent in Milly and Kay in *IB*, although in this rather loosely constructed story little is made of the contrast. The two women here are sisters and not in any specific way rivals. They are simply different, Kay being outgoing and socially active while Milly remains domestic and depressed. Kay is represented as attractive: she spends one night with Surrogate in his luxurious flat and the next with Jules in a comfortable hotel. Milly is drab, and spends her nights joylessly with the pathetic Conrad. The contrast becomes more significant in *EM*, where Loo and Kate compete for the hero's attentions, a competition which extends into the cultural opposition between the England which has "made" Anthony and the cosmopolitanism of Krogh. Here again there is a difference of class and station between the two women. Kate may, in the past, have earned her own living, but her work as we see it is managerial and far from menial. Now, as Krogh's fiancée, she has power and status. Loo's bourgeois English background is poor in comparison. Loo herself is kept under close parental control and has only limited freedom of action. She does manage a few hours with Anthony, but is soon recaptured by her parents and taken back to Coventry.

In *CA* the hero finds himself between Rose Cullen and Else. Rose is sophisticated and self-determining, with a wealthy fiancé and numerous powerful friends. She has freedom of movement herself, and is able to organize a similar facility for the beleaguered hero. Else, on the other hand, is still a child and is obliged to work as a maidservant. She is in many ways an echo of Rose in *BR*. It is interesting that, although D has no sexual interest in Else, the story nonetheless hints at sexual rivalry between the two women. Rose is pointlessly jealous over D's innocent concern for Else's welfare, and Else's sexuality is further suggested by the rather coy scene in which she removes her clothing in D's bedroom. If the purpose is not to raise the idea of Else's sexuality, this piece of business is redundant. The concealment of the papers could have been accomplished in any number of ways without it. As it is, the connotations of the action are even underlined by the peeping tom observations of Mr. Muckerji.

An element of sexual rivalry, real or implied, is present between the two women in most cases. It occurs most obviously in *HM*, between Helen and Louise. Louise, to whom the hero is married, turns out to be a woman of self-possession and common sense, despite the picture we initially get of her through Scobie's eyes as feeble and incapable. Louise shows her true colors when she returns from South Africa to bring her erring husband back to heel, and in the scene where she punches the importunate Wilson on the nose. Louise is a mature married woman with a social position as an officer's wife, which she is anxious to maintain. Helen is little more than a schoolgirl whom events have left alone and without immediate means of support. Recently widowed, she is in a fragile state, obliged to consider how to earn her future livelihood, and prey to the attentions of Bagster. She is not particularly attractive, but her helpless dependence captures Scobie's interest.

HM is the novel in which Greene comes closest to the traditional sexual triangle, but traces of it remain, with echoes of the same contrasted female types, in most of the other middle and late novels. In *TC*, for instance, the hero is carrying on a fairly routine relationship with Martha, a mature married woman, wife of an ambassador, who runs her husband's household and offers sanctuary within it to the likes of Jones. She is not in any way dependent upon the hero, and appears to survive the termination of their affair with much the same sang froid that Louise accepts the death of Scobie. Meanwhile, however, Brown has recourse from time to time to a prostitute, Tin Tin. We don't see much of her, but enough to discover that she is young, girlish, and virtually a slave to her employment. Nothing comes of the relationship, nor does Tin Tin, like such other members of her group as Else and Coral Fellows, meet a violent end. Yet she is briefly present, and Brown's attempt to meet her is made the occasion—and any number of other occasions could have been contrived to do as well—of the discovery that Jones has become a favored guest of the Haitian government.

Plarr's emotional life follows much the same pattern as Brown's. He has unhappy affairs with the wives of prominent local men—the lady we meet in the story, the latest of the line, is Señora Escobar—and at the same time becomes fascinated by a girl in a brothel. As a native girl available to the highest bidder Clara echoes Phuong, and in her loveless marriage to the antagonist she is reminiscent of Marie Rycker. She is little more than a girl, and when her husband is taken away she becomes potentially dependent upon the hero, whose child she is carrying. One of the reasons Plarr is so anxious to secure Fortnum's safe return is to avoid the claim Clara would have upon him if she were left, like Helen Rolt, a young widow. There is a hint of the same pattern in *EA* where the hero, his affair with another man's wife terminated by her decision, and subsequently by her death, seeks consolation with the easily acquired Sylvia; and he does this, significantly, on his way to his former lover's cremation.

If we admit "offstage" characters, who can, like Kite and Carson, be quite important in a Greene novel, we can see the same positioning of the hero between two contrasting rival women in several further cases. In *QA* Fowler is caught between Phuong, whom he needs to secure by marriage, and Helen, the absent wife to whom he is still legally bound. Helen appears only in name and through the texts of her letters, but her power of decision remains crucial. It lies with Helen to determine whether or not Fowler can keep Phuong by offering to marry her. Phuong, on the other hand, merely responds to circumstances and makes no decisions. She is, in any case, manipulated by her sister. If Fowler is going away and cannot marry her, Phuong will accept Pyle's offer. If she has any personal feelings in the matter they are not expressed. While Helen is a free woman, Phuong is entirely subservient to her situation.

For all its superficial differences, *BC* is structurally very close to *QA*, and it includes a vestigial trace of the same patterning of female characters. Marie succeeds Phuong as the child-woman willing to unite herself to the man most likely to afford her a comfortable western lifestyle. She suffers from ill treatment and is virtually dependent upon others. Querry, meanwhile, self-exiled from Europe, is pursued by a letter from a woman he left behind who has emotional (if not legal) claims upon him. In this way the letter from Toute-à-toi, asserting a bond from which the hero wishes to escape, parallels the correspondence with Helen in *QA*. There is even a trace of the same pattern in *OM* (written between *QA* and *BC*), where Wormold transfers his affections gradually from his absent exwife to Beatrice, with whom he settles at the end.

The pattern in which the hero struggles to loosen the bonds of a prior, perhaps matrimonial attachment in order to commit himself now to the younger, weaker woman requiring his support, can be traced back through *HM* to *MF*. Scobie, having in Louise's absence formed a tie with Helen, finds the marital reins suddenly tightened when Louise returns. Unable to make a choice, Scobie dies. In *MF* Rowe is initially bound by a sense of guilt to the memory of his dead wife. The events of the story enable him to escape this binding guilt and successfully transfer his affections to Anna. In a sense, therefore, Rowe is at first held in restraint by Alice but, in the course of the story, wins his freedom and a new bride.

Most interesting with respect to the female roles are *BR* and *PG*, the two novels in which the heroes are dedicated to celibacy and in which, therefore, we might expect the women to be less important. Indeed, there are here no entanglements of the straightforwardly romantic kind, but even in these unlikely cases we can still discern the hero as distinctly flanked by two contrasting women, one childlike and vulnerable, the other mature and dominating, each trying to influence his moral course of action.

Pinkie has in Rose a heroine who belongs clearly to the "working girl" group. She is young, somewhat naive, and until her marriage with Pinkie entirely dominated by others—her parents and her bullying employer. She attaches herself to Pinkie as unthinkingly as Phuong to Fowler, Else to D, or Marie to Querry. The other major female figure in *BR* is Ida. There is, of course, no suggestion of any personal bond between Ida and Pinkie, and the rivalry between Ida and Rose has therefore no intrinsic sexual element. Their antagonism over Pinkie is moral, Ida wanting to bring him to account for his actions, particularly for the murder of Hale, while Rose wants to protect him at almost any cost.

Although Ida and Rose are not sexual rivals in the usual sense, the hostility between them, as between their counterparts in several of the other novels, is imaged partly in sexual terms. Ida is not only the story's self-appointed detective and agent of conventional rectitude, but she is also a woman of considerable sexual appetite and attraction. She is portrayed as displaying an aggressive sexuality which men, like Hale and Phil Corkery, find almost intimidating. She has the exaggerated attributes of a fertility goddess. She is never long without a male companion, whom she tends to overshadow so completely that the reader often forgets his presence. The scene of Ida's disrobing in the hotel bedroom is the focal point for currents of sexual imagery associated with her throughout the novel. Rose, on the other hand, is neither especially attractive physically nor much concerned over sexuality. While Ida shows the kind of sexual appetite associated with Lucy (in *MW*), Kay Rimmer, or Martha, the unattractiveness of Rose, and her evident view of sex as a not over-important element in human relationships, associates her with girls like Coral Musker, Marie Rycker, and Phuong.

The Priest in *PG* is an older man and no longer personally interested in sex. Yet the circumstances of his story still place him between two very different female figures, each with some influence upon him and together corresponding to the contrasting pairs of women we find in other novels. These are the two women who successively give shelter to the Priest in the first stage of his journey, before his meeting with the *mestizo* adds new impetus to his wanderings. One is Maria, the woman with whom he had cohabited some seven years ago, the mother of his child; the other is the girl, Coral Fellows.

Coral has associations with a number of the "working girls." She shares a name with Coral Musker, although by itself this means little, since Greene frequently reuses names. Her schoolgirl qualities, her pedantry and her evident enthusiasm for the correspondence courses she is following, link her to Helen Rolt. Like Rose in *BR*, she is a daughter of incompetent parents who leave her to face the problems of life without guidance. Like these other girls, exposed to work and responsibility at an early age, Coral has developed a kind of practical wisdom which goes along with a naivety in personal matters: she manages her father's plantation, but thinks it might be helpful to teach the Priest the morse code. Like Else, she is anxious to befriend and protect the middle-aged hero, and like Else she apparently pays for this with her life.

Marie, on the other hand, exhibits some of the qualities of the more mature type. She tends to dominate the Priest, giving him instructions and, at one point, berating him quite cruelly. She does indeed protect him, giving him her bed in a manner reminiscent of Lucy hiding Andrews from his pursuers. The Priest is even a little nervous lest Marie should make sexual demands: when he takes shelter in her hut he asks "doubtfully" about the sleeping arrangements, "afraid of claims" (2.1). The Priest's affair with Maria is a thing of the past, but the business of the bed in the hut brings the memory to life. Coral's sexuality, on the other hand, remains a thing of the future. In the second of the two episodes in which we see her, she experiences the onset of menstruation as she stands by the spot in the barn where the Priest had earlier lain (1.4). Although, of course, there is nothing sexual on the literal level between Coral and the Priest, this deliberate indication of Coral's sexual maturity in association with the Priest's sleeping place makes her metaphorically his virgin bride. There are other hints which reinforce this suggestion: the Priest's concern at the thought of men knocking at Coral's window, of whom he might himself be one (1.3); and Coral's attempt to question her mother about the Virgin birth (1.4). There is, in this way, a metaphorical contrast between the mature and maternal Maria and Coral's young virginity.

Something comparable to the antithesis of Elizabeth and Lucy in *MW* occurs in most of Greene's novels. Its importance varies from case to case, being relatively minor in *OM* and *BC*, but obviously central in *HM*. An arrangement of corresponding pairs is given on the following page.

MW	Elizabeth	Lucy
ST	Coral	Janet
IB	Milly	Kay
EM	Loo	Kate
BR	Rose	Ida
CA	Else	Rose
PG	Coral	Maria
MF	Anna	Alice
HM	Helen	Louise
EA	Sylvia	Sarah
QA	Phuong	Helen
OM	Beatrice	Wormold's exwife
BC	Marie	Toute-à-toi
TC	Tin Tin	Martha
HC	Clara	Señora Escobar

In a number of these cases the situation is a version of the traditional sexual triangle, with the hero caught between the two women, or in the process of transferring his affection from one to the other. This is clearly true of *MW*, *HM*, *QA*, *OM*, and *HC*—and the pattern can also be traced in *TA* where Henry moves gradually from his vague friendship with Miss Keene to his betrothal in Paraguay to the daughter of the chief of customs, although neither of these ladies has any active role in the story. In other cases, where the triangle is not literally sexual, it still involves the hero's affections, except in *ST* (where it is Myatt, not Czinner, who stands between the two women) and *IB* (where only one of the women has any significant dealings with the hero). In virtually all cases the ultimate purpose is moral, the two women representing respectively contrasting views or ways of life relevant to the hero's course of action.

The single feature within the action of the stories which most clearly differentiates these two female types is that, whereas the one frequently demands sympathy, "pity," or even physical rescue from an oppressive situation, the other, more self-sufficient type is herself protective, often giving the hero shelter or assistance in his dealings with his enemies.

Lucy unknowingly gives Andrews protection when he takes refuge in her bed after his encounter with Cockney Harry: "I shall be safe with her tonight," is his thought as he makes up his mind to accept her invitation (2.9). Kate's protectiveness towards Anthony, stemming from their school days, prompts her to find him employment with Krogh. Rose Cullen helps D avoid his pursuers at several points, and it she who arranges his final escape. She does this by means of her influence over Forbes, much as Kate exerts her influence over Krogh on Anthony's behalf. Maria in *PG*, with a faint echo of Lucy, gives the fugitive Priest a bed where he will be safe for a night. Louise is protective of Scobie, both in her resentment of his not being given promotion and, more significantly, in her return from South Africa in an effort to rescue him from adultery. Sarah's care for Bendrix is manifested in her bargain with God which, if taken at face value, may be said to have saved his life at the cost of her personal happiness. Martha not only tends Brown's wounds after his beating but also, through her husband, is mistress of a house which serves as a sanctuary for political refugees: Brown never quite has to claim this asylum for himself, but he escorts Jones there and is a frequent visitor.

Ida is an exception who proves the rule: although Pinkie is beyond the pale of her maternal instinct, she is concerned with what she sees as the salvation of Rose, and her retrospectively protective feeling towards Hale is a central driving force in the action. Although Ida offers no protection to the hero she does exhibit a form of the unshakeable possessive interest in him which is paralleled in some of the other novels. Ida's remorseless pursuit of Pinkie, like that of an avenging fury, has something in common with the embarrassing possessiveness of Toute-à-toi and Señora Escobar, women who will not allow their heroes to forget past indiscretions. This, again, is related to the wifely hold exercised by Louise over Scobie and over Fowler by the absent Helen.

While the stronger women are often protective to the point of possessiveness, the weaker ones tend to exert merely passive claims for emotional support and material assistance. Probably the clearest and most extreme case is that of Else, who attaches herself to D with instantaneous and dog-like devotion, and for whom he feels increasingly responsible as she incurs, by helping him, ill treatment from his enemies, who eventually kill her in an attempt to hinder his mission. D feels pressure to do something about Else, arousing Rose's jealousy in his efforts. The news of her death is for him a turning point (comparable to Ali's death and its effect upon Scobie), determining him to hound his enemies even though he can no longer hope to complete his original assignment.

The image of Else, requiring D's assistance against Mrs. Mendrill and K, is echoed in several other instances in which a young heroine is somehow held or threatened by a grotesque adult pair. An obvious case is the scene in which Pinkie successfully bargains for Rose with her hostile, moody father and mother, thereby securing her escape from Nelson Place. This, in turn, recalls Loo and her anxiety to escape with Anthony, however temporarily, from the restrictive supervision of her parents. A more literal rescue is effected by Raven, when he manages to get Anne away from Acky and Tiny. Acky and Tiny are perhaps anticipated by Jennings and Mrs. Butler, the oppressive, older, guardian-like figures in Elizabeth's cottage. Jennings is recently deceased, but his presence is still felt; and Mrs. Butler's malicious evidence is largely responsible for the release of the smugglers and the revelation of Elizabeth's involvement with Andrews. Fainter echoes are Mr. and Mrs. Fellows, whose self-involved negligence is surely a factor in Coral's death, and the obnoxious Mr. and Mrs. Peters from whom Coral in *ST* is rescued by Myatt.

Acky the defrocked priest, the guilt-ridden Jennings seeking reassurance from his Bible, K the would-be professor, each with a dangerously vindictive female companion, and each pair jealously guarding and restraining an innocent young woman: the features common to these cases also call to mind the underworld beneath the garden where Javitt and Maria guard the photographic image of Miss Ramsgate. *UG* gives a plainer view of the imagery behind the stories. Essentially, the hero faces danger, represented by the two demonic figures, male and female, of whom the man in each case offers a dubious kind of teaching, while the woman, distinctly unfeminine as she is, presents a more overt threat of imprisonment or death. The hero's goal, however, which justifies the risk, is the "daughter" of this pair, whose flight into the daylight upper world they cruelly restrain. The hero must learn the old man's lesson, locate the girl, and facilitate her escape, avoiding the old woman's clutches.

While the hero's rescue of the girl has echoes of the mythic world of *UG* in several of the novels up to and including *PG*, from *MF* onwards the rescues tend to be more strictly literal affairs, involving the removal of the girl from possible danger and, usually, the displacement of a dubious rival. Scobie saves Helen from loneliness and the unwanted attentions of Bagster. Fowler is impelled by the realization that Pyle's bombs might have hurt Phuong, as well as by his wish to preserve her from marriage to Pyle. Plarr becomes, in Clara's eyes, a desirable alternative to her tedious marriage with Fortnum. Castle, with crucial assistance from Carson, has already rescued Sarah from persecution in South Africa, and now, confronted with "Uncle Remus," tries to save all black Africans from political oppression. In *BC* the rescue motif is made only more prominent by Querry's unwillingness to participate in it. He has no notion of taking Marie away from Rycker, but she contrives and takes advantage of a situation in which he is made to appear to have done so. On the other hand, it must be added, there is no gesture towards any such rescue in *TC*, where Brown leaves Tin Tin just as he finds her, or in *PG*, where the Priest remains ignorant, until too late, of Coral's danger. In these few cases the appeal of the female victim is mute and remains unheeded.

The root of the distinction and opposition between the two female types is moral, and is revealed, in the more expanded cases, in the actual or potential influences exerted by these women upon the conduct of the hero. The stronger, protective women are generally benign. Even Ida may be said to be so, in the sense that she strives for "right" and "justice" and in defense of victims like Hale and Rose. Ida is hostile towards Pinkie only because, uniquely among Greene's heroes, he has made a deliberate, overt commitment to evil. These women, however, usually display limitations, particularly in their failure to appreciate long-term moral implications, a failure which tends in practice to result in their influencing the hero to ignore wider claims upon his sympathies. The weaker, more dependent type, on the contrary, usually represents humanitarian demands, the duty to take whatever action may be possible to alleviate suffering. In the later novels, from *HM* onwards, the role of these weaker women, from Phuong to Clara, is generally very passive, consisting in the often tacit appeal of a distressed young woman to a man who may be able to help her. Earlier figures of this type, from Coral Musker to Coral Fellows, not only make the appeal of endangered innocence but also, in most cases, offer some articulation of moral values. The moral influence of the weaker female tends, very broadly, to run counter to the hero's involvement with the antagonist, while that of the stronger woman is either neutral or such as to encourage the hero along the course of action which the antagonist represents.

Kate Farrant is a clear instance of the stronger type exerting a morally negative influence which favors the hero's association with the antagonist. She is the driving force of the story, having somehow won Krogh's affections and persuaded Anthony to join her in Krogh's employ. Evidently she wants only Anthony's good, but her plan, as events reveal, is not one he can follow. He is not personally suited to Krogh's world, and he soon decides to leave Kate and follow Loo back to England. However kindly meant, Kate's plan ignores Anthony's moral nature and draws him to his death. Loo, on the other hand, answers Anthony's needs. She is possibly the least attractive among the successors of Andrews's Elizabeth, being generally shallow and vulgar; but she represents for Anthony, despite its limitations, the England that "made" him and to which, rather than stay with Krogh, he must return.

Loo is provincial, and in Kate's eyes she is "common." She exhibits a "crude innocence" but represents, again from Kate's point of view, what Anthony needs to be "saved" from: "the lights behind the bicycles, the leaves on Warren Street pavement, the port in the Ladies Bar" (1.3). Loo, in short, exemplifies what Greene himself labeled the "seedy" and which his critics saw as one of the features of Greeneland. This is "England," opposed to the sophisticated, modern internationalism of Krogh's. But, for all her provincialism and vulgarity, Loo retains a fundamental honesty, a bedrock of integrity, which is answered in Anthony by the limit beyond which he will not go. "There were things he would not do" (1.1), and it is this sense of a broad but unshakeable morality which separates him, in the end, from Kate and Krogh. Loo has a comparable moral sense, and uses it as a basis for an important judgement. "It's not respectable what you are doing," she says to Anthony of his association with Krogh (4.1). Later Anthony finds that Loo was right, and he decides to join her rather than stay with Kate in Sweden. Kate, in the end, is the rich man's whore, like Lucy, while Loo is Elizabeth's 1930s equivalent: a shopkeeper's daughter, ordinary but fundamentally honest. Anthony belongs to Loo's England.

There is a comparable sense in *BR* that the hero belongs to the same world as the weaker woman, and not to that represented by the stronger. Pinkie's country is the underworld of urban gangsterism, and its effective opposite is Ida's world of bourgeois complacency and physical security. Rose comes from the same place as Pinkie, and in her Catholicism she shares with him a view of life. Pinkie's interpretation of Catholicism, of course, is not the same as Rose's, but his outlook on life has, in many ways, more in common with hers than with Ida's. Pinkie feels that Rose "belonged to his life, like a room or a chair: she was something which completed him" (4.3). Ida "belonged to the great middle law-abiding class, her amusements were their amusements, her superstitions their superstitions... she had no more love for anyone than they had" (3.1). She has no experience of Nelson Place: "*She's* never lived there," Rose observes (3.3). Confronting Pinkie and Rose, Ida acts "as if she were in a strange country: the typical Englishman abroad. She hadn't even got a phrase book" (4.3).

The dichotomy between Rose and Ida is not a matter simply of social background but also, and more fundamentally, of morality. And just as in *EM*, in the end, Loo's moral values are vindicated over Kate's, so here are Rose's over Ida's. Ida talks a great deal about "right" and "justice," and she appears to be disinterested. Her motivation and its improbability are what make her something of a problematic and unsatisfactory character. In the end, as Phil Corkery observes, she pursues right and justice, not for their own sakes or from any love for the victims, but only "because it's fun" (7.6). The narrative constantly derides her energetic activity: she is compared to "a warship going into action, a warship on the right side in a war to end wars, the signal flags proclaiming that every man would do his duty" (4.2). She is representative of the thinking of "the great middle class," but that thinking is exposed as being a mere muddle, based indiscriminately in conventions, mysticism, and sentiment: "the Bible, where it lay in the cupboard next the Board, the Warwick Deeping [and] *The Good Companions*" (6.1).

For all her naivety, Rose opposes Ida's shallow conventionality with strong human feelings of love and loyalty. Both Pinkie and Ida recognize that Rose is "Good" (with a mysterious capital G—4.3). The difference between the two women is nowhere clearer than in the ending. Ida is left, poised over her Ouija Board, wondering whether to recall one of her former lovers (7.10), while Rose talks with a priest about divine mercy and emerges with a hope, however short-lived, of redemption. She passes the final judgement on Ida at the same time, observing that Ida "doesn't know about love" (7.11).

The ending of *BR* is bitterly ironic, since Rose is carrying Pinkie's recorded message. Rose's fate is not untypical, as a good number of the female characters of her group end up victims, suffering for their involvement with the hero. Elizabeth is murdered, as also are Else and Coral Fellows; Coral Musker, apparently on the brink of death, falls prey to Mabel Warren; and Helen Rolt is left helpless in the clutches of Bagster. Members of the other group tend, on the contrary, to be survivors. They may be, as in most cases, left lonely or isolated by events, but they generally retain their resilience and powers of self-determination.

The two contrasting types can also be traced in *PG*. Maria, the stronger, more dominating of the two, first attached herself to the Priest out of pride. "It's not everyone who's a priest's woman," she says (2.1). There is consequently a suspicion that she manipulated the situation and even played for her own ends upon the Priest's weakness. It is at any rate evident that, now the affair is over, she has little feeling left for her former companion. She shows no tenderness, and after one night's shelter, little concern for his future. Coral Fellows, on the other hand, is genuinely concerned for him and affirms a responsibility to help. "We couldn't let them catch him," she says categorically, in the face of her parents' indifference (1.3). The suggestion that she and the Priest should communicate by means of the morse code may be ludicrous, but Coral is at least trying to aid him, and the suggestion is taken up later, in the Priest's dream, when Coral appears an as angel bringing him "news" (3.4). While Maria contributes to the Priest's degradation, Coral offers moral support.

Like Else, Coral appears to meet her death as a result of her alliance with the hero. The circumstances of Coral's death are not made clear, but if we assume it to have been unrelated to the Priest it becomes a merely sentimental addition to the story. Only if Coral dies in some way as a consequence of her desire to shelter the Priest do the facts of her death, and the business of the Priest's subsequent return to the scene, have meaning. A comparable element of self-sacrifice can be seen in the cases of Elizabeth, Coral Musker, and Pinkie's Rose.

The earliest novels are content with broad moral contrasts. Elizabeth plainly appeals to Andrews's better self, while Lucy arouses his baser instincts. Coral Musker sacrifices her chance of freedom as she pauses to help the injured Czinner, with the result that the shallow Janet steps easily into her place at Myatt's side. Milly's painful efforts to come to terms with Jim's plight contrast strongly with the hedonistic life Kay pursues meanwhile. Anne Crowder is alone in *GS*, without a counterbalancing female character; but she is evidently herself of the same type as Coral Musker (whom she closely resembles), and she is in a number of ways an index of the story's moral truth. She is "straight" and "loyal" (3.2), and she at once feels a due sense of "repulsion" when she learns of the murders Raven has committed (5.2). Anne's loyalties, however, never really waver, and her entanglement with Raven remains largely circumstantial. She remains, consequently, perhaps the simplest of these early heroines.

There is greater complexity in *CA*. Else here plainly represents the weaker, victimized, self-sacrificing female type, echoing Pinkie's Rose and, in her immature devotion to the hero, anticipating something of Coral Fellows. She also represents, much as later do Phuong and Clara, the oppressed poor for whom, in the context of the novels' political themes, the heroes show some sympathy. Else serves to direct the hero towards the stance he eventually takes, a stand against Benditch and, more generally, against the political forces of oppressive power and privilege. Rose Cullen is initially Else's opposite: a member of the privileged class, Benditch's spoilt daughter, living a life of self-indulgent luxury. Rose is true to her type in becoming possessively protective towards D, and therefore instinctively hostile in her feelings towards Else.

In the end, however, Rose moves beyond the limitations of her initial role to provide D with real help and to unite her fate with his. In this she goes far beyond what the stronger females are usually willing or able to do. (One thinks, for instance, of the way in which each of Louise Scobie, Helen Fowler, and Martha Pineda finally lets her man go his own way with only a metaphorical shrug.) Rose is Benditch's daughter, and her initial task in the story is to facilitate the hero's access to her father, the antagonist, much as Kate serves to introduce Anthony to Krogh, and as Louise's whining drives Scobie to accept dealings with Yusef. Her role as Benditch's daughter is prominent in the first half of the story, during which she does what she can to help D along the road which leads him to his meeting with her father. Once this meeting has proved abortive, however, Rose disappears for a while from the action. When she returns at the end, as D's companion in his escape, we see more clearly why, from the beginning, it has been emphasized that, although Benditch's daughter, she has dissociated herself from her father. Whereas Kate remains with Krogh, therefore, and Martha with her husband, in the morally simpler framework of *CA*, Rose is uniquely able to make the final leap from the side of the antagonist to that of the hero, achieving what is rare in Greene, a happy ending.

In *MF* Alice, Rowe's sick wife whom he has killed out of pity, is the focus for the sense of guilt which is blighting the hero's life when the story opens. Insofar as Hilfe works upon this sense of guilt to achieve Rowe's submission, using his remorse and his record as a convicted murderer against him, the memory of Alice works to further Hilfe's influence over the hero. Despite the fact that she is Hilfe's sister, Anna works in a contrary direction. She tells Rowe that Hilfe's people are "bad" (1.7.2) and tries on several occasions to help or warn him. She narrowly escapes the fate of Else and Coral Fellows, as it is only Rowe's quick action which saves her from Hilfe's bomb. Anna is Rowe's guide, leading the hero away from the pull of the "Ministry of Fear."

OM follows the same pattern, but in a comic vein. Wormold is loosely bound to his exwife by sentimental ties. She never enters the story, except as a factor in his memory. When Beatrice arrives and becomes his partner in spying, simply by helping him and occupying his attention, she gradually displaces his exwife in his thoughts. She is the one who speaks plainly at the end, when they are interviewed by their superiors in London. After this, Wormold rescues her from a threatened posting to Jakarta and offers her marriage. Wormold's exwife, therefore, stands for his old life in Cuba, the context in which he became Hawthorne's agent. Beatrice, although another employee of Hawthorne's people, supports Wormold in his rebellion against his masters and accompanies him as he embarks on a new life in England.

In *HM* it is Louise who first drives Scobie to incur an obligation to Yusef. This she does by making demands which, as she herself later admits, are unreasonable and selfish. She does not, of course, consciously will Scobie's moral compromise, but the compromise is the direct outcome of the pressures to which she subjects him. Later, as the possessive aspect of her nature asserts itself and she returns from South Africa to interrupt Scobie's affair with Helen, she is the occasion of his further slide into corruption. Unaware that Louise already knows what he is trying to hide from her, Scobie allows himself to be blackmailed and then conspires with Yusef to ensure Ali's silence.

While Louise exerts a generally negative moral influence on the hero, comparable to that of Kate upon Anthony or of the memory of Alice upon Rowe, Helen fails to achieve very much along the lines of the positive moral assertion offered by Elizabeth, Loo, Coral Fellows, and Anna Hilfe. Helen and most other later members of the weaker group remain young, naive, and easy prey to others, but lack the capacity for decisive, independent action and clear moral statement. They remain largely mute and passive, allowing themselves to be managed by others, and even handed about like pieces of property.

Helen is carried into the story on a stretcher, established in a government hut, and becomes an object of tacit contention between Scobie and Bagster. She has virtually no direction of her own future. Phuong is managed by her sister and, in the course of the story, is mechanically transferred from Fowler to Pyle and back again as events unfold. Tin Tin and Clara are both impoverished young women earning their livelihood in brothels. Clara is taken away by Fortnum, who marries her; and she is then seduced by Plarr, whom she seems to prefer but who has no intention of marrying her. Marie is treated like a servant by her husband. She is the most dynamic of these later child-women, in her bid for freedom and her attempt to attach herself to Querry; but even here the action is impulsive and irresponsible, conceived with the single short-term aim of getting herself back to Europe. Marie remains like Helen, Phuong, and Clara in her failure to involve herself realistically in the moral issues of the story.

These women are quite shallow, unsophisticated characters, with limited powers of assertion and a tendency to lose themselves in trivial, even childish amusements: Helen's stamps, Phuong's magazines, Marie's cheap fiction, Clara's gaudy sunglasses. They manifest positive action only in trying to please the man to whom they wish to attach themselves. Their moral significance arises not from what they say or do but from what they represent in terms of oppressed humanity claiming sympathetic attention. In this way the weaker woman in the later novels generally serves as a stimulus prompting the reluctant hero to involve himself in humanitarian action.

The role of the stronger woman, where both are present, changes accordingly in the late novels. Most of the novels following *MF* and *HM* portray a hero in the process of moving, or attempting to move, from attachment to a mature woman, usually a wife or mistress, to a new relationship with a younger, more dependent woman who is claiming his protection. While, following Phuong, the weaker women tend to become passive indicators directing the hero's sympathies to the sufferings of their respective peoples (the Vietnamese, the South American peasants, black South Africans), the stronger women become conversely something of a retarding influence, holding the hero back in a former, less responsive, and more selfish way of life.

There is perhaps also a sense, in the late novels, that the failure of the hero's relationship with the stronger woman may be a reflection of his shortcoming, particularly of his inability or unwillingness to accept personal commitment. His turning instead to a younger, more dependent woman, to whom he has at first no very binding obligations and whom he may not feel the need to treat as an equal, may be further symptomatic of weakness. The moral impulse of the story is then towards his making a proper commitment to this second woman. The heroes who do so, like Fowler and Wormold, survive happily, whereas those who fail, like Brown and Plarr, do not.

Scobie is another case of such failure. His initial compromise, undertaken in order to send Louise away, arises from motives not entirely selfless: Scobie is more at peace without Louise and finds her presence a burden. When she has gone he meets Helen, whose utter helplessness and dependence attracts him. He is not initially bound to her, as he is to Louise, as her appeal is unspoken and his attention to her voluntary. Ironically, however, he finds that his kindness and affection towards Helen begin to turn into a bond of much the same kind as holds him to Louise. Helen's mute appeal becomes more pressing and eventually vocal, and Scobie finds himself then with another human obligation no less demanding and troublesome than the first.

> "You are so careful always," she said, and now he realized what was happening and why he had thought of Louise. He wondered sadly whether love always inevitably took the same road.... He knew from experience how passion died away and how love went, but pity always stayed. (2.3.1.1)

The duality suggested here, between a relationship entailing commitment and responsibility and one which, however passionate or kindly, might stop short of these less romantic qualities, is part of what is acted out between the rival pairs of women in several of the late novels, particularly in *QA* and *HC*, and more sketchily in *TC* and *TA*. Scobie, like several of the late heroes, fails in his attempt to reconcile the two.

In *QA* Fowler is still married to Helen at the beginning, and in the course of the story he succeeds in obtaining from her his release, the divorce which enables him to marry Phuong. However reluctantly, he does offer Phuong the full commitment of a formal marriage, and this is clearly the precondition for the degree of personal happiness he enjoys at the end. Helen ties him to his old life, a life in which he had evidently been something of a philanderer, rootless, and not very contented. His flight to the remoteness of Saigon is his attempt to get away from all that. His old marriage still binds him, but as he becomes more committed to his new home and its people he is allowed to untie this last knot and make a new start. Phuong is not only a rather helpless girl looking out for the man most likely to provide for her, but also, in Fowler's eyes at least, a representative of an innocent, victimized people. In *QA*, as in *HC*, the hero's willingness to engage himself in action on behalf of suffering humanity goes along with his personal affair with a young female drawn from among the oppressed. Fowler is finally spurred into action by witnessing the bomb attack in which Phuong herself could so easily have been a victim.

Querry in *BC* is breaking free from his former life in Europe, the surviving claims of which are represented in the story by Toute-à-toi. This life has been a moral failure, both in his work, where he has in a sense betrayed his vocation, and privately, where he has had a succession of affairs which have hurt others without bringing him any lasting happiness. He escapes to the jungle, where he is faced with a mute appeal for help and sympathy from Marie Rycker. This he ignores as far as he can, but finds himself nonetheless going through the motions of abducting and seducing her. His actual innocence of any intention to take advantage of Marie or to interfere in any way between her and Rycker, on a purely literal level, is a virtue; but symbolically she is repeating the kind of claim for sympathy and support which he has evidently turned his back on in the past, and on this level Querry's failure to respond is a serious shortcoming. While it remains true that Querry's deliberate elopement with Marie is hardly imaginable as a satisfactory, or even possible, ending to the story, his failure to respond to her, echoing his callous attitude to the women he had known in Europe, is a failing; and his failure to see what Marie has in mind prevents him from anticipating the situation which results in his death.

Querry's case must be compared on the one hand to that of Fowler and on the other to that of Plarr. Fowler achieves a degree of contentment because he moves far enough from his initial position of cynical isolation to offer marriage to Phuong. Plarr, however, fails to turn his "obsession" with Clara into anything more: his determination to save Fortnum is dictated in part by his reluctance to have Clara left on his hands, and he dies in trying to preserve the husband who will save him from having to take responsibility for the widow. In the general pattern of the late novels, the weaker woman represents the call for human sympathy, and the hero's failure to respond, even if he is hindered by such circumstances as her marriage to another man, is a decisive factor in his fate.

Martha in *TC*, a woman of the stronger type, represents the unsatisfactory life Brown is attempting to lead as a hotelier in Papa Doc's Haiti. Aware of the ultimate untenability of the position, Brown has already tried, unsuccessfully, to quit; and his attempt to sell the Haitian property is at the same time an effort to end his affair with Martha. The unhappiness of this relationship is clear, not only from the way the couple seem inevitably to lapse into bitter argument, but also from the inescapable presence of the ironically named Angel, who stands for Martha's commitment to her family. Even had Brown wanted a permanent and committed relationship with Martha, she would not have been able to agree. Brown evidently needs to move on, but rather like Querry he fails to develop any realistic alternatives. Frustration over his affair with Martha drives him, on one occasion, to the brothel where, for the first time in two years, he sees Tin Tin. She appears "all in white . . . like a bride at a church door"(1.5.3);

but she occupies only a few lines, and the story does not explore the possibility that Brown might take the hint and make this potential "bride" his own. There is in *TC* only a fleeting glimpse of the young native woman, found by Fowler and Pulling but overlooked by Plarr and Brown.

Henry Pulling finds his bride at the very end of *TA*. She is the chief of customs' daughter, a girl whom Pulling will marry in the next year when she turns sixteen. She is not only his reward but also an integral part of the new life he is undertaking, since alliance with the customs office will be essential to his success as a smuggler. Here is the comic equivalent of the young bride offered to the hero as a bridge to a new life. Henry's old life is represented by his alternative mate, Miss Keene, an older woman occupied with tatting and church bazaars. Barbara Keene, to whom Henry had almost proposed, would have bound him to his dahlias and suburban retirement and made impossible his travels with Augusta.

Heroes in these later novels—Fowler, Querry, Brown, Pulling, and Plarr—tend initially to seek in the girlish women to whom they turn their attentions an easy alternative to the complex demands of a fully adult sexual relationship. In the comic situation of *TA* this does not matter: Henry will no doubt be happy enough with his child bride in the slightly unreal and heavily euphoric world in which he is to settle. In the serious novels, however, there is an implicit requirement, particularly clear in *QA*, *BC*, and *HC*, that the hero accept the transformation of his lighthearted affair into a permanent relationship with mutual obligations. Fowler must marry his mistress, Querry finds his innocent and unthinking sympathy for Marie turned into alleged adultery and paternity, and Plarr sees himself similarly on the verge of having to shoulder the burden of care for Clara and their unborn child. In each case the cynical, unfeeling hero falls under pressure to accept responsibility for a young bride.

Plarr initially sees his relations with Clara very much as Fowler has, in the past, viewed his association with Phuong. Neither man supposes the woman to have any feeling for him beyond a liking for the protection and material comforts he can provide, and neither man will admit to love for his partner. Querry is similar in failing to see Marie's growing feeling towards him. Plarr distinguishes sharply between "love," of which he thinks himself incapable, and "obsession," in terms of which he accounts for his interest in Clara (2.3). His first meeting with her, in a brothel and reminiscent of the circumstances under which Brown meets Tin Tin, emphasizes that what he is seeking in this child-woman is not adult love but a deliberate alternative.

> There was something clinical in a brothel which appealed to Doctor Plarr.... Only in television dramas did emotions of love, anxiety or fear infiltrate into the wards. His first years in Buenos Aires, while his mother complained, dramatized and went over his missing father's fate, and the later years when she became volubly content with sweet cakes and chocolate ices had given Doctor Plarr a suspicion of any emotion which was curable by means as simple as an orgasm or an eclair. (2.2)

Like Phuong and Marie, therefore, Clara represents the requirement that the hero develop the faculty for love, not only by concerning himself in the wider field of human suffering, of which she is an individual case, but more particularly in a personal relationship.

The two last novels, *HF* and *CE*, do not display their female characters in contrasting pairs, as do most of the others, but there are still continuities in the female roles. Each of these two stories presents a leading female character who shares with the "working girls" of the early novels a relative dependence and helplessness, a largely passive role, and a liability to fall victim to untoward circumstances. As in *HC*, the lady has in each case already been rescued by the antagonist before the action opens: Fortnum has taken Clara from the brothel and married her; Carson has secured Sarah's escape from South Africa; and the Captain has somehow (the circumstances never become fully apparent) taken Liza from the clutches of "the Devil." The hero's task in each case becomes essentially to maintain the security in which this prior rescue has placed the heroine: Plarr, in Fortnum's absence, has to look after Clara; Castle has to save (not Sarah herself but) Sarah's people from "Uncle Remus"; and Baxter is directly charged with Liza's protection while the Captain is away.

As in *HC*, so in *HF* and *CE*, the antagonist has become a largely benign figure, and the woman's role is to induce the hero, if she can, to act along the humanitarian lines which the antagonist has established. Just as Fortnum's love for Clara sets Plarr a standard, so the Captain's love for Liza is Baxter's example. Again, Carson's care and self-sacrifice in working for the welfare of black Africans, constantly recalled in the story by Sarah's presence as Castle's wife, establishes the line which Castle must take when confronted by Muller. We should therefore count Sarah Castle and Liza among the successors of Elizabeth, Pinkie's Rose, Phuong, and Clara, not only as dependent women in need of the hero's protection but also as important monitors, indicating for the hero the required course of action, reminding him of the humanitarian imperative.

6. Detectives and Villains

At the moral heart of a typical Greene novel is the hero's decision to act in concert with the antagonist, to join his enterprise or follow his example, and thereby to engage himself in some morally significant undertaking. Although the antagonist may occasionally, like Carson, be benign, and is rarely without some redeeming features of personal warmth or good intent, it is generally true that the line of action into which he draws the hero involves something illicit, underhanded, even simply illegal.

The world of the antagonist, towards which the hero is drawn, is characteristically covert, and this is evident, in many cases, from the behavior and status of the antagonist himself. He is usually one to whom secrecy is vital. Carson, Hilfe, and Pyle are secret agents; Carlyon, Yusef, Augusta, and the Captain are all engaged in smuggling; Sir Marcus, Lime, and Benditch are profiteers involved in illegal plots and deals; Calver is an outlaw trying to evade capture; Jones hides his true past and lives by fraud; Krogh perpetrates fraud on an international scale; even the relatively inoffensive Fortnum, beneath his consular veneer, conceals alcoholism and incompetence. Literally or metaphorically, the antagonist belongs to an underworld, whether it be Javitt's subterranean tunnels or Kite's criminal fraternity. The hero's entry into this world provokes, in most cases, the specific reaction of another important character, one who is, or who assumes the role of, a detective determined to uncover what is being concealed. Once the action of the novel has been set in motion by the hero's movement towards the world of the antagonist, a further impetus is provided by the need to avoid or deceive this "detective" who is now on the trail. Thus there lies, at the heart of a typical Greene plot, a kind of detective story.[68]

Greene's use of detection as a motif is another of the several important ways in which his plots are indebted in conception to those of Conrad, and particularly, in this case, to *The Secret Agent*. Like Conrad, Greene employs a very much modified form of the classic detective story. In the classic type, exemplified by Conan Doyle and Agatha Christie, the detective is the hero, a hero descended from the legendary figures of old romances, a man of special powers who goes about the world using his gifts to right wrongs and rescue the unjustly accused. In the modern, popular detective story, the hero's quest usually becomes a puzzle to be solved, and the reader is encouraged to ally himself with the hero in unraveling the clues and resolving the problem. Greene, on the other hand, has no interest in the process of detection—indeed, in Greene the reader usually knows the truth from the outset, and he watches the frequently baffled detective make slow approaches to an already revealed end. Greene's detectives are not his heroes, nor is their task the main concern of the novels. What these figures do is add a crucial impetus, keeping the action moving by preventing the hero from enjoying in peace the fruits of whatever compromise he has effected. Having somehow involved himself in a dubious line of action, the hero finds he must go on: like the Priest he must keep moving, like Pinkie he must commit more crimes to conceal those already committed, like Plarr he must continue to help the terrorists. The hero may have the option of simply disengaging, of stopping whatever he has begun doing; but it is usually the case that his doing so would risk exposure or discovery by the detective. The detective is, in a sense, the fuel which keeps the plot in motion, preventing the hero from simply "getting away with" whatever he has done.

The number and prominence of these detective figures in Greene's fiction are striking. The list includes not only detectives in the stricter sense—policemen and private investigators—but also spymasters, soldiers, investigative journalists, and even occasional private individuals who simply set themselves to uncover the truth behind suspicious activity. There is usually one such

Detectives and Villains 241

character in each novel, but in some cases there are several involved in different episodes of the story, and occasionally, as in *CA*, we have to be content with an anonymous police presence manifested from time to time in different unnamed officers. Here again a preliminary list may be helpful.

MW Mr. Farne and Sir Henry (prosecutors in the trial of the smugglers)
ST Hartep and Mabel Warren
IB The Assistant Commissioner
EM Minty
GS Mather
BR Ida
CA The police pursuing D, and Mr. Muckerji
PG The Lieutenant
MF The police pursuing Rowe, and Mr. Prentice
HM Wilson
TM Calloway
EA Parkis (hired by Bendrix, who is himself the chief detective here)
QA Vigot
OM Segura
BC Parkinson
TC Concasseur
TA Sparrow, Colonel Hakim, O'Toole
HC Perez
HF Daintry
CE Martinez

In most of these cases the detective is pursuing or investigating the hero himself or occasionally (as in *TA*) the activities of the antagonist through the hero. The Assistant Commissioner is therefore an exception in that his assignment is not to investigate Conrad, of whom he knows nothing until the action is virtually over, but rather to report on the effects of Jim's sentence. Parkis is also an apparent exception, in that he is hired by the hero to investigate someone else, and the largely ineffectual Rennit and Jones from *MF* may be mentioned here as in the same case; but Rennit and Jones do actually contribute to the police investigation of Rowe, and even Parkis finds that he has spent some of his time reporting on the activities of his employer.

The business of detection in a typical Greene novel, however, is more complex. In most cases it is a dual process, for while the hero is being investigated or pursued by some kind of detective, he is himself often engaged in the investigation and potential exposure of the activities of the antagonist. The hero renders himself suspect by acting in accord with the antagonist, but his action, typically, has been undertaken without full awareness of its implications. The hero consequently embarks on an investigation of his own, a process which is often both a gradual discovery of what the antagonist is really up to and at the same time a reappraisal of his own moral position.

In *MW*, for instance, Andrews's association with Carlyon makes him a smuggler, and the action on the beach from which Andrews makes his escape lays him open to the charge of complicity in the murder of the exciseman. He is therefore, when we first see him, in flight from the law. Already, however, he has begun the process of exposing Carlyon by writing the letter revealing the smugglers' plans, and he is therefore also in flight from the smugglers, who now suspect his treachery. The two movements come together in the courtroom where Andrews squares himself with the law by giving evidence against the smugglers: in revealing the truth about them he also clarifies his own position by distancing himself from them. Truth is exposed here as the hunted man surrenders and declares himself, and at the same time uncovers and betrays the secrets of the antagonist. The story does not end here because the courtroom episode raises a number of claims which have to be satisfied, and this is done as Andrews then retraces his steps, by way of Lucy and Elizabeth, to his final confrontation with Carlyon.

This dual process of detection is subject to considerable variation and metaphorical displacement in the serious novels, but continues in the "entertainments" to appear in ways very similar to its original statement in *MW*. In *GS* Raven, acting under orders which come ultimately from Sir Marcus, commits murder in the opening pages. When he is paid for this in stolen money, he becomes a fugitive from the law and, at the same time, begins a quest for vengeance against the criminal employers who have betrayed him. As he acquires further information, chiefly from

Anne, Raven's pursuit of personal revenge becomes involved with higher motives, aiming not only at the death of Sir Marcus but also at the exposure of the plot and the prevention thereby of war and great suffering. Again the movement of the story comes from a dual process of investigative pursuit: while Mather leads the police hunt for Raven, Raven draws upon all his resources to avoid arrest while tracking down his employer. Again, as in *MW*, both movements conclude simultaneously, this time when Mather corners Raven just as Raven shoots Sir Marcus. Raven's own death at this point precipitates the exposure of the antagonist's plot.

CA follows a similar dynamic pattern. The "confidential agent" D is on a mission to conclude a deal with Lord Benditch. His mission is of doubtful legality and therefore requires secrecy. Although D and his cause are portrayed sympathetically, it has to be borne in mind that Benditch, like Sir Marcus, is a profiteer, and that the proposed export of coal is illegal, contravening the British policy of neutrality. However humane his aims, in his dealings with Benditch D is still acting against the law. D's initial need for discretion turns into actual flight from pursuit when his enemies contrive to place him under suspicion of involvement in a series of crimes from theft to murder. (He is in fact responsible for the death of K, and it is chiefly on this account that he has to leave the country at the end. Fortunately the reader is unlikely to waste much sympathy on K.) Meanwhile D becomes increasingly eager to strike back at his opponents, and his anger finds a focus when he learns they have killed Else. As with Raven the movement which begins in a desire for personal vengeance is subsumed in a wider need to expose the antagonist's plot. After the death of K, D is less concerned with avenging Else and more anxious to prevent the export of coal to his enemies. His attempt to reveal the truth to the miners corresponds to Andrews's testimony in court, and in both cases the truth becomes lost under local prejudices. In the end, however, D's exposure of Benditch is successful: like Raven, he leaves such chaos in the wake of his flight that official attention is drawn to the plot and its evil consequences thus prevented. D is therefore another instance of the pursuer pursued, and like Raven he is apprehended just at the point where his own effort to expose truth is rewarded with success.

MF begins as Rowe pursues the mystery of the cake. He soon encounters resistance and enlists private detectives to help him. He is also apparently assisted by Hilfe; but Hilfe is really plotting to hinder Rowe's investigation, and he contrives that Rowe, very like D, soon falls under suspicion of a crime (the "murder" of Cost) and so becomes a fugitive from the law. The police pursuit of Rowe is at first purely imaginary (because Cost has not been killed), but later Rowe is sought by the police in connection with the disappearance of Jones and as one of those involved in the bombing at the Royal Court Hotel. By this time Rowe has been captured and hidden away in the asylum. Even there, however, he continues his detective work, speculating on newspaper reports, examining marks in Forrester's books, and eventually penetrating the sick bay to discover the truth about Major Stone. When Forrester, presumably in an effort to restrain him, tells Rowe that he is a murderer, Rowe runs away and gives himself up to the police.

This point in *MF* corresponds to the courtroom scene in *MW*: Rowe surrenders himself to the authorities and reveals what he knows of the activities of his enemies. Although Rowe is not "wanted" for the murder referred to by Forrester, the information he gives the police identifies him as the man sought in connection with other mysteries, and this helps Prentice to unravel more of the plot, and particularly the parts played in it by Forrester and Cost. It remains for Rowe to conclude the detective work himself and make the identification of Hilfe as the arch-villain. The confrontation with Hilfe at the railway station corresponds to Andrews's last meeting with Carlyon and Raven's shooting of Sir Marcus.

In the matter of "detection," as in other respects, *MF* tends to be more sophisticated than the earlier "entertainments." Rowe is not actually sought for the reasons he believes, nor is he himself aware until near the end of the real nature of the plot which he has been instrumental in uncovering. Detection is here bound up metaphorically, chiefly by way of the asylum episode, with self-discovery and revaluation of the past. The structural similarity remains nonetheless. It remains true also that the hero's association with the antagonist is the root of both branches of the dual process of detection. Rowe is pursued by Hilfe's agents from the moment he leaves the fête with the cake, and he is himself on Hilfe's track from the point soon after where Poole attempts to poison him. It does not matter that Rowe has no personal association with Hilfe except as a result of accident, his winning of the cake. In this highly symbolic story Rowe is already associated with Hilfe at the start by a state of mind, a yearning for moral simplicity (which Rowe locates in his boyhood), represented later in the story by the false innocence of Forrester and Hilfe, a moral simplicity that lends itself to Nazi ideology. The truth which Rowe has to reveal here is not just the existence of Hilfe's plot but also the negative way of thinking which underlies it, and into which he had himself fallen after his wife's death.

The pattern of detection seen in *MW*, *GS*, *CA*, and *MF* is more faintly, or only partially present in the other early novels, *ST*, *IB*, and *EM*. In *ST* there is no antagonist figure, and consequently, while the hero, Czinner, remains subject to pursuit and liable to exposure, he is not himself engaged in the exposure of anyone else. (He may have done this formerly, in giving evidence at the Kamnetz trial, but this business is not presented in the novel.) His purpose is simply to join and lead a preplanned popular uprising. This becomes a criminal purpose once he has crossed the border into Yugoslavia, and he is then liable not only to exposure but also to arrest and execution. He is pursued at first not by police but by an investigative journalist, Mabel Warren. Mabel spots him in Cologne, follows him onto the train, searches his baggage and finds evidence of the planned uprising, confronts him, and telephones news of his presence back to her London office from Vienna. The appearance of her report in the British press next morning results in Czinner's arrest when he reaches Subotica. The business of detection in *ST*, however, concerns only Czinner and is not found in the other threads of the plot. (Grünlich is a fugitive from justice, but he is not actually pursued.)

There are several matters of detection and exposure in *IB*, but—as befits a novel constructed deliberately as a collage—they are only coincidentally related. The story begins as the Assistant Commissioner is given an investigative task: to report on the likely repercussions of Jim's reprieve or execution. This investigation provides the containing frame for the mosaic of the novel, but it is related only tangentially to the hero, Conrad. By pure chance Conrad sees the Assistant Commissioner in the street and later, in his derangement, pursues him as a representative of the system which has unjustly condemned Jim. Conrad might be said to be engaged upon exposure of this injustice, but such a way of speaking does not take us very far: he is pursuing the wrong man, and his actions are quite ineffectual. Neither is he himself pursued: it is only his paranoia, and later his sense of guilt, which make him act like a fugitive. The real elements of detection are in the background: Conder's reporting on the communists, and the Assistant Commissioner's investigation of a murder case, leading to the arrest of the perpetrator.

The idea of exposure, of the revelation of concealed truth, still looms large in *IB*: most of the central characters are engaged, directly or indirectly, in some effort to discover and present the truth about Jim's case. There is not only the Assistant Commissioner's report but also the attempt involving Kay, Surrogate, and Caroline Bury to bring moral pressure to bear on the decision; there is the petition (handed around but ultimately discarded by Jules); and there is Milly's attempt, involving Mrs. Coney and Conder, to win sympathetic publicity. The point of all this in *IB* is ironic futility: the report is never written, Lady Caroline proves powerless, the petition is never presented, the publicity is negligible. In the end, the truth of Jim's sad case remains known only to his widow, the Assistant Commissioner, and the prison chaplain.

The pattern of detection established in *MW* reappears more clearly in *EM*. Anthony's association with Krogh brings him into contact with an immense financial empire. As Anthony begins to penetrate this institution, eventually discovering that it rests upon fraud and violence, so he himself falls under the scrutiny of the watchful freelance journalist Minty. Anthony's "investigation" of Krogh (carried out quite perfunctorily, like all of Anthony's undertakings), begins with his examination of the man's wardrobe, encompasses informal, offstage conversations with junior employees, surreptitious glances at papers left on Kate's desk, and concludes with his interview with young Andersson. Krogh is, of course, a fraud, but so is Anthony, as the reader is several times reminded through the matter of his Harrow tie. The business of the tie is significant because it associates Anthony's habitual petty deception with Krogh's large-scale fraud. Anthony wears a tie which claims unmerited status, while Krogh's ties are merely tasteless. Anthony selects new ones for him, but Krogh sends them back to the shop. Minty's investigation of Anthony begins with suspicions about the Harrow tie and ends with his presence as an unobserved witness at Anthony's death.

Minty may have been, as Greene records, an afterthought in the story's evolution (*WE*.1.6), but his presence is nonetheless important. However "seedy" his appearance, he is genuine where Anthony is not: Minty really did go to Harrow. His preservation of a living spider under a glass in his room may image his role as an observer of life. His main business is to watch Krogh: "Minty keeps an eye on him, watches, records, perhaps now and then puts a drawing-pin on his chair" (3.2). The primary purpose of the "Harrow dinner" section (3.2) is to show Minty as an acute observer of human nature; yet his observation of Anthony yields no practical result, and Anthony's fate is entirely independent of Minty's information. Nonetheless, the very presence of this watcher as a "spare cog" in the story's mechanism is indicative of the importance Greene attached to the "detective" role, to the figure who observes the hero while the hero himself works towards exposure of the antagonist.

Detection is clearly the major impulsive power in the plot of *BR*. It is Ida's determination to uncover the truth behind the death of Hale from which almost everything follows, and it is her constant and unrelenting presence that keeps events in motion. Here again the ultimate cause is the antagonist's influence, in this case that of the deceased Kite, since it is to avenge Kite that Pinkie kills Hale and so attracts Ida's attention. Pinkie himself is not concerned to expose any kind of truth, but rather, in keeping with the moral inversion of his creed, his belief in Evil, to ensure its continued concealment. Hale disclosed a hidden truth and betrayed Kite, and Pinkie kills him for it. Most of Pinkie's subsequent actions, in response to the pressure of discovery represented by Ida, are similarly directed at concealment, including his dealings with Rose, the killing of Spicer, the removal of Drewitt, and the suicide pact.

BR is unusual in that it gives the detective role to one of the female characters. This was perhaps why Greene found Ida a difficult character to bring to life, because she has to be at once an embodiment of maternal, sexual comforts, and a serious threat to Pinkie's position. It was a combination Greene did not attempt again. *PG* returns to a simpler situation, in which both hero and antagonist are outlaws simultaneously hunted by the same agent of authority, the Lieutenant. The Priest's story begins as he turns his back on escape and elects to remain within the state where he is a hunted man, and it ends with his capture. In between the Lieutenant makes great efforts to track him down—searching the Fellows' farm, taking hostages, combing the villages, and keeping the *mestizo* as a witness to identify the fugitive.

While the Lieutenant's pursuit of the Priest is evident, it is not the case that the hero undertakes any kind of literal investigation or exposure of Calver. There is, however, a sense in which confrontation with Calver is the Priest's metaphorical goal, his achievement of which ends his flight. Moreover, if we accept the invitation to read symbolism into Calver's name and to see him as a kind of redemptive savior, then it follows that the hero's task, as a priest, is to discover and reveal the truth which Calver represents. This, in the end, he does, by giving up his own freedom to bring salvation to another and by accepting a martyr's death.

HM returns us to firmer ground and a clearer statement of the pattern of detection. Scobie is a policeman, and his chief work as such, besides investigation of routine petty squabbles among the natives, is the prevention of smuggling. The foremost smuggler is Yusef who, rather like Sir Marcus and Lord Benditch, is trying to make a profit from the war. Scobie's pursuit of Yusef's diamonds is constant (the affairs of the Portuguese Captain's letter, Pemberton's suicide, and Tallit's parrot are all part of it) and the level of its success is indicated by Yusef's evident anxiety to divert Scobie with offers of bribery, friendship, and eventually blackmail. Meanwhile Scobie himself is watched by Wilson, an undercover investigator reporting to his superiors in the government hierarchy. The story opens with Wilson's arrival and concludes with his discovery, from the diary, that Scobie's death may well have been suicide. What Wilson chiefly suspects is that Scobie is in league with Yusef, and while this is untrue at the outset it becomes increasingly the case as the story progresses. Ironically Wilson never discovers the real nature of Scobie's involvement with Yusef, any more than Scobie ever succeeds in exposing Yusef's involvement in diamond smuggling, but it is against the background of this dual process of detection that Scobie's personal tragedy is acted out.

Lime in *TM* is another wartime profiteer. His boyhood friend Martins comes to Vienna at Lime's invitation. When Martins finds Lime is supposedly dead and suspected of criminal activities he begins his own investigation, becoming, in Calloway's words, an "amateur detective" (6). Martins's initial aim is to exonerate Lime, but as he discovers the truth his purpose changes and he helps the police in Lime's capture—being, again in Calloway's words, "the only person who could persuade Lime to come over," to come back into the British sector where he could be arrested (13). Meanwhile Martins himself is being observed. Calloway follows him from the cemetery and has him watched by plainclothes police. Martins falls briefly under suspicion of involvement in the murder of Koch. Calloway, the narrator, keeps a police file on him, and even opens the story with a quotation from it. Here agin, much as *MW*, *GS*, and *MF*, the hero is at first himself suspected but in the end helps the authorities to a discovery of the real criminals. The shooting of Lime by Martins echoes Raven's shooting of Sir Marcus and Rowe's complicity in Hilfe's suicide. It also anticipates Fowler's part in the death of Pyle.

EA is a love story and therefore does not follow the pattern of action between hero and antagonist evident in most of Greene's other novels. Even so, it is a love story told very much in terms of detection. The story is essentially Bendrix's effort to uncover the truth about Sarah, and particularly about her reasons for suddenly rejecting him without explanation. The novel opens with Henry's idea of hiring a detective to follow Sarah, an idea taken up by Bendrix, who employs Parkis. Parkis's investigation is interspersed with retrospective episodes from the early stages of the "affair." From the beginning Bendrix feels "like . . . a detective" in his relations with Sarah. "Even in the moment of love, I was like a police officer gathering evidence" (2.1). "Even before the days of Mr. Parkis I was trying to check on her" (2.2). After Sarah abandons him Bendrix is all the more in the dark about her real nature, and hence his eagerness to hire a detective. Parkis's reports, delivered at intervals through the first half of the novel, gradually yield information—a scrap of a letter and an address to which Sarah pays clandestine visits. Bendrix himself penetrates this household in "disguise" and meets Smythe. Then Parkis obtains Sarah's diary, which makes clear for the reader as for Bendrix much that had been mysterious in Sarah's behavior. Even so, Bendrix's detective work does not end here. Within a few pages of the end of the extract from the diary Sarah dies, leaving her lover to become the involuntary recipient of several further testimonies concerning her. This new information, which comes variously from Smythe, Sarah's mother, and Father Crompton, reveals yet more of the meaning and implications of Sarah's actions.

The element of detection is integral to *EA*. It is not merely that Greene chose to tell the story of the "affair" in terms of Bendrix's investigation, but that the story, without this element, is unimaginable. Bendrix's investigation arises from the fact that Sarah's life is largely concealed from him, particularly in the crucial matter of her vow on the occasion of the bomb. It is a brute fact of the story that, on this occasion, Sarah leaves Bendrix without any explanation, and that it is only through Parkis's work and from the stolen diary that Bendrix discovers what has happened to end the "affair." Had she told Bendrix, although he would still no doubt have felt bitterness, and would probably have continued to "badger" her for some time, there would have been nothing to investigate, and what is left of the novel's story becomes banal. Yet it is nowhere clear just why Sarah does not explain herself to Bendrix, which would seem, given her decision, the humane—not to say courteous—way to proceed. In the end one is driven to the conclusion that Sarah's concealment of her reasons is an authorial imperative, rather than a natural development of character and situation. The story depends upon Bendrix being made to search for answers which are, rather artificially, being withheld from him by Sarah.

The full pattern of detection is restored in *QA*, where once again the hero investigates and exposes the actions of the antagonist while himself being investigated by a suspicious police detective. In the real time of the novel these two investigations are consecutive, the one leading up to and the other following Pyle's death; but in the narrative, with its frequent time shifts, they run concurrently. The novel opens, on the night of Pyle's death, with the beginning of the police investigation and Vigot's first interview with Fowler. Then follows Fowler's retrospective narration of his relations with Pyle, punctuated by several further interviews with Vigot in the days following the murder. The story ends with a three page "coda" between Fowler and Phuong following what is clearly to be Fowler's last meeting with Vigot. Vigot's investigation of Fowler therefore frames the narrative.

Fowler's investigation of Pyle begins with suspicion of his involvement in "secret" activities (2.1). He is puzzled by the story of the crates of plastic and questions Pyle about them. He witnesses an obviously prearranged meeting between Pyle and a Caodaist officer at Tanyin. Following promptings from Dominguez, Fowler visits Mr. Heng and is shown the molds, which he is later, after the "bicycle bombs," able to identify and link with Pyle. Following Mr. Heng's information he searches Mr. Muoi's premises and finds the equipment which makes the bombs. He deduces, from overheard conversation and Pyle's own words, that the Americans are behind the big explosion. He has, at this point, gathered enough information to apprehend the whole picture of Pyle's activity and its consequences, and he arranges with Mr. Heng the plan which results in Pyle's murder.

OM is the story of Wormold's venture into espionage, which causes him to investigate in particular the economic and military affairs of Cuba. The story begins as he reluctantly accepts the task, and it ends when the job is terminated by his expulsion from the island and return to London. Instead of real espionage, however, in this comic novel the hero follows the suggestions of the dreamer Hasselbacher and embarks upon a purely mock investigation, fabricating in his reports both the information he supplies and the sources (or "agents") from whom he supposedly obtained it. To this end Wormold pretends to recruit agents and then invents the story of secret installations in the mountains. As the other side begins reacting by blackmailing Hasselbacher and killing Raoul Wormold's investigation turns necessarily to the anticipation and evasion of his concealed enemies. He attempts to rescue Teresa and warn Sanchez, and he tries frantically to discover the identity of his intended assassin at the dinner. At last he uncovers Carter and kills him, at the same time effecting his one real act of espionage in obtaining a copy of the police list of known agents—although even this comes to nothing, since his attempt to convey the information to London is a failure.

Meanwhile Wormold's acting out of Hasselbacher's fantasy brings him to the attention of the authorities. He is questioned by the police in Santiago. He is questioned again after his visit to Professor Sanchez. By this time Segura has realized what is going on, and his suspicions are expressed during the two games of checkers he plays against Wormold. In the end, after the deaths of Hasselbacher and Carter, Segura puts a stop to Wormold's activities and obliges him to leave the country.

The dual process of detection is absent from *BC*. Querry is pursued and reported upon by Parkinson (a remote descendant of Mabel Warren); but only in vague and figurative terms could it be said that Querry himself undertakes any kind of investigation or exposure. Indeed, it is the virtual passivity of the hero which most distinguishes *BC* as singular among Greene's novels. Like most of the heroes, Querry is in flight, a man pursued; but his flight is voluntary and, while other heroes are, at the same time, engaged in some mission, usually attempting the exposure of the antagonist, Querry has no purpose beyond the completion of his own physical and spiritual withdrawal.

BC, like *EA*, is a novel written very much to expound a thesis, to exemplify a spiritual problem. It asks what becomes of the man without faith who rejects worldliness and, in the manner of the ascetic saints, seeks the furthest remove from earthly pleasures. In *EA* the question concerns the fate of an unbeliever who prays in a moment of crisis and finds prayer apparently answered. Both novels are intellectual explorations of problems in moral philosophy, expanded stories of much the same type as "A Visit to Morin." Intriguing and brilliant as they are, both these novels are flawed: most readers will remain unconvinced by Sarah's vow and by Querry's renunciation. It is surely no coincidence that these are the two among Greene's mature novels which deviate most from the patterns of action he develops in the others.

The dual process of detection reappears in *TC*. The story opens as Brown is given the task, by the captain of the *Medea*, of reporting on Jones. Brown overtly rejects this imposition, but in the event the novel which develops, and of which Brown is the first-person narrator, is precisely his account of the career of Jones in Haiti. Brown does not intentionally investigate Jones, but he constantly witnesses, and the text of the novel is his report. He visits Jones in prison and later sees him at the brothel and in a passing car, reconciled to the authorities. When he later falls from favor Jones comes for help to Brown, who conveys him to the safety of the embassy. Here Brown watches Jones become, apparently, his rival for Martha's attentions, and therefore contrives his escape to join the rebels. On their journey to the mountains Brown learns a good deal more about Jones, and he learns more still, across the border, when he is told how Jones died. Jones is Brown's alter ego, and Brown's revaluation of Jones at the end of the story, represented by the monument he helps to erect, is an indication of the progress the hero has made in self-knowledge.

Brown himself meanwhile comes under hostile scrutiny from the Haitian authorities, represented by Concasseur. He first encounters Concasseur's gaze when he goes with the Smiths to visit Jones in prison. The events which follow are never fully explicit, but it appears that Jones gains his release by offering the Haitian authorities a fraudulent arms deal—fraudulent because, as they eventually discover, Jones is unable to deliver the goods. While this offer is under negotiation Jones is also approached by the rebels, seeking the arms which Jones has let it be believed he can obtain. Concasseur learns that Jones may be dealing with the rebels: he tells Brown, for instance, of Philipot's visit to Jones, and he clearly suspects that Brown, as an associate of both Jones and Philipot, may be a mediator in the business. Brown is therefore questioned and beaten by Concasseur. Concasseur keeps Brown under surveillance and is able to intercept him with Jones at the cemetery, precipitating the encounter which results in Concasseur's death and Brown's flight across the border.

TC belongs with *QA*, *TA*, and *CE* as a novel which consists of the hero-narrator's report of his observations on the character and activities of his antagonist, activities which are in all cases illegal, although not entirely unsympathetic. *TA* is the story of Henry's dealings with Augusta from their first meeting (the first, at any rate, since his infancy) up to his decision to unite his fortunes with hers in Paraguay. The interim is occupied by his gradual discovery of her history, particularly the stories of her relationships with a succession of men, and of her present illegal activities. Henry eventually uncovers the nature of Augusta's dealings with Mr. Visconti, who turns out to be a successor of Sir Marcus, Lord Benditch, and Harry Lime, as one who makes money from illicit opportunities arising from a state of war. More important, however, is the fact that Henry's investigation of Augusta, like Brown's of Jones, is also a process of self-discovery. In the end he finds that she is his real mother and that true self-fulfilment lies, for him, in the adoption of her attitude to life, particularly her concept of "fun."

Henry's association with Augusta brings him at once to the attention of the law. There is no single officer or detective in *TA*, but a succession of agents of various national forces observing and pursuing Augusta—and Henry, insofar as he is her unwitting accomplice. There are Sparrow and Woodrow in London, Colonel Hakim in Istanbul, O'Toole on the boat to Paraguay, and the police in Ascunción.

HC and *HF* form a pair in which the detection motif is subtly altered in a way which goes along with the altered nature of the antagonist's role in these two stories. When the antagonists become innocent victims there is nothing much concerning them for the heroes to expose. Fortnum is doing nothing in particular of which he need be greatly ashamed, and Carson, being dead, is doing nothing at all and is represented as having been entirely honorable. Consequently the relation of hero to antagonist in these novels has nothing of the element of pursuit or exposure but develops instead the idea of self-exploration through increasing understanding of the antagonist's true nature, a motif which can be traced back to *TA*, and perhaps even to *QA*. In *HC* and *HF* the hero reappraises his own values as a direct result of his dealings with the antagonist.

Plarr's story opens at the point of Fortnum's capture and ends with his own death in an attempt to save Fortnum's life. There is much retrospective material in the narrative, but most of Plarr's actions between these two points are concerned with Fortnum, being either efforts to obtain his release, to pacify his wife, or to attend him in captivity. Initially Plarr sees Fortnum as a weak, almost contemptible man, a man whose job is something of a fraud (since he is neither a real nor a very efficient consul), who relies unduly upon alcohol, and whose wife is unfaithful. Yet Plarr is where he is, as the opening pages tell us, because of the unresolved question of his father's fate; and in the course of the novel Fortnum becomes symbolically the father Plarr has lost. As Plarr is forced through circumstances (his part in Fortnum's capture, his relationship with Clara, his duty to Fortnum as his patient, and later his shared confinement with him in the hut) to reconsider, he comes to see the man's weaknesses in a new and more sympathetic light. Fortnum becomes the imprisoned father whom Plarr has waited all his life to release. By accepting death in Fortnum's place Plarr finally exorcizes his father's spirit. "Detection" is not the most appropriate word for it, but Plarr's relationship with Fortnum is clearly a learning process, essentially a matter of self-discovery which is the precondition for the feeling of resolution achieved by the novel's ending.

Plarr's association with Fortnum, and his part in the consul's capture, are suspected by the policeman Perez. Perez uncovers the fact of Plarr's affair with Clara and believes that this may have influenced Plarr to become covertly involved in dealings with the kidnappers. Perez questions Plarr several times and eventually corners him with the kidnappers in the hut. In the end Perez's men shoot Plarr but conceal the true facts of his death under a false story.

As in *HC*, so in *HF* the hero's task is not to investigate or expose the antagonist but rather to discover or vindicate a kind of human truth which the antagonist exemplifies. Although he does not accept communist ideology, Castle has seen in Carson's particular practice of it a germ of human kindness. Because of his personal debt to Carson and, more widely, because of his belief that communism may be the only means to end oppression of black South Africans, he has become a double agent, passing secret information on African affairs to Moscow. As the story unfolds Castle's task becomes specifically to expose, by revealing it to the east, the anti-black conspiracy of the western powers known as "Uncle Remus." In finally achieving this he "identified himself truly for the first time with Carson" (4.2.4), a move which corresponds to Plarr's symbolic acceptance of death in Fortnum's place in *HC*.

HF is in some ways particularly close to the pattern of *OM*. The hero's investigation in both cases is perfunctory: Wormold fabricates most of his information, while Castle is simply presented with all that he needs. He is assigned to interview Muller, who then obligingly gives him, by mistake, a set of notes revealing the full extent of the nefarious plan. In both stories the hero's energies are devoted not so much to investigation (or mock investigation in Wormold's case) as to fathoming the machinations of others in the web of intelligence and counterintelligence in which he has become entangled. To the London interludes in *OM*, showing the discussions between Hawthorne and his chief, correspond in *HF* the several chapters of meetings among Daintry, Perceval, and Hargreaves. Both novels represent the hero's idiosyncratic pursuit of human values against a background of a deadly, largely ungovernable, and ultimately unprincipled bureaucratic machine. As Wormold gradually realizes that his venture into espionage has provoked the forces which kill Raoul and Hasselbacher, and which threaten himself and Beatrice, so Castle discovers that his actions as a double agent have attracted the notice of Hargreaves and Perceval, who have mistakenly killed

Davis on that account and who are planning to deal with himself in similar fashion.

The action of *HF* is precisely concerned with the investigation and exposure of Castle. The novel opens with Daintry's security check, and progresses through the mistaken identification of Davis as the "leak" to the belated realization that the culprit must, after all, have been Castle. Daintry's final interview with Castle is followed immediately by his report that Castle is the traitor; but before he can be apprehended the hero is conveyed to Moscow. The main action ends here, with Castle's task completed and his escape made good. Part Six is an expanded "coda" of the kind often present in Greene's novels, showing the effect of the action upon the chief survivors.

Even in *MQ*, which is a different kind of novel and where we might not therefore expect it, the dual pattern of investigation persists. Monsignor Quixote is sent off by the Bishop of Motopo on a quest, "to go forth like . . . Don Quixote on the high roads of the world" and to "tilt at windmills" (1.1). Exactly what he is seeking is never stated openly, but it becomes clear to the reader in the long first Part that Quixote is reviewing the major ideological and spiritual questions of his life. While pursuing with Sancho a running debate on the relative merits and inner meanings of Marxism and Catholicism, Monsignor Quixote visits a succession of politically, intellectually, or spiritually significant sites: the tomb of Franco, the University of Salamanca, the grave of Unamuno. In the shorter second part Quixote embodies in action the wisdom he has acquired, opposing the subjection of faith to materialism, becoming in this way a martyr, and finally performing the mass in which the two great institutions of the modern world, communism and Christianity, are reconciled.

Monsignor Quixote's quest is an investigation only in a metaphorical sense, and therefore only loosely comparable to the campaigns of detection undertaken by heroes such as Andrews or Castle. There is no antagonist figure in *MQ* to be exposed. The pursuit of Monsignor Quixote himself, however, remains a literal part of the story. His activities, almost from the start, are regarded as suspect by such representatives of authority as Father Herera and members of the Opus Dei; and before long he is being sought by the police. The pursuit is only suspended during the brief episode in which Monsignor Quixote is forcibly kept at home by Father Herera. It resumes on his escape, and is concluded only in the final phase of the action, when the police catch up with his car and oblige him, dying, to take refuge in the monastery.

The pattern is again clear in Greene's final novel. *CE* is the story of Baxter's dealings with the Captain, from their first meeting in Baxter's boyhood to the Captain's death. Even as a boy Baxter is curious about the Captain and seeks information concerning him from Liza and by hunting for newspaper accounts of his activities. At the time of Liza's death Baxter discovers a good deal more, both by reading the letters the Captain had written to Liza and by questioning his own natural father. When he joins the Captain in Panama, Jim's information about the Captain acquires value, as it is sought by Quigly, who offers Baxter rewards in return. Baxter does finally ally himself with Quigly and contribute to the exposure of the Captain's activities, although the Captain's suicidal flight is prompted more by the news of Liza's death than by fear of discovery. Baxter himself, precisely because of his known association with the Captain, is under police surveillance from his arrival in Panama. In the end, when the Captain disappears, he is called in for questioning by Colonel Martinez; and afterwards Martinez is left puzzling over the manuscript Baxter has left which tells the Captain's story.

The detectives or investigative figures in Greene's novels are united by their common role in the pursuit of the hero with a view to his exposure, but not by personal characteristics. Personally they vary widely. Some are policemen or soldiers, while others are journalists, secret agents, or even private individuals driven by personal compulsion. Some, like Daintry and Vigot, are pleasantly human, while others, like Wilson and Parkinson, engage little sympathy. Nor are these various detectives impelled by any single common motive. Daintry and the Assistant Commissioner believe in law and order, Ida has a broad notion of justice, the Lieutenant acts upon socialist ideals, Wilson is motivated at least in part by jealousy, while the journalists—Mabel,

Minty, and Parkinson—seem each to be working from some sense of personal bitterness or frustration.

While there is not here a character type, there is among the detectives a common role or function in the pattern of action, consisting in the pursuit of the hero with a view to his capture or exposure, a purpose of which the hero, rarely free from guilt, is well aware and anxious to frustrate. To this extent many of Greene's novels involve inverted detective stories—"inverted" because the hero is not the leading detective but the guilty party whom it is the detective's object to uncover. Because of this inversion Greene's novels eschew the simple moral dualism of popular detective fiction, just as they also avoid the conventional ending in which the triumphant investigator reveals the truth he has uncovered.

In crime fiction, almost by definition, the detective is the hero whose task is to vindicate truth and justice against his criminal adversary, who is therefore the story's villain. The very notion of "crime" as the ideological basis for the fictional world implies a simple moral dualism, and the detective hero is an agent of "good" if only in the plain negative sense that the activities of the adversary he confronts are self-evidently wrongful ("criminal"). Things are never so straightforward in Greene. Greene's detectives are not his heroes but are opposed to the heroes, and the heroes' activities are rarely simply either good or bad. Consequently the detectives become themselves morally ambiguous. Just as the hero, enmeshed in the contradictions of the human situation, tends at once to be acting both rightly and wrongly, so those who take on the task of preventing him can be seen as at once right and wrong in so doing.

The moral ambiguity of the detective role is apparent from the portrayal of most of the characters assigned to it. Despite their position in the pattern of events as the hero's opponents, some of them are presented, like Vigot or Daintry, as sympathetic, not only in character but also in their goals. Most of those who are less personally sympathetic, like Ida and the Lieutenant, have redeeming features in what they would claim to be good intentions. The more embittered investigators, like Minty and Wilson, have at least their human weaknesses and are, in the end, more pathetic than really dangerous. Among the group it is probably only of Concasseur and Perceval that one would say they have deliberately placed themselves beyond human consideration and moral restraint.

Frequently Greene creates a gradual distinction, in the course of a story, between the man and the detective role he has taken on. In this way the character, who may at first appear as a potential villain insofar as his purpose is to frustrate the hero, defeats expectation by personally avoiding villainy and developing some degree of sympathy for the hero. Segura is a clear case. At first sight he is a threatening, predatory presence (at Milly's birthday party), known as the Red Vulture and said to torture prisoners and carry a cigarette case made of human skin. In the end he becomes amiable, allows Wormold to make him drunk and steal his gun, and permits Wormold and his entourage to leave Cuba unharmed. His revelation that the skin of the cigarette case is that of the man who tortured his father to death turns macabre sadism into a kind of retributive justice. While his local reputation for violence remains intact, Segura acts towards the hero with gentleness and courtesy. Something of the same happens in the case of the Lieutenant. His rigid idealism expresses itself in brutality as he applies the policy of shooting innocent "hostages." Yet there is a human side to him, which comes to the fore in his personal dealings with the Priest, who pronounces him "a good man" (2.3). The Lieutenant gives the Priest money when releasing him from prison, treats him with consideration when he is captured, and is even prepared to break the law to procure him a visit from a confessor.

On a smaller scale something similar happens in *CA*. Here the police are initially allied with the enemy, working in L's interest to inhibit D's freedom of movement. Yet in the end they prove kindly. It is a policeman who rescues D after the explosion, and in police custody he is given welcome food and rest. Again, in *TA*, the agents of authority (Sparrow, Hakim, and O'Toole) are initially suspicious of Henry and anxious to trap him, but by the end the local agents of law enforcement have become friendly. They joke with him at parties, and he is about to marry the daughter of the chief of customs. Similarly, in both *TM* and *MF* the police move from initial suspicion of the hero to active cooperation with him in the exposure and capture of the antagonist.

Surprised at the personal gentleness of their pursuers, several heroes enter into significant discussions with their detective inquisitors, even to the point of experiencing an urge to confide in them and confess. Fowler wishes he could tell Vigot the whole truth (4.1), Querry does, in a sense, "confess" to Parkinson, and Castle as good as does so in his final talk with Daintry. Very similarly, the Priest, finally captured, engages in a long discussion of fundamentals with the Lieutenant. Baxter in a way confesses to Martinez by leaving his manuscript for the police to find.

The brutality continues nonetheless. The Lieutenant shoots the Priest, Mather's men shoot Raven, and Perez apparently shoots Plarr. Ida is a factor in Pinkie's death, Henry is beaten by the police in Paraguay, and the British police prosecute D. Jim remains in his cell, and Perceval kills Davis. What remains remarkable is the number of Greene's law enforcers who are anxious, in the end, to distance themselves personally from the results they or their organizations have produced. Perez merely conceals the truth, but Daintry resigns rather than condone, and the Assistant Commissioner is "half inclined" to do the same. Sir Henry Merriman thinks of retirement after the trial (*MW* 2.8), while the Lieutenant experiences depression, "as if life had drained out of the world," after he has caught the Priest (3.4). There is a distinct lack of elation among these detectives, even when they have succeeded in tracking down their man.

Most of them do indeed suspect the right person, even though they may lack conclusive evidence, or fail to catch the culprit before he makes an escape or meets some other fate. Greene's detectives share with their more effective colleagues from popular fiction something of an instinct for things not quite right, an instinct which leads them to pursue suspicions which the common mind would be inclined to dismiss. Thus Minty instinctively latches onto Anthony, Ida knows Pinkie is somehow involved in Hale's death, Wilson is the only person who thinks of mistrusting Scobie, Vigot knows Fowler is somehow implicated in Pyle's murder, Segura suspects the apparently innocuous Wormold, Parkinson cannot accept Querry's plain account of himself (ironically, since it is, as far as Querry is concerned, true), Concasseur thinks Brown is Jones's associate long before he becomes so in fact, and Perez is sure Plarr knows more about Fortnum's capture than he will admit. Few of the heroes escape retribution: apart from the comedies of *OM* and *TA*, D, Martins, and Fowler are the only ones to survive in anything like equanimity. The abiding impression left by Greene's detectives, however, is not their skill in uncovering hidden truths and exposing the perpetrator to justice, but rather the chasm which remains between the truths they discover and the deeper truths which, in every case, elude them.

One of the functions of the detective is to provide the narrative with an extra driving force, a sense of urgency, through their actual or metaphorical pursuit of the hero. No less important, in most cases, is the detective's role in focusing the reader's attention, in the closing pages, on the discrepancy between what is publicly knowable of the hero's story—which is roughly what the detective has himself discovered—and the very different inner meaning which the reader will be in the process of drawing from the novel as a whole. An obvious, perhaps rather heavy handed instance is that of Ida who, after the main action has ended, returns home and reviews the business in conversation with Clarence. "I wonder you don't feel bad about that," says Clarence, referring to her part in Pinkie's death.

> "Somebody else would have been dead if we hadn't turned up."
> "It was her own choice."
> But Ida Arnold had an answer to everything. "She didn't understand. She was only a kid. . . . Anyway, she's got me to thank she isn't dead. . . ."
> "You're a terrible woman," Clarence repeated; he was a little drunk, "but I got to give you credit. You act for the best."
> "He's not on my conscience, anyway."
> "As you say, it was him or her."
> "There wasn't any choice," Ida Arnold said. She got up; she was like a figurehead of Victory. (7.10)

This proliferation of beery platitudes, coming as it does immediately before the final scene of Rose's visit to the priest, presents the reader very precisely with the questions which need to be considered: what is the extent of Rose's understanding, was there really "no choice" over Pinkie's fate, and what is the value of Ida's "victory"? The novel, of course, is not dogmatic, nor even very specific, in offering answers. This is not its purpose. The object is, more widely, to make the reader aware of a moral complexity in human affairs which eludes the simple categories of conventional wisdom.

A number of the endings featuring the detective character are closely comparable. In *HM*, for instance, we have (in 3.3.1.1) Wilson and Louise looking through Scobie's diary after his death. Wilson is not a bad detective. He knows about Scobie's affair with Helen and the money borrowed from Yusef, and he even spots the false entries in the diary. There is nonetheless an immense irony in the glib observation here that Scobie's secrets "were never very secret." As this section of the narrative shows, Scobie's entire private world of compassion remains unknown to the surviving characters, which compassion, as the reader remembers, extended even to the planets (2.1.1.3). What was for Scobie "the heart of the matter," is lost to Wilson and Louise in the entirely superficial issues of an extramarital affair and the acceptance of bribes.

More thoughtful men than Wilson, like Daintry and the Assistant Commissioner, are bitterly angered by the discrepancy they partly perceive between the official, public verdict on the hero's case and the underlying human considerations which have not come into account. Similar again is Minty's bitterness when he realizes that the facts of Anthony's murder will remain concealed and that his friend will be remembered only as a thief. The less thoughtful, more callous investigators simply conceal or distort the evidence, like Parkinson in his articles and Perez in his report, again underlining the discrepancy between what is commonly passed as truth and the human reality.

The same kind of discrepancy emerges from the conclusion of *PG*, preceded by a lengthy discussion, almost a debate, between the hero and his captor. The Lieutenant is courteous and considerate, and is allowed to make a number of strong points against institutional Catholicism, but the Priest, with his references to the spiritual dimension of life, wins the moral argument. His subsequent execution by the Lieutenant's men, anticipating the murder of Plarr by Perez, is another attempt—vain, as the conclusion reveals—to suppress a complex truth in the interest of ideological simplicity.

The case is slightly different when, as in *QA*, *TC*, and *CE*, the hero is telling his own story. Here the final word rests with the hero, attempting to vindicate a complex moral reality against the ignorance and incomprehension of the wider world. In *TC* Brown asserts his unity with Jones in the matter of the memorial and in the quoted words of the funeral sermon for Jones's men. In *QA* Vigot has proved both personally sympathetic and a good detective—he has, for instance, discovered the fact of Pyle's last visit to Fowler. Fowler wishes he could tell Vigot the truth about this, and then proceeds to relate it to the reader. Vigot, the representative of official truth, remains unable to prove what he suspects and is left ignorant of the tangle of motives behind Fowler's action. *CE* ends with Colonel Martinez holding Baxter's manuscript, which has just been translated for him. Martinez is therefore potentially in possession of all the available information, since, except for the brief coda of Part Four, Baxter's manuscript is the text of *CE*. It is clear, nonetheless, that Martinez will never understand the implications of the document he holds. *CE* concludes with his statement of uncertainty: "The vital question remains—what or who is King Kong?" The reader knows that King Kong represents the Captain's protective love for Liza. Failing to see this, Martinez, like Wilson, remains wholly ignorant of the heart of the matter.

In *TM*, where uniquely Greene makes the detective character the narrator, the outcome is much the same as in *QA*. Calloway simply surrenders his narrative position to the hero at the novel's climax, and Lime's death is related by Martins, a page of text in inverted commas introduced simply by the words: "Martins told me later"(16). This device not only enables Martins, like Fowler and Brown, to have the last word (there remains in *TM* only the very brief scene in which Calloway tells of Martins's departure after Lime's second funeral), but also allows the reader to come away from this story, as from most of the others, with the sense that the hero, in the end, had a deeper insight than the detective into the human issues revealed. When Martins ends his piece of quoted narrative by telling how he shot Lime, Calloway interrupts with a kindly, "We'll forget that bit." Martins, however, knows better and replies, "I never shall." The full implication of Lime's death is secret or privileged information which Calloway will conceal or ignore but which Martins will guard and remember.

Through the figure of the detective, towards the end of most of the novels, Greene draws attention to the question of truth. The detective, in most cases, has done his best and has come up with either a practical solution (typically a bullet) or a version of events which will satisfy those to whom he reports. The plain inadequacy of the detective's level of interpretation, even when he is himself kindly and well intentioned, directs the reader to the more complex realities which the story has revealed.

7. Conclusion

The typical Greene plot opens with the hero either, as in the early and middle works, distressingly enmeshed in the turmoil of life, or else, as in the late novels, living in hermit-like withdrawal from a world which he has already tried and found uncongenial. In either case he stands, as it were, on the brink of action, whether this be simply to seek alleviation of his own difficulties or, as in the late novels, to engage himself in the human cause. The Greene novel typically covers this action, the cycle of the hero's response to the miseries of life, from its origin in his personal past to its end, which is usually a tragic catastrophe but which occasionally, in the lighter-hearted stories, achieves a comic integration.

The hero's crucial action is taken under the influence of the antagonist, and the story proper normally has its roots in the first meeting or association between these two. The morally significant action of the hero, which is the focus of the plot, is typically a direct response to the antagonist. The ways in which this influence is exerted on the heroes vary considerably from case to case. In several novels the antagonist assumes a parental or quasi-parental role, or becomes a guide or mentor for the hesitant hero. In such cases he may actually direct the hero, whether as his leader (Carlyon), employer (Krogh), creditor (Yusef), parent (Augusta), or foster parent (the Captain). In other novels the association between the main characters may be more subtle, involving some kind of alter ego relationship. Here, as in *PG*, *HC*, and *HF*, the hero approaches the antagonist metaphorically, imitating him in some significant respect or adopting a point of view which he represents.

The course of action taken by the hero under the antagonist's influence always entails moral difficulties. The antagonist himself is often either a criminal or engaged in covert activity which sets him outside the law or beyond the pale of conventional morality. On the other hand, he is rarely a plain villain and is usually distinguished by an element of personal kindness or charm. He frequently professes good intentions, and in several cases among the late novels his conduct, although unconventional and not entirely legal, is seen in the end to be the best course to take. The limitation of the antagonist's point of view lies not so much in its potential conflict with law or conventional values (neither of which are absolute in Greene's world), but rather in its tendency to result in cruelty, to cause or permit avoidable death or suffering. Only in the last novels, notably in *HC*, *HF*, and *CE*, does the antagonist remain innocent in this respect, while the burden of responsibility for suffering is diverted to other characters (to Leon, Muller, and the Devil).

The starting point of the hero's story is his association with the antagonist, which may occur quite suddenly, but which is more often, as in *HM* and *QA*, a slow process, or even, as in *MW*, *BR*, and *HF*, one which has been accomplished in the past, before the main action begins. What might be called the story's turning point, the hero's reaction against or confirmation of this initial association, comes when he is confronted with its moral consequences. This point is typically sudden and dramatic, and in many cases it involves an innocent victim. The victims are very important, although as characters they may have only minor roles, because of their dramatic impact and function as clear moral indicators. It is usually through the victim that the ills inherent in the antagonist's courses come to light, and it is often when confronted with the victim, not infrequently a corpse, that the hero realizes the moral implications of the line he is himself taking. In most cases, if not directly the cause of the victim's fate, as Pinkie is, the hero shares responsibility for it, either as an accomplice, like Scobie, or by simply allowing the continuation of a situation he might have prevented, as does Fowler for a time.

In the dynamics of a typical Greene plot there are therefore two main motions, directly contrary in the early novels, but becoming more complementary in the late stories. In the first motion, which may already have begun when the novel opens, the hero approaches the antagonist and acts under his influence. In the second, after a turning point, there is either a rejection and contrary motion away from the antagonist or, in the late novels, a renewed impulse leading to affirmation, to an open confirmation of the hero's unity with the antagonist.

From this duality of motion arises, in a typical novel, the dual process of detection. The hero's initial movement, towards the shady world of the antagonist, makes him an object of investigation or pursuit, usually by a policeman or journalist. At the same time the hero normally begins his own investigation of the antagonist, the process which generally leads to the turning point, the confrontation with the victim. As a result of this the hero has to decide whether to change or continue his direction, whether to turn against his antagonist or affirm their unity.

From these motions arise also the betrayals which critics have observed to be characteristic motifs in Greene's stories. In fact these betrayals are of two quite distinct kinds. First there is the disloyalty to accepted or institutional codes, of which the hero may be guilty in his initial association with the antagonist. Thus Andrews breaks the law when he joins Carlyon and becomes a smuggler, Scobie betrays his trust as an officer in his dealings with Yusef, and Castle becomes a traitor in becoming a double agent. Of a very different kind is the personal betrayal of the antagonist, which occurs in a number of the novels as a result of the hero's change of direction. Thus Anthony's decision to return to England constitutes a threat to Krogh, Martins betrays Lime to the police, and Fowler conspires to arrange the murder of Pyle. Again, however, in *BR*, *PG*, and most of the late novels, the hero's final movement is to identify with the antagonist, not to betray him. Even in these cases, however, some trace of the betrayal motif often remains. Thus Brown intends to abandon Jones to his fate, not to join him; Plarr provides the information which, albeit unpredictably, leads to Fortnum's capture; Castle had intended to break off his contact with Carson's people; and Pinkie's marriage to Rose is potentially a betrayal of Kite.

The female characters discussed in Chapter 5 may also be placed in relation to these two movements or phases of the typical Greene plot. The weaker type tends to act, in the early novels, against the antagonist's influence. In the later novels the women of this type serve rather as an additional incentive for the hero to affirm his acceptance of the antagonist's lead. Women like Phuong and Sarah Castle represent an oppressed humanity whom the hero, by emulating the antagonist, may be able to assist. The weaker type is therefore relevant chiefly to the second phase of the hero's action, his decision after the turning point to reject or commit himself to the antagonist's line of action. The stronger type bears rather upon the first phase. In most of the early and middle novels she encourages the hero in his initial movement towards the antagonist. In the late novels, however, her influence tends to operate in a more plainly negative way, holding back the hero from committing himself openly to renewed action, binding him to old habits or obligations which he has outgrown.

The dynamic pattern just outlined evolves and changes through the series of Greene's major novels, and the main phases distinguishable in its development are closely congruent with the three stages of Greene's work outlined in Chapter 1. In the early novels the hero is initially an unhappy, usually disadvantaged individual who turns to the antagonist in hope of a quick solution to his problems, seeking security, guidance, and support. Later he discovers the inhumanity consequent upon the antagonist's activities and attempts to dissociate himself from his former ally and protector. This turn involves considerable personal risk and so reveals the hero's unexpected moral fiber—"the man within." Little more is involved, however, since all these stories are very compressed, and the entire action is completed within only a few days.

The middle novels are marked by a new expansiveness which allows for both a greater emphasis upon the hero's past and a much more detailed presentation of his growth and development in the course of the action. The hero now begins with a yearning for a kind of lost innocence which, in each case, he identifies with a period in his personal past. He forms an initial association with the antagonist in the hope of recovering something of the "peace" he sees himself as having lost. In the course of the ensuing events, however, it becomes clear that the results of this association are not acceptable, particularly because the "peace" in question stands to be gained at the cost of others' suffering. The outcome varies: in *HM* and *MF* the hero rejects his antagonist; but Pinkie, with his inverted morality, refuses in the end to abandon the memory of Kite; and the Priest, in the highly metaphorical context of *PG*, may be seen as achieving a final identification with Calver.

The rather naive heroes, typified by the immature Pinkie, the unworldly Priest, and the simple-hearted Scobie, are replaced by cynical, world-weary men such as Fowler, Querry, and Brown. Accordingly the yearning for lost innocence gives way to an impulse towards withdrawal and inaction. As his story opens the late hero is trying to preserve a kind of innocence or integrity by abstaining from involvement in a generally corrupt and vicious world. The antagonist here offers him a self-comparison and may be seen as an alter ego with whom the hero needs, in some significant respect, to identify. In the first phase the hero examines the antagonist and perhaps begins cooperation with him, but with reservations and limitations. After the turning point, in most cases, he recognizes the need for involvement, and the action he subsequently takes can be seen as an emulation of his antagonist. Thus Fowler in the end adopts Pyle's policy of covert conspiracy with native forces, Brown appears at Jones's side as an active opponent of Papa Doc, and Castle reveals himself as, like Carson, a communist agent. Only Baxter, a generally negative character, refuses.

There is a tendency for the antagonists in the last novels to become progressively less threatening, until in Fortnum, Carson, and the Captain we have men who are almost wholly benign. The last three novels then form a subgroup in which responsibility for the evils inherent in purposive action is diverted from the antagonist and placed on the shoulders of a secondary antagonist, a new figure who now undertakes the violence and deception which, in earlier novels, had been an integral part of the antagonist role. In each of *HC*, *HF*, and *CE* the two antagonists (Fortnum and Leon, Carson and Muller, the Captain and Quigly) are mutually hostile, the more benign being in danger as the potential victim of the other. The hero's task now becomes in effect to choose between them. (With hindsight, we can see the splitting of the antagonist role anticipated in *TA*, where Mr. Visconti does the real dirty work behind the scenes, while his partner, Augusta, appears to care only for "fun.") In these novels the sound hero steers a careful course and ends shoulder to shoulder with his mentor. Thus Plarr opposes Leon's terrorism and allows himself to become a prisoner alongside Fortnum, and Castle accepts that he must stop Muller and does so by identifying with Carson and defecting to Moscow. Only the unsound Baxter makes the wrong choice and aligns himself with Quigly against the Captain.

The novels of Graham Greene move between two fixed moral points. One is the belief that life is inherently uncongenial and involves the average man in unavoidable fear and suffering. This provides the starting point, the initial fictional state from which the hero is impelled to escape, either by striving or withdrawal. The other fixed point is the categorical imperative of human compassion. This provides the moral goal of the novels, the final standard by which the hero's actions are to be judged.

Along with these two primary constants go several associated points. Conjunct with the first is the fact of irreducible moral complexity. In Greene's fictional world there are no final answers to the problems underlying human unhappiness. Characters who believe they have such answers are men like Hilfe, Pyle, and the Lieutenant. They may well intend to do good, and may even achieve good results within limited contexts; but any good they do in one quarter is offset by suffering caused in another. For this same reason, the novels finally reject any ideological systems, whether Marxist or Catholic. Such ideologies may be fine in theory and may indeed promote human welfare in some ways, but in their inevitably institutionalized forms, Greene shows, they also become, at best comically inept, at worst cruelly oppressive.

The possibility of a transcendental solution is left open, although the opening left is so narrow as to be all but invisible in most novels. There are, however, allusions at the endings of *BR*, *PG*, and *HM* to "divine mercy," and there are gestures towards the same direction in a few other cases, particularly in *MW*, *EA*, and *MQ*. Far from being dogmatic assertions of salvation (or damnation), however, these allusions do no more than raise questions.

From the irreducible complexity of the human situation follows also the point, which might be taken as the motto of the middle novels, that innocence is not enough. The attempt to avoid human problems by imagining or creating for oneself a realm of moral simplicity, from which evil and suffering can be artificially excluded, is shown to be illusory in that it is itself ultimately productive of harm. The point applies most obviously to the seekers of lost innocence: Pinkie, the Priest, Scobie, and Rowe, men upon whom it is incumbent that they should abandon their ideals of pure life and accept entanglement in the human world. It applies also to the late heroes, to Fowler, Querry, Brown, and Plarr, who attempt to simulate a kind of personal innocence by merely abstaining from morally significant action.

Individual moral action becomes an imperative. Greene does not believe in institutional solutions. The police and the media are fallible in the investigation of human truths. Institutions, whether administered from Moscow or from Rome, cannot reach the heart of the ordinary man. Situations continually arise in which the individual is called upon to act in some humane cause. The only heroes who finally turn their backs upon the call of humanity are Pinkie and Baxter, both of whom meet apocalyptic ends, falling like Lucifer in trails of smoke from great heights.

The hero's action, which, in the context of Greene's hostile universe, is often futile, is to be judged more by intention than by tangible result. The motive must be humanitarian: it must be either (as in the comic novels) a deliberate celebration of the human capacity for "fun," or (as in the serious novels) a response to the cry of the suffering victim. In the end it is the depth of conviction of Greene's humanitarian feeling which secures his place among the major writers of the twentieth century.

Notes

1. For bibliographical details, see R. A. Wobbe, *Graham Greene: A Bibliography and Guide to Research* (New York: Garland, 1979).
2. "The Basement Room" was made into a film released in 1948 under the title *The Fallen Idol*. This title was then used in subsequent editions of the story. (The film appeared in America under yet another title, *The Lost Illusion*.)
3. For bibliographical details, see J. Don Vann, *Graham Greene: A Checklist of Criticism* (Kent: Kent State UP, 1970); and A. F. Cassis, *Graham Greene: An Annotated Bibliography of Criticism.* (Metuchen, NJ: Scarecrow, 1981.)
4. Norman Sherry, *The Life of Graham Greene. Volume One: 1904–1939; Volume Two: 1939–1955; Volume Three: 1956–1991* (London: Jonathan Cape, 1989, 1994, 2004).
5. The first significant book-length study of Greene in English, Kenneth Allott and Miriam Farris, *The Art of Graham Greene* (London: Hamish Hamilton, 1951), notes "the remarkable family likeness they [the novels] bear to each other," and develops a number of points of resemblance arising from Greene's fundamental pessimism (14–19).
6. The generic ancestry and makeup of Greene's novels, with particular reference to Conrad, is discussed in Robert Pendleton, *Graham Greene's Conradian Masterplot* (London: Macmillan, 1996).
7. The phrase occurs in *MW* 2.9 and is employed as heading for the introductory chapter of Allott and Farris (1951).

8. Norman Macleod, " 'This Strange, Rather Sad Story': The Reflexive Design of Graham Greene's *The Third Man*," *Dalhousie Review* 63 (Summer 1983): 217–41.
9. There is nothing inherently wrong with this biographical approach, which is particularly feasible in Greene's case because of his avowed importation of so much autobiographical material into his novels. There is, however, a caveat. Much of the biographical information upon which criticism has tended to rely, especially information about his early years, comes largely from Greene's own autobiographical writings, particularly from *SL* and the opening pages of *LR*. It should be remembered that Greene, like Conrad (in this respect, as in many, his literary mentor), was not in maturity above representing his past life in terms of his fiction. Greene had been writing novels about men in some ways like himself for many years before he turned to autobiography. It might therefore be reasonable to read his autobiographies in terms of his novels rather than *vice versa*.
10. E.g., Roger Sharrock, *Saints, Sinners and Comedians: The Novels of Graham Greene* (Tunbridge Wells: Burns & Oates, 1984).
11. As is suggested in Marie-Beatrice Mesnet, *Graham Greene and the Heart of the Matter: An Essay* (London: Cresset, 1954), 81. Cf. Evelyn Waugh's comment that only a Catholic could understand *HM* (in his review of *HM*, "Felix Culpa," *The Tablet* 191 (June 5, 1948); reprinted in *Commonweal* 48 (July 16, 1948), and in Samuel Hynes (ed.), *Graham Greene: A Collection of Critical Essays* (Englewood Cliffs, NJ: Prentice Hall, 1973).
12. "Henry James: The Religious Aspect," in *Collected Essays* (1969).
13. Gene D. Phillips, "Graham Greene: On the Screen," in Hynes (1973), 175. A generally negative view of the use of Catholic themes in Greene's middle novels is given in D. S. Savage, "Graham Greene and Belief," *Dalhousie Review* 58 (1978): 205–29.
14. There is a useful review of critical attitudes to Catholicism in Greene's novels in S. K. Sharma, *Graham Greene: The Search for Belief* (New Delhi: Harman, 1990), 7–24.

15. Greene suppressed, by refusing to reprint them, two of his early published novels, *The Name of Action* (1930) and *Rumour at Nightfall* (1931). He also left unpublished several early novels in manuscript: *Anthony Sant*, renamed *Prologue to Pilgrimage* (1923–24), *The Episode* (1925–26), and the unfinished *Fanatic Arabia* (1936).
16. For detailed discussion of Bruckner, see Robert Simpson, *The Essence of Bruckner*, 2nd ed. (London: Victor Gollancz, 1977).
17. E.g., R. W. B. Lewis, "The 'Trilogy' of Graham Greene," *Modern Fiction Studies* 3 (Autumn 1957): 195–215; reprinted with minor changes as part of his *The Picaresque Saint: Representative Figures in Contemporary Fiction* (Philadelphia: J. B. Lippincot, 1959), 270–74; and in Hynes (1973).
18. Greene's plays of this period are *The Living Room* (1953), *The Potting Shed* (1958), *The Complaisant Lover* (1959), and *Carving a Statue* (1964).
19. Phillips in Hynes (1973),173.
20. It is, in a way, absurd to call *TM*, written after *HM*, an "early" work; but on the structural criteria applied here it belongs with the "political thrillers" of the first period rather than with the much more complex narratives of the middle phase. Its exceptional nature, as a relatively simple story among the much more profound works of the wartime era, doubtless arises largely from its original conception as a basis for a film script.
21. The hero of *PG* has no personal name. To avoid confusion and to distinguish him from other priests in Greene's fiction, he will here be referred to as "the Priest," with a capital P.
22. A recent study of the theme of childhood deprivation in Greene's fiction is P. N. Pandit, *The Novels of Graham Greene: A Thematic Study in the Impact of Childhood on Adult Life* (New Delhi: Prestige, 1989).
23. Sherry (1989), 430.
24. Francis L. Kunkel, *The Labyrinthine Ways of Graham Greene* (New York: Sheed and Ward, 1959), 80–81, observes Greene's tendency to explore "the development of a character in a shed of some kind" and concludes that "Greene employs

the shed as a device which permits his protagonists to shed their burdens."
25. Greene was aware of the weakness of the barn scene in *ST*. See his diary entry for June 6, 1932, quoted in Sherry (1989), 415.
26. See for example the letter quoted in Sherry (1989), 577.
27. In *WE* 1.4 Greene says that the key scene of *GS* is the one "in an empty house," but this is surely a slip. In the house (*GS* 1.3) there is little exchange between Raven and Anne before they are interrupted. Only later, in the railway shed (5.1), where they spend much longer together, do they achieve significant communication.
28. This description of Pinkie parodies Wordsworth's "Ode on Intimations of Immortality": "But trailing clouds of glory do we come/From God, who is our home:/Heaven lies about us in our infancy!" These lines express the neoplatonic view that the newborn spirit, just come from the eternal, is still close to God and initially free from human corruption—a view usually seen as opposed to Christian belief in "original sin."
29. Sherry (1994), 293–301, usefully summarizes early critical reactions to *HM*.
30. For the reasons given in this paragraph, I dissent from Francis L. Kunkel's view that (whereas Rose is realized "in the past as well as in the immediate present") Scobie "is realized almost exclusively in the present" (Kunkel [1959], 70). References to Scobie's memories of past peace and to his daughter may be few and brief, but they remain effective and important in our understanding of the character.
31. Scobie's offer to forfeit his own peace in return for the girl's being granted peace (2.1.1.3) clearly echoes the Priest's prayer for his daughter, in which he offers his own soul to damnation in return for her salvation (*PG* 2.1). Amazingly there are critics who invite us to see those prayers as accepted at face value (e.g., Henry J.Donaghy, *Graham Greene: An Introduction to his Writings* [Amsterdam: Rodopi BV, 1983], 41). We are asked to suppose that God agrees to release a child

from damnation in return for the eternal torment of an innocent—or at least unselfish—man, an idea which makes nonsense of whatever theological reference the novels may include by rendering God the moral inferior of every human character. The god who would accept such an arrangement would be indistinguishable from the Nazis in *The Tenth Man*, anxious to take any victim regardless of the means of his selection. Greene's point, of course, is not that God accepts the deal, but that Scobie and the Priest, in their distress and compassion, offer it sincerely.

32. George Orwell, "The Sanctified Sinner," in the *New Yorker* (July 17, 1948), reprinted in Hynes (1973).
33. T. S. Eliot, "Little Gidding," III.
34. T. S. Eliot, "The Dry Salvages," III.
35. The significance of *JM* and *LR* as essays in "self-discovery" is discussed in Jeffrey Meyers, "Greene's Travel Books," in Jeffrey Meyers (ed.), *Graham Greene: A Revaluation* (London: Macmillan, 1990).
36. Greene liked to give the impression that Conrad's influence was something he grew out of as he was writing his early novels (*SL* 11.4), but the truth is surely that he rather grew into Conrad as he matured. Greene's first three published novels mimic superficial aspects of Conrad, especially a tendency to lapse into lush prose and a preference for romantic adventures involving smugglers and revolutionaries. Greene's mature work settles down to a serious grappling with central issues of Conrad's major fiction, particularly the question of action in a world where corruption is pervasive and moral compromise inevitable. Thus the "journey back" in the middle novels has its archetype in *Heart of Darkness*; the withdrawn heroes of the later novels are echoes of Heyst in *Victory*; the central idea for *OM* comes from *The Secret Agent*; and *The Tenth Man* is so close to *Under Western Eyes* that one wonders whether this was not the real reason Greene "forgot" about it for so many years. Pendleton (1996) examines Greene's debt to Conrad, and comments (87) on the specific closeness of *The Tenth Man* to *Under Western Eyes*. Stephen K. Land, *Conrad and the Paradox of Plot* (London:

Macmillan, 1984), looks at Conrad's presentation of a fictional world in which action and compromise are required of the hero, but in which action provokes reaction so that happy resolutions are very rare.

37. *OM* is a clear example of what Northrop Frye calls "the second phase of comedy" (Northrop Frye, *Anatomy of Criticism: Four Essays* [Princeton: Princeton UP, 1957], 180.)
38. Greene says that the idea for *OM* came from his wartime observation of agents in Portugal who fabricated information (*WE* 8.2). That Conrad remained a deeper source is suggested by the name "Stott" and the hero's large-bosomed wife, elements of "Nobody to Blame" which come directly from *The Secret Agent*.
39. Neil M. Ewan's *Graham Greene* (London: Macmillan, 1988) is a general study of Greene that gives particular attention to the place of comedy and irony in his fiction.
40. The broad structural resemblances between *TC* and *QA* have often been observed—e.g., in Richard Kelly, *Graham Greene* (New York: Ungar, 1984), 84.
41. The imagery surrounding parenthood, and especially fatherhood, is examined in Daphne Erdinast-Vulcan, *Graham Greene's Childless Fathers* (London: Macmillan, 1988).
42. "Seems, madam! nay, it is; I know not seems" (*Hamlet* I.ii).
43. As a historian Greene knew the name Visconti as that of the family which ruled Milan from about 1277 to 1447, and hence the several references in *TA* to the aristocratic connotations of the name. The arms of the family were a blue serpent on a white field, devouring a man whose head and arms protruded from its jaws. Their enemies called the serpent a snake, and hence references to Mr. Visconti as a viper. Greene first encountered the name in Marjorie Bowen's *The Viper of Milan*, which he read as a boy (*WE* 9.3).
44. Brian Thomas, *An Underground Fate: The Idiom of Romance in the Later Novels of Graham Greene* (Athens: U of Georgia P, 1988), 176, points out that *HC* continues from *TA* the theme of the hero's search for a lost father.
45. E.g., Donaghy (1983), 101.
46. Erdinast-Vulcan (1988), 85–99.

47. Published in *Nineteen Stories* (1947).
48. The name Buller also occurs in *HM* 2.1.1.4, in the story which Scobie supposedly reads to the boy in hospital in Pende. Here, with no contextual allusions to South Africa or British imperialism, the name has no particular connotation.
49. Baxter does, of course, have the opportunity to alter his earlier drafts as he writes the later additions, and he even admits to making corrections to the earlier texts. We must assume, however, that such revisions were minor, or else there ceases to be any point to the elaborate business of the gaps in a document several times put aside and then continued. If Baxter is allowed to have made extensive alterations with hindsight, he might just as well have written the whole story in one go.
50. There is a particularly close link between early antagonists in Greene, characters such as Carlyon and Krogh, and the character of Lingard in Conrad's *Almayer's Folly* and *An Outcast of the Islands*. Lingard is given to patronizing weak young men who turn against him when he proves unable to satisfy their expectations.
51. I take "she" here to refer to Rose, whose presence has been irritating Pinkie on the previous page. It could conceivably refer to Ida, however, who has been mentioned a few lines before by Dallow.
52. This is one of the very few places where Greene uses a word or phrase which, lifted from context, might be taken to imply a homoerotic element in the hero-antagonist relationship. Left in context the implication remains very weak. The haymaking with supposed homosexuality between Andrews and Carlyon, and between Scobie and Yusef, in various places in Michael Sheldon, *Graham Greene: The Man Within* (London: Heinemann, 1994), seems to me to rest on dubious evidence and to contribute nothing helpful to a reading of the novels.
53. The lines of the "epitaph" are from Rilke's *Die Sonette an Orpheus*, Erster Teil, 5.
54. An early use of the term "Greeneland" is in Arthur Calder-Marshall, "The Works of Graham Greene," *Horizon* (May 1940).

55. John Spurling, *Graham Greene* (London: Methuen, 1983), 73–74.
56. Coincidences include, for example, D's encounter with Rose at the point of his arrival in England, Raven's meeting with Anne (who just happens to be the fiancée of the detective who is pursuing him), and the several chance encounters in *TA*. Ironic twists include the reappearances of the *mestizo* in *PG*, Louise's unexpected return in *HM*, Marie's false accusation in *BC*, and Muller's arrival on Castle's doorstep in *HF*.
57. Examples include Mrs. Bellairs's telling of Rowe's fortune at the beginning of *MF*, the rather similar business with the Brighton tealeaf reader in *TA*, and Ida's luck with the horses, which provides the economic foundation for her protracted pursuit of Pinkie in *BR*.
58. This has been done persuasively in Thomas (1988).
59. Allott and Farris (1951), 14–19, give a synopsis of pessimistic tendencies in Greene.
60. The lines, from Browning's "Bishop Blougram's Apology," are quoted in *SL* 5.2. *SL* was published in 1971, but there is no reason not to extend Greene's remark about the applicability of this "epigraph" to the novels he was to write after this date.
61. Francis L. Kunkel concludes that Greene is "half-Manichean," the other half being Pelagian (Kunkel [1959], 20). A Manichean sees the universe in terms of the struggle of two opposing principles, which are independent of each other, neither being subordinate. In moral terms this is a very simple view, akin to that of Rowe's boyhood, in which everything is reducible to either good or evil.
62. These remarks occur in "The Lost Childhood" and "Henry James: The Religious Aspect," both included in Greene's *Collected Essays*.
63. Greene's novels are not, of course, unique in this respect. A comparable irreducible moral complexity lies at the root of much of Conrad's fiction. Most popular storytelling, on the other hand, remains dualistic. A sophisticated embodiment of the Manichean view in modern fiction is Tolkien's *Lord of the Rings*.

64. See Judith Adamson, *Graham Greene: The Dangerous Edge* (London: Macmillan, 1990). Greene was impressed, at different times, by both communism and Catholicism as potential solutions to social and political problems. His approach, however, was ultimately pragmatic rather than doctrinal, and he tended to be more impressed by active individuals than by ideas.
65. Evolutionary allusions crop up in Greene's novels in the years from 1955. Pyle's father collects Darwin manuscripts. Doctor Colin subscribes to a notion of progressive evolution. Even Mr. Visconti refers to evolutionary theory. Leon's theology derives broadly from Teilhard de Chardin's Christianized Darwinism and is close to some of Javitt's ideas.
66. A recent instance is Sharma (1990), 7–8.
67. Allott and Farris (1951), 95, for instance, comment upon the similarity among Coral Musker, Milly Drover, Loo, and Anna Hilfe.
68. William M. Chace, "Spies and God's Spies: Greene's Espionage Fiction," in Meyers (1990), touches on the theme of this chapter in his discussion of the importance ascribed to processes of information gathering (or spying) in a number of Greene's stories.

Index

Adamson, Judith, 281
Allott, Kenneth, 273, 280, 281
Another Mexico, see *The Lawless Roads*
Anthony Sant, 275

"Basement Room, The," 131–32, 141, 166, 273
The Basement Room and Other Stories, viii, 5
Baudelaire, Charles, 67. 68
Beethoven, Ludwig van, 5
Berkeley, George, 100
Bowen, Marjorie, 192, 278
Brighton Rock, viii, 2, 6, 7, 22, 23, 24, 26, 28, 29, 31, **34–36**, **37–39**, 41, **42–49**, 50, 52, 54, 55. 57, 68, 69, 70, 75, 79, 113, 122, 129, **142–46**, 157, 180, 182, 185, 189, 198, 219–20, 227–28, 247–48, 262–63, 267, 268, 272, 280
Browning, Robert, 190, 280
Bruckner, Anton, 5, 275
Buchan, John, 21, 27
Buller, Sir Revers, 123—24
Burnt-Out Case, A, viii, 3, 6, 7, 72, 79, **89–98**, 114, **164–65**, 167, 172, 180, 189, 198, 218, 221, 225, 234–35, 236, 252–53, 280
Byron, George Gordon, 6th Baron, 67, 68

Calder-Marshall, Arthur, 279
Calles, Plutarco, 39
Captain and the Enemy, The, ix, 2, 3, 6, 103, **125–29**, 131, 132, 140–41, 166, 167, **178–79**, 189, 210, 237–38, 254, 258, 264, 267, 271
Carving a Statue, 275
Cassis, A. F., 273
Catholicism, 3–4, 6–7, 71, 197, 198–99, 271, 281
Cervantes, Miguel de, 109, 134
Chace, William M., 281
Chrêtien de Troyes, 68
Christie, Agatha, 240
Comedians, The, ix, 6, 7, 72, 79, 89, 96, 98, 100, **101–9**, 110, 111, 113, 114, 117, 134, 143, 165, **167–70**, 171, 172, 173, 179, 180, 181, 189, 191, 198, 201, 214, 217, 225, 234, 235–36, 253–54, 264, 278
Communism, 114, 174, 197, 198, 281

Complaisant Lover, The, 275
Confidential Agent, The, viii, 2, 3, 6, 7, **24–25**, 26, 27, 29, 31, 32, 34, 39, 40, 42, 55, 69, 129, 143–44, **146–47**, 167, 176, 180, 189, 195, 196, 216, 230, 241, 243–44, 245, 260
Conrad, Joseph, 1, 15, 71–72, 78, 87–88, 120, 134, 240, 274, 277–78, 279, 280

Darwinism, 202–3, 204, 281
"Destructors, The," 2, 70
Doctor Fischer of Geneva, ix, 6, 103, 125, 129, 137, 143, 159, 167, **176–78**, 180, 204
Donaghy, Henry J., 276–77, 278
Doyle, Sir Arthur Conan, 240

Eliot, Thomas Stearns, 277
End of the Affair, The, viii, 2, 6, 7, 37, 55, **72–75**, 80, 113, 119, 129, 136, 183, 198, 211, 213, **249–51**, 252, 253, 272
England Made Me, viii, 3, 5, 7, **20–21**, 24, 26, 31, 32, 33, 69, 127, 132, **141–43**, 147, 160, 177, 180, 189, 216, 226–27, 245, 246–47
Episode, The, 275
Erdinast-Vulcan, Daphne, 278
Ewan, Neil M., 278

Fallen Idol, The, 273
Fanatic Arabia, 275
Farris, Miriam, 273, 280, 281
Fleming, Ian, 21
Fielding, Henry, 109
Forster, Edward Morgan, 59
Francis of Assisi, 68
Frye, Northrop, 278

Getting to Know the General, ix
Gun for Sale, A, viii, 3, 6, 7, 11, 17, **21–24**, 26, 27, 29, 33–34, 40, 55, 69, 70, 114, **143–44**, 147, 196, 229, 242–43, 245, 249, 276

Heart of the Matter, The, viii, 3, 6, 7, 24, 26, 37, 39, 52, **61–67**, 70, 75, 79, 96, 113, 129, 132, **154–58**, 168, 189, 198, 209, 216–17, 219, 221, 222, 226, 231–32, 233–34, 248–49, 263, 267, 270, 272, 275, 276, 279, 280
Honorary Consul, The, ix, 6, 72, 79, 89, 103, **113–19**, 120–21, 122, 127, 134, 135, 146, 165, 167, 168, **171–75**, 180, 183, 187, 189, 200–201, 217–18, 222, 234, 235, 236–37, 238, 254–56, 266, 267, 271, 278
Human Factor, The, ix, 6, 79, 89, **119–25**, 144, 146, 165, **171–72**, **174–76**, 180, 183, 189, 200, 237–38, 254–57, 266, 267, 271, 280
Hynes, Samuel, 274, 275

"Innocent, The," 122
It's a Battlefield, viii, 5, 10–11, 15, **18–19**, 21, 24, 27, 32–33, 87, 113, **140–41**, 145, 146, 171, 173, 180, 182, 185, 189, 200, 215–16, 222, 245, 246

James, Henry, 4, 192
Jone, Heribert, 199
Journey Without Maps, viii, 67, **70–71**, 90, 277

Kelly, Richard, 278

Kunkel, Francis L., 275–76, 280

Labyrinthine Ways, see *Brighton Rock*
Land, Stephen K., 277–78
Lawless Roads, The, viii, 274, 277
Lewis, W. B., 275
Living Room, The 275
Loser Takes All, viii, 6, 129, 137, **159–60**, 176, 177
Lost Illusion, The, 273

Macleod, Norman, 274
Man Within, The, viii, 3, **13–14**, 15, 18, 24, 32, 96, 125, 127, 131, 132, **137–40**, 145, 146, 147, 158, 160, 172–73, 185, 215, 220, 221, 222, 242, 243, 245, 246, 249, 267, 272, 273
Marx, Karl, 198, 271
May We Borrow Your Husband?, 6
Mesnet, Marie-Beatrice, 274
Meyers, Jeffrey, 277, 281
Ministry of Fear, The, viii, 2, 7, 24, 26, 27–28, **36–37**, 39, 41, 52, **54–61**, 70, 79, 127, 129, 146, **150–53**, 155, 157, 158, 161, 162, 180, 187, 189, 198, 209, 219, 225, 130–31, 232, 244–45, 249, 260, 270, 280
Monsignor Quixote, ix, 2, 6, 7, 11, 67, 87, 96, 98, 101, 110, 113, 114, 125, 129, 134, 137, 183, **198–99**, 204, 257–58, 272

Name of Action, The, vii, viii, 14, 275
Nineteen Stories, 279
"Nobody to Blame," 87, 278

Orient Express, see *Stamboul Train*

Orwell, George, 66–68, 277
Our Man in Havana, viii, 6, **87–89**, 96, **98–100**, 107, 110, 111, 119, **163–64**, 191–92, 200, 218, 221, 222, 231, **251–52**, 256, 260, 262, 277, 278

Pandit, P. N., 275
Pendleton, Robert, 273, 277
Philby, Kim, 119
Phillips, Gene, D., 274, 275
Potting Shed, The, 275
Power and the Glory, The, viii, 2, 6, 7, 11, 24, 26, 27, 37, 39, **49–54**, 55, 57, 68, 70, 75, 79, 113, 122, 129, 146, **147–50**, 151, 152, 155, 157, 158, 168, 171, 175, 180, 186, 189, 191, 193, 197, 198, 200–201, 219, 220–21, 223, 225, 228–29, 248, 263–64, 266, 268, 270, 272, 275, 280
Prologue to Pilgrimage, 275

Quiet American, The, viii, 3, 6, 7, 11, 17, 25, 72, 79, **80–87**, 89, 91–92, 102, 114, 117, 120, 129, 143, 153, 158, 159, **160–63**, 165, 169, 172, 173, 180, 181, 200, 201, 207, 218, 222, 234, 235, 236, **251**, 254, 256, 264, 267, 278

Reed, Carol, 25
Rilke, Rainer Maria, 279
Rumour at Nightfall, vii, viii, 14, 275

Sackville-West, Edward, 72
Savage, D. S., 274
Sense of Reality, A, ix, 165

Sharma, S. K., 274, 281
Sharrock, Roger, 274
Sheldon, Michael, 279
Sherry, Norman, ix, 273, 275, 276
Shipwrecked, The, see *England Made Me*
Simpson, Robert, 275
Sort of Life, A, ix, 274, 277, 280
Spurling, John, 280
Stamboul Train, viii, 2, 5, 10, **14–18**, 19, 21, 22, 27, 32, 114, 136, 146, 183, 189, 215, 222, 224, 245, 276
Stopes, Marie, 45

Teilhard de Chardin, Pierre, 114, 281
Tenth Man, The, viii, 6, 11, 87, 277
Third Man, The, viii, 2, 3, 7, **25**, 26, 74, 129, 158–59, 180, 181, 195, 200, 207, 211, 249, 260, 264–65, 275
This Gun for Hire, see *A Gun for Sale*
Thomas, Brian, 278, 280
Tolkien, J. R. R., 280

Tolstoy, Leo, 150, 152, 197, 198
Travels with My Aunt, ix, 2, 6, 72, 87, 96, 101, 103, 104, **109–13**, 114, 132, 135, 167, **170–71**, 177, 189, 200, 222, 234, 236, 241, 254, 256, 260, 262, 271, 278, 280

"Under the Garden," ix, 2, 5, 72, 114, 131–32, 141, **165–67**, 180, 186, **202–6**, 208–9, 210, 224–25

Vann, J. Don, 273
"Visit to Morin, A," 253

Wagner, Richard, 68
Waugh, Evelyn, 274
Ways of Escape, ix, 276, 278
Welles, Orson, 25
Wobbe, R. A., 273
Wolfram von Eschenbach, 68
Wordsworth, William, 70, 71, 276

Yonge, Charlotte M., 56